DATE DUE			

CLASSICAL GREEK ARCHITECTURE
THE CONSTRUCTION OF THE MODERN

For Micha Levin

Copyediting: Susan Schneider

Design: Alice Leroy

Typesetting: Thomas Gravemaker, Studio X-Act

Proofreading: Chrisoula Petridis

Color Separation: Dupont, Paris

Bibliography and captions: Sancra Ras

Plans and diagrams: Jan Willem Ter Steege

Distributed in North America by Rizzoli International Publications, Inc.

Simultaneously published in French as *Architecture Grecque Classique*
© Éditions Flammarion, 2004
English-language edition
© Éditions Flammarion, 2004

www.editions.flammarion.com

04 05 06 4 3 2 1

FC0442-04-IX
ISBN: 2-0803-0442-9
Dépôt légal: 09/2004

Printed in Italy by Canale

Alexander Tzonis
Phoebe Giannisi

CLASSICAL GREEK ARCHITECTURE
THE CONSTRUCTION OF THE MODERN

Flammarion

Acropolis, Athens. View of the entrance.
Photograph by Lucien Hervé.

CONTENTS

View of the Acropolis, Athens.
Photograph by Frédéric Boissonas.

PREFACE

Classical Greek architecture has not ceased to fascinate. The intention of this book is to try to explain why. More than inventions of pleasant forms, ancient Greek buildings were essays towards the discovery of the mind construing space. Their achievement rivals that of Classical tragedy, Euclidean geometry, and Hippocratic medicine. Like them, Classical Greek architecture was created by recruiting, reinterpreting, and recombining numerous preexisting products—many of which originated outside the Greek realm. Like them, Classical Greek architecture developed a new system of the world, natural and social, which was rule-based. However, unlike them, this new system did not lead to any final theory, but to endless different possibilities of new worlds. What its *nomos* delivered to us was the *construction of the modern*—that is, freedom.

Two kinds of documents have been used in this book: drawings by archaeologists and photographs. I have chosen to concentrate on images by photographers who worked on ancient Greek architecture during the first half of the twentieth century. While from an archaeological point of view the restoration of some of the buildings during this period is no more satisfactory, these pictures were preferred because of the better conditions of the sites that surrounded the buildings at that time. In addition, although each of these photographers had a different pictorial style, all share a special rigor in the representation of spatial structure, which is vital to the representation of Classical Greek space and is rare among contemporary photographers.

The book opens with a photograph by Lucien Hervé. Hervé was the photographer of Le Corbusier, and no other photographer has captured to the extent of Hervé the sense of the tragic and system that one finds in Le Corbusier's work. His book *La Plus Grande Aventure du Monde, L'Architecture Mystique de Cîteaux,* edited and introduced by François Cali, was published by Arthaud in 1956. It was introduced by Le Corbusier, who praised the photographs for celebrating at the same time the old material—"stone . . . the man's friend"—and the modern material—*béton brut*—both materials sharing the same plastic qualities. The rigorous geometric structure, the high contrast between light and shadow, and the smooth tones of gray printed in *héliographie* of Hervé's images established a new way of representing architecture photographically. Soon after, Serge Moulinier, who had worked with Hervé previously, was to apply the same graphic idiom in his *L'Ordre Grec, Essai sur le Temple Dorique,* a book conceived and edited once more by François Cali and published by Arthaud in 1958. Our book uses some of Moulinier's photographs.

Frédéric Boissonas (1858–1944) was a Swiss photographer who, like Hervé, was admired by Le Corbusier. He used a special large camera, well suited to architecture, to take his photographs of the Acropolis. Maxime Collignon published many of Boissonas's photographs in his book *Le Parthénon* (1912). It was from this publication that Le Corbusier selected many illustrations for his famous manifesto, *Vers Une Architecture* (1924), to demonstrate the "mathematical order" and "revolutionary" spirit of the Parthenon.

The photographs of Delphi were taken before the Second World War by Georges de Miré and were selected from the archive of the École Française d'Athènes. From around the same period are the photographs of the Propylaia and the Acropolis by Walter Hege (1893–1955), selected from the archive of the German Archaeology School of Athens. Waldemar Deonna (1880–1959) was a Swiss archaeologist, professor at the University of Geneva and amateur photographer. The photographs included here were selected from his archive at the Musées d'Art et d'Histoire de la Ville de Genève. They were taken between 1904 and 1907, while Deonna was working in Greece hosted by the École Française d'Athènes. I have resorted to my own photographs to demonstrate specific issues presented in the text, only in the absence of material easily available from photographic archives.

Many of the ideas in this book have been developed over a long time, in fact from my years as a student of A. K. Orlandos and D. Pikionis in Athens. Many other ideas originate from my work on Renaissance and seventeenth-century Classicism, and I would like to acknowledge my debt to J. Ackerman, L. Lefaivre, and to those who attended the lectures on that subject and debated

View of the Acropolis, Athens.
Photograph by Frédéric Boissonas.

"You will find a spring on the left of the halls of Hades . . . . In front of it are guards.
You must say, 'I am a child of Gaia and of starry Ouranos . . . I am thirsty and perishing . . .
give me without delay cold water flowing forth from the lake of Memory.'"
Orpheus from Petelia, fourth century B.C.E.

WHY CLASSICAL GREEK ARCHITECTURE TODAY?

"Though they had eyes to see, they saw to no avail; they had ears, but understood not... as in dreams... without purpose they wrought all things in confusion... without knowledge to build brick-houses facing the sun, nor to work in wood... they dwelt... in sunless caves... and made everything without judgment till I taught... numbers... letters... flaxen-winged seafaring vehicles to wander over the ocean." Aeschylus, *Prometheus Bound,* 447–469.

It might seem strange in our age of dramatic change—where identity, diversity, and ecology are key issues, and the emancipation of non-Western cultures is one of the most globally widespread movements—that classical Greek architecture should still be such a gripping subject. Yet it is precisely because we live in a period of such significant change that exploring classical Greek architecture is so compelling, despite its reputation as a conservative, closed, and standardizing system, seeking complicity with the West in its first efforts to establish a global empire.

We bring to this exploration not only a desire to learn about the forms and forces that shaped buildings belonging to a bygone era, but also our concerns and aspirations about how buildings, cities, and landscapes are transforming the physical and social fabric of our lives today. Far from being merely a splendid collection of static monuments, the architecture of Greek antiquity is about creativity, intelligence, and the human ability as a community to construe and construct the world. In this respect, the study of ancient Greek architecture is bound up with heuristics and politics—in the broadest sense of the word—and its long-vanished history may prove to be a most relevant tool for a new way of thinking in our time. Indeed, what makes the study of this subject so very exciting is the fact that the Parthenon *is* our contemporary.

This approach is fraught with paradox and challenge. To be able converse with the Parthenon or Propylaia of the Acropolis of ancient Athens, involving them in the intimacy of our contemporary problems, we have first to be

Olympus.
Photograph by Frédéric Boissonas.

distanced from them. In other words, we have to determine just how different and alien they are, and also to what extent our current perception and memory of these products of antiquity is tainted by reconstructions by intervening generations. Whenever a memory is evoked, it is remodeled by the beliefs and desires that gave rise to it. Thus, we need to be aware that ancient Greek architecture today is perceived through the kaleidoscope of concepts and models pieced together by past researchers who, like us, were driven by the ideas and interests of their time—even if they claimed to view the contribution of ancient Greece outside the confines of a given cultural context.

This is why Oswald Spengler, the German philosopher, mathematician, and great popularizer of the history of culture, saw in Greek architecture only a quality of the serene order of a statue, being "statuesque." Writing as the First World War[1] was coming to an end, he was anxious to grasp the violent, revolutionary, and chaotic events of his time.

Likewise, another German philosopher, in his own anxiety during January 1943[2] about "the planet in flames," emphasized the Greek contribution running parallel to the German mission, both being "people of poets and thinkers" endeaovoring to "save the West"—the uniqueness of "thinking Greekly" being to stand against both the "Orient" and vulgar Western "liberalism." There is a long tradition of this kind of reductive, purist approach to ancient Greek culture, circumscribing it as an "authentic" product of a pure race with an uncontaminated past. Similarly, ancient Greek buildings are often seen as miraculous creations of the genius of a heroic people of Northern descent, from those lands overshadowed by mysterious "snowy Olympus," *nifoendos Olympou*. A standard American scholarly tomeof the 1940s covering the history of architecture[3] describes this event concisely as the "coming of [people] . . . speaking a language which belongs to the Aryan linguistic group, that . . . were blond . . . [having] their own gods . . . and especially a sky god, Zeus . . . The migration . . . seems to have had two chief strains . . . Ionians and . . . Dorians . . . and each created the Doric and Ionic orders."

None of the above interpretations of ancient architecture takes into account the fact that the unique characteristics of the Greek "miracle" lay in the unprecedented level of literacy that allowed not only abstract representation, data storage, and logical thinking, but also the unparalleled processing and exchange of knowledge between groups.[4] Neither do they consider the fact that this miracle was made possible through the introduction of Semitic symbols taken from a foreign people across the sea, the Phoenicians; nor that even the god Zeus,[5] or at least some aspects of his divine identity, originated in the mountains of Palestine. Equally absent is the Greek concept of *polis*—not as an abstract ideal or a physical accumulation of settlements, but as a concrete institution and legal, political mechanism that structured human relations and interactions, largely favoring the fusion rather than the cleansing of cultures and peoples. Finally, they ignore the web of reciprocities and circulation of goods, skills, and theories that the Greeks constructed with other groups through dialogue or conflict.

The Mediterranean.
Photograph by Frédéric Boissonas.

The Mediterranean.
Photograph by Frédéric Boissonas.

However, another approach to Greek culture and, in particular, Greek architecture, will enable us to investigate their emergence and evolution as networks of communities both embedded within a region, and scattered over the "water-washed islands" or coasts of the "wine-dark," *oinopi ponto,* of the Mediterranean Sea. This sea—strictly speaking also including the Black Sea—was more dangerous than the territory of snowy Olympus; on the other hand, it could be easily crossed in "deep blue-bow . . . black hollow ships," thus ensuring that far-flung communities would remain closely interlinked.

In addition to these physical means of enabling Greek communities to expand were the institutional instruments that facilitated deployment while supporting cohesion—the most important of which being the sanctuary of Delphi. According to the *Homeric Hymns To Pythian Apollo,* it was founded by Apollo, who himself laid the foundations of the main temple, and invited "people from all over the world" to come to question him, promising to "give them advice and answers." The sanctuary was located "beneath . . . Parnassus" in a spectacular site—"a foothill turned towards the west: a cliff hanging over it from above, and a hollow, rugged glade running under . . . near by a sweet flowing spring," as the hymn describes it. The physical characteristics of the site helped to launch it as the most important mechanism for instigating and regulating Greek networks—not only because of its imposing sublimity, evoking "feelings of awe and mystery,"[6] but also due to its location, removed from the territorial orbit[7] of already-established communities, with their parochial, vested interests.

While many other activities occurred in Delphi—as well as in Olympia and other more modest sanctuaries—the promotion and maintenance of the web of communities remained a central function. Architecture was a dominant feature in all of these sanctuaries, both as the offspring of this human intercourse and as an enabling agent.

The ancient Greeks themselves would not subscribe to such view. Greek authors did not hesitate to acknowledge the links between their own and foreign cultures, as well as their cultural debts, even after the emergence of an explicit "East-West divide" that occurred with the Persian wars.[8] Even Homer—one of the great architects of Greek identity—in the *Odyssey* refers to the carpenter-builders (*tektona douron*) as men with a craft (*demiourge*), traveling "all over the boundless earth." Technical experts, like the poets, musicians, law makers and early philosophers—the sophists—travelled extensively across the mediterranean. Greek culture and architecture were conceived and constructed by such "cosmopolitan" technicians, who were seldom rooted in one place. It was a situation not dissimilar to that of Paris at the beginning of the twentieth century, New York in the late 1930s and early 1940s, or even Paris at the time of Colbert and Louis XIV.

Most ancient Greeks concerned with cultural politics did not worry unduly about authenticity or being the first to reach a goal in the way that, for example, many Europeans did during the nineteenth century with the rise of the nation states. Ancient Greeks appear to have set greater store by innovation (*kainotomia*), resourcefulness (*polymechania*), and by gaining prowess (*aristeuein*) in a

Aerial view of the Treasury of Athens,
Temple of Apollo and the theater, Delphi. Photographer unknown.

Treasury of the Thebeans: triglyph and metope, Delphi.
Photograph by Georges de Miré.

Treasury of Athens, Delphi.
Photograph by Georges de Miré.

competitive framework. They would not hesitate to extract, recombine, and fuse existing knowledge, whether regional—as in the magnificent Homeric synthesis of linguistic forms drawn from Mycenaean, Aeolic, Ionic, and Attic "theme blocks" fitting into larger metric schemata and formulas—or foreign, as in the epic poetry of the Homeric epoch recruiting motifs and personae from *Enuma* and *Elish Erra*.[9]

Indeed, Herodotus, whose writings included precious descriptions of Egyptian architecture, was attacked by Plutarch as being a "friend of the barbarians" in *De Malignate Herodoti* for his notorious generosity in crediting non-Greeks with the origin of most Greek achievements. However, Plutarch himself in his book *On Music* made explicit reference to such circulation of knowledge in the emergence and early evolution of Greek lyric poetry and music, acknowledging the introduction

of the flute from Asia, the lyre from Thrace, the double-flute from Egypt, and of formal types and schemata in music. He also painstakingly discussed how these imports led to inventions, as in the case of Olympus—both importer to Greece of a new norm, *nomos*, of harmony, and creator of new modes of music within Greece itself. Even Aristotle considered it normal that the craftsmen should be immigrants and non-citizens, and, as their names suggest, the potters and vase painters of Athens were undeniably foreign.[10]

What appeared to worry a significant number of Greeks was the extent to which artists, importers or autochthonous creators—whether authentic or not—were breaking with tradition, thereby constituting a severely punishable act of impiety. Plutarch discusses in his *Spartan Institutions* the case of the great musician Terpander who dared to add a single string to his lyre in Sparta; for this he was

Omphalos (Navel of the Earth), Museum of Delphi.

fined, had his instrument confiscated, and had "the strings that brought the number beyond seven" cut off ceremoniously with a knife. He also tells in the *Life of Pericles* of the prosecution of Phidias for impiety that, even if its political motivations were clear, almost led to Phidias' impeachment. Even intellectuals such as Aristophanes were critical of the admirers of poetical innovation, the *philokainoteroi*, in their violation of the boundaries of traditional harmony, *exarmonious*. The great challenge facing all artists of ancient Greece—architects included—was to maintain a delicate balance between the agonistic urges of their culture and the forces of tradition.[11]

Renovations

Starting with Homer, the Greeks themselves began the rewriting of ancient Greek history. The reconstruction of the architectural past of ancient Greece by the Greeks, with all of the above-mentioned implications of discriminating memory, may have started later, in the Hellenistic period. This was the time of the movement of "antiquarian scholarship," whose legacy included the return of a revised version of the palm capital style in the upper inner columns of the Pergamene Stoae of Athens.

Vitruvius' *On Architecture*, a Latin work by a Roman author, is the earliest text we have that contains extensive passages claiming to state the origins of Greek architecture. Pausanias' *Guide to Greece* and Pliny's *Natural History* also contain historical information. None of these texts was conceived with the idea of writing history as Herodotus, Thucydides, or Plutarch dealt with other subjects. All of these texts had an enormous impact in

View of the Temple of Apollo and the theater, Delphi.
Photograph by Waldemar Deonna.

shaping the perception of Greek architecture, not only by supplying isolated data, but also by developing categories and models through which the overall picture of Greek architecture could be framed.

An event of physical restoration may mark the beginning of modern efforts to reconstruct the architecture of antiquity. Still standing today, close to Ponte Rotto in the midst of ancient Roman ruins, is the Casa dei Crescenzi. A strange building, it is a collage of antique friezes and medieval brick walls, in which are entrenched half columns in the form of an ancient colonnade. Erected in the middle of the twelfth century by Nicolaus Crescenzi,[12] a citizen of Rome aligned with the local popular Republican Party, this hybrid building integrating ancient fragments and design schemes in a modern tower structure was apparently intended to commemorate the victory of the local Roman party over the papacy. Evidence of this is the inscription on the façade in Leonine hexameters: "*Romae veterems renovare decorem.*" From a contemporary architectural point of view, Creszenci's design was imaginative; however, as a "historical reconstruction," it was archaeologically naive. It reveals how ignorant, or perhaps indifferent, even the inhabitants of Rome were at that time with regards to the architecture of antiquity. However, it also manifests the beginnings of *renovatio*, a cultural movement linking a political program of renewal with the image of revival of ancient architecture. This movement has deeper roots. It first appeared around the year 1000, during the Dark Ages in Western Europe when, to quote Giorgio Vasari,[13] "the arts declined by the day to the point that they lost entirely design perfection." "Only formless and inept things" were produced and only buildings that were "rude," "inferior,"

Temple of Hera, Olympia.
Photograph by Frédéric Boissonas.

and "devoid of arrangement," were erected. Nonetheless, the sense of despair and fear that the "death of the human race" had arrived (Focillon, 1969), so predominant during this period, was increasingly coupled with a sense of hope for the rebirth of the world of excellence that was antiquity. This was a belief shared by imperial courts and—as was apparent in the case of Creszenci—regional parties, legitimizing a new political order by identifying it, by analogy, with an old heroic regime. Architecture through "renovation" of ancient structures—known as *renovatio*—played a key role in constructing this identity. Interestingly, a similar movement seems to have appeared in Greek history at the time of Homer, forging a Hellenic identity through reconstruction of the past. Numerous texts followed.

For his limited *renovatio*, Crescenzi cannibalized actual fragments from ancient Roman buildings.

However, for most people around Europe, ancient structures were not immediately available. The only sources at hand for the "program" of *renovatio* were ancient texts; the fundamental conceptual system of the time prescribed adherence to texts, rather than recourse to empirical observation.

Greek texts were available in Western Europe even during the "darkest" years of the Middle Ages. The Muslim invasion disrupted both Eastern and Western trade networks,[14] but did not destroy them.[15] Taking over from the Christians in matters of commerce, it was the Jews who maintained a flow of information, transported manuscripts to Western Europe, and, together with the Arabs, translated ancient Greek texts. Thus, several ancient Greek theoretical works that played an important role in the movement of *renovatio* in architecture—such as Aristotle's *Poetics*, Heron of Alexandria's *Mechanics*, and much of the work of

Plato and the Platonists including Timaeus[16]—were made available in the early Middle Ages.

The most significant text providing direct information on ancient Greek architecture was neither by a Greek, nor written in Greek. As we have already seen, Vitruvius' *On Architecture*, was a true encyclopedia of architectural knowledge with an abundance of information on the design, construction, and functional organization of buildings, cities, machines, and ancient Greek architecture. Seventy-eight of Vitruvius' manuscripts were scattered among the medieval libraries of Cluny, Murbach, Melk, Reichenau, Sankt Gallen, and others,[17] but we know very little how they were consulted, if at all. However, Poggio Bracciolini and Cencio Rustici's "rediscovery" of the Sankt Gallen manuscript circa 1416 was considered one of the most significant events marking the climax of the early phase of *renovatio* and the beginnings of the Renaissance.

Vitruvius' text covered knowledge from philosophy, natural science, physiology, and acoustics to medicine. His ideas were strongly influenced by Lucretius, from whom he inherited a materialist outlook, despite later claims that he foreshadowed Christian cosmology and theology. Vitruvius had a universal appetite for mastering technological and scientific knowledge, which he sought to impart to all architects. Yet he lacked a predilection for history or rhetoric. If he recommended a knowledge of history for architects, it was only for practical purposes to allow them to explain to "inquirers" why they use a certain ornament. Thus, in contrast to Plutarch's work *On Music* that gives a detailed historical account of *armoniai*—"modes," tonal scales, or other kinds of music—Vitruvius' discussion of Doric, Ionic, and Corinthian kinds of architecture provides only sparse speculative or anecdotic references.

His story of the architectural invention of the Corinthian capital has all the ingredients of a memorable legend, even if the text of the narration lacks lyricism. Starting with the observation of a high, slender column, it goes on to explain its conception as imitating the slim figure of a virgin (*virginalis gracilitatis imitationem*) and that it was inspired by a specific virgin from Corinth who had died. Later on, he describes the configuration of the capital as being designed in imitation of the basket containing the unfortunate young girl's favorite playthings, which had been left on the grave after the funeral by her nurse and was covered with acanthus leaves that had sprouted up around it the following spring.

Not only does this moving story encapsulate in one plot three major ideas—life, death and ceaseless renewal—but it is also about poetic creativity inspired by the drawing of unexpected analogies from everyday reality, and the victory of art over death. In addition, there was something "romantic" about the Corinthian capital—the preferred kind of capital of the Romans, as well as of many Western European architects for centuries to come—in that it was the creation of one man, Callimachus, moved by the tragic end of a young girl, "just ready for marriage." In defense of the story, some archaeologists have suggested that Vitruvius based his fable on the most probable historical fact that the Corinthian capital was first applied to funerary votive columns. Others have

Capital of the Tholos of Epidauros, sculpted by Polyclitus the Younger.

associated the Callimachus of the Vitruvian story with the historical figure of a smith working in Athens on the Acropolis in the temple of Erechtheion—the argument being that the form of the Corinthian capital was first cast in iron. However, as we will see later, the dates do not correspond, because the capital appeared earlier in Bassai, and Vitruvius himself clearly states that Callimachus worked as a marble carver (*artis marmorae*).

Equally ahistorical is the Vitruvian explanation of the form and proportions of other kinds of Greek architecture, which he based on anthropomorphic analogies. The same is true of his rationalization of the members and details of the Doric temple, designed as imitating (*imitatione*) in stone earlier forms of carpentry construction. Vitruvius analyzed in great detail the pros and cons of the details of the triglyphs—the vertical bands of the Doric frieze—being imitations in sculpture of

windows within a post-and-lintel timberwork. His arguments are highly convincing because he constructed them with the same standard of rigor and rationality that he brought to the construction of buildings. His plan, stated in the preface of the Fourth Book of his text, was to reduce architectural knowledge to "a perfect order" (*perfectam ordinationem*), and thereby define the order of the organization of buildings within which nothing was allowed to float "inchoate like atoms," and where everything followed on rationally and intentionally (*inventa ratio, habet rationem*). Being a materialist empiricist, he believed that artifacts should be modeled on nature (*naturae deducta*), rather than invented subjectively. What cannot happen in nature, he declared, may not be obtained by force in a designed product. Vitruvius argued rationally as a designer, but he did not pay attention to historical considerations. The path that history took was much more intricate, torturous, full of trial and error, and at times—like the wanderings of Odysseus—less logical in its adventures. The knowledge of such a path may be more relevant for us today than the reductive short cuts of probing reconstructions of the past.

Vitruvius' intentions, when writing his *Ten Books on Architecture*, were very different from those of Herodotus, Thucydides, or Plutarch in their historical writings. Vitruvius's goal was immediate and practical: to construct a canon based on rationality (*disciplinae rationes*) capable of serving the "huge scale" construction program of the new empire. We do not know precisely how successful he was during his life. However, the influence of his *On Architecture* on the development of the theory

Hephaisteion, Athens.
Photograph by Walter Hege.

Corner of the Parthenon, triglyph.
Photograph by Czako.

Parthenon architrave, east side.
Photographer unknown.

and methodology of architecture since the Renaissance was enormous. Any historical shortcomings and the way of glossing over the exchanges between regions and ethnic groups[18] that generated the various types of plans and kinds of architectural members were irrelevant to this success. Interestingly, the only time that Vitruvius discusses in detail the relation between building and its environment is when he deals with the "regional kinds" of building (genera aedificiorum) to be found in a region (regionum) as products of the different physical conditions and climate[19]—the North dictating one extreme type of architecture, the South another extreme, and the "temperate" region (the superior area inhabited by the Romans), a superior architecture. From this he drew the conclusion that the Romans legitimately ruled the world (terrarium imperii).

Finally, Vitruvius treated the Doric, Ionic, and Corinthian kinds of architecture—which he calls genera—as independent entities in the Aristotelian sense of species, gene,[20] characterized by primary characteristics like members, mele parts, mere, and secondary characteristics such as shape. Vitruvius developed a similar conceptual structure with membris and partis, and proceeded to deal with their characteristic attributes by focusing on the relationship between them, which accounts for the terms proportion and symmetry employed. Gradually, as we move towards the nineteenth century, the analogy between "natural kinds" and Vitruvian genera preserved in modern times in Italian and French translations was to disappear, with the concept of genera being translated as that of the "orders of architecture."

As we will see later, the Aristotelian-Vitruvian analogy appeared to provide an extremely accurate reflection of the conceptual system of architecture developed by the ancient Greeks. However, it failed to capture the interaction between the kinds of architecture within the framework of a system. This system of spatial intelligence, one of the great inventions of Greek architecture that was to have enormous repercussions in the future, lies beyond the Aristotelian paradigm of the "natural kinds."

Vitruvius' influence is felt today because, with the exception of the mainly descriptive texts by Pausanias and Pliny, none of the vast number of ancient Greek texts has survived. Vitruvius himself, in the preface to the seventh book of his treatise, acknowledged his debt to the writings of Greek authors now lost: Agatharchus, Democritus, and Anaxagoras on perspective; Silenus on Doric proportions; Rhoecus and Theodoros on the Ionic temple of Hera at Samos; Chersiphron and Metagenes on the Ionic temple of Diana at Ephesus; Pythios on the Ionic temple of Athena at Priene; Iktinos and Carpion on the Doric temple of Athena on the Acropolis at Athens; Theodoros of Phocaia on the Tholos at Delphi; Philo on the proportions of temples and the arsenal in the harbor of Piraeus; Hermogenes on the pseudodipteral Ionic temple of Diana at Magnesia and the monopteral temple of Dionysos at Teos; Arcesius on Corinthian proportions and the Ionic temple of Asclepius at Tralles, and Pythios on the Mausoleum. This was a long list of authors and Vitruvius stressed that there were also other "less famous" authors who wrote important books on "symmetry" and "machinery" that he did not list.

It would appear that Greek architects, in contrast to the Romans, developed their thinking and promoted their work via writing, employing their rhetorical capabilities to the full. Cicero in *De oratore* refers to Philo, the architect of the Arsenal of Athens, not only as having written about "the theory of his work," but as having done so with great eloquence—a considerable compliment coming from one of the greatest experts of rhetoric in history. Since none of these Greek writings has survived, we are grateful to Vitruvius for having preserved at least some of this knowledge. However, it is difficult to assess to what extent we can rely on Vitruvius' text to find out what these lost writings contained. Not only he was removed chronologically by several centuries from the period of so-called Classical Greek architecture, but his knowledge of Greek was also fairly limited. In addition, contrary to Philo, Vitruvius was a not an eloquent writer. Indeed, he brought Alberti—the great theoretician and architect of the Renaissance—to the point of despair, declaring that Vitruvius' writings only led to confusion and that it would have been better for those interested in the architecture of antiquity if he had not written at all.[21]

Unlike Vitruvius, Alberti was deeply involved with the theory of rhetoric and had an excellent knowledge of the Greek authors available at that time. Nevertheless, there was very little he could improve upon in the history or theory of ancient Greek architecture, which he believed had its beginnings in Asia and was "brought to perfection in Italy." Like most of the authors of the Renaissance, he did not care to differentiate between Greek and Roman architecture, but bundled both together under the name "ancients." Moreover, he had an additional reason not to recommend Vitruvius. Interested in improving the state of architecture of his time, he was in search of concrete rules of design that he thought could be more safely extracted by studying and documenting the precedents of successful buildings of the past.

However, given the limited means of representation then available, and what for us today are idiosyncratic standards of exactness[22] in copying a building,[23] it was very hard to document ancient monuments in as useful a manner as Alberti desired. This becomes clear in a rare early visual record of ancient Greek architecture in the drawings by one of Alberti's contemporaries, Cyriaco D'Ancona.

Cyriaco was a merchant born in 1391 in Ancona, an Italian city claiming to have been a Dorian colony. At the time of Cyriaco, the city still adhered to the strange tradition of commemorating its Greek ancestry with an annual parade of foreign slaves through its streets to present offerings at the old acropolis. Cyriaco traded in Greek wine, carpets, precious stones, and young slaves between Italy and the Ottoman Empire. He himself lived with a young Greek slave. However, he was also involved in the commerce of ancient medallions, statuettes, and most importantly manuscripts. Cyriaco ended up keeping many of these manuscripts, including one by Vitruvius. During these trips, he took extensive notes, copied ancient Greek inscriptions, corresponded often in ancient Greek with friends, and sketched ancient Greek

Drawing of Parthenon façade.
After Cyriaco D'Ancona.

buildings. Cyriaco visited many historical Greek sites—Delos, Paros, Delphi, Corinth, and Athens twice, in 1436 and 1444—staying in the Propylaia, transformed into an Italian palazzo. Most of these documents, comprising six volumes entitled *Commentaries,* were destroyed by fire in 1514. The few that have survived include a sketch of the Parthenon and a copy of one of his drawings on the same subject, made by Giuliano da Sangallo, now lost.

Two major illustrated treatises of the Renaissance—the *Treatise on Architecture* (1451–64), by Antonio Averlino, known as Filarete (c. 1400–69), the first architectural treatise written in a modern language, and the *Treatises on Civil and Military Architecture* (c.1474–82) by Francesco di Giorgio Martini (1439–1501)—continued to provide drawings of canonical columns and capitals based on the authority of Vitruvius' text, rather than on the documentation of real buildings. They perpetuated Vitruvius' claims about the origin of the configuration of the ancient Greek stone temple from the primitive wooden building. Moreover, following imperatives to construct a syncretist culture synthesizing Christian doctrines with the writings of antiquity, they reinterpreted, amplified, and applied Vitruvius' proportions of the Doric, Ionic, and the Corinthian styles of architecture as derived from the model of the human body.

Perhaps no other book of the Renaissance supplied a more total and vivid vision of the political-cultural *renovatio* than the lavishly illustrated *Hypnerotomachia Poliphili.* Reusing information provided by the drawings of Cyriaco D'Ancona and the universe of ancient texts available at that time, the book (published in 1499 and completed in 1467) was signed by a mysterious Francesco Collona. Recently attributed by Liane Lefaivre to Alberti, it employed approximately thirty thousand Greek words and provided a cornucopia of images of a new way of life—a model for the courts of the time. The book offered a reinterpretation of Greek culture and architecture, in contrast to medieval models with emphasis on sensual gratification, luxury, and aesthetics. This was an image of antiquity that dominated Europe up until the time of

The five kinds of architecture.
After Serlio, 1537.

Winckelmann in the nineteenth century and, to some extent, still persists today.

Very different is the image of antiquity in the 1511 edition by Cesare Cesariano[24] (1483–1543) of the original text by Vitruvius, accompanied by a wealth of illustrations, a translation (the first into a modern language), and commentaries approximately ten times longer than the text itself.[25] While paying constant tribute to Vitruvius's authority, Cesariano in his lengthy commentary took countless liberties to demonstrate the universality of architectural rules, such as presenting the ground plan and façade of the late medieval Gothic cathedral of Milan as an example of classical Vitruvian composition. On the other hand, because of his profound humanistic knowledge of ancient texts (a member of the erudite Milanese group), his theory of architecture was the best qualified for reconstructing the architectural thinking of antiquity. Characteristically he was the first to draw a diagram of architectural styles, placing them in line, and was also a pioneer in the development of an explicit representation of the partitioning of the ancient temple, absent from Vitruvius. Sebastiano Serlio (1475–1564) in his *Books on Architecture* (1537–75),[26] the first work to exploit the possibilities of new techniques of graphic representation and mass printing in architecture, repeated the idea of aligning in the same table the different kinds of architecture, which he called "manners" or "orders." Applying a uniform scale to all columns to enable their comparative analysis, he arranged them from left to right, from the strongest to the lightest, thereby expressing unequivocally the order of the styles of architecture

first invented in Greece. However, the text lumped Greeks and Romans together under the name "ancients"—a custom that was to continue until the seventeenth century.

Even with these innovations, Serlio was severely criticized by the next generation as being too servile to the authority of Vitruvius. Andrea Palladio[27] (1508–1580) and his student Scamozzi began to demand a return to the "source of the Orders," the original buildings, in what Frear de Chambray (1650) in France called "the best book available on the subject." A significant moment in the history of the documentation of ancient monuments occurred when Colbert,[28] eager to establish normative rules of architecture—preferably based on the precedent of the "ancients"—for the building program of Louis XIV he directed, and losing patience with the endless debates of the architects, decided to send Antoine Desgodetz (1653–1728) to Rome to record, compare, and to identify these norms if they existed. Applying new techniques of documentation, it did not take Desgodetz long to succeed in recording a large number of buildings. His findings were published in 1682 in *Les Édifices antiques de Rome,* together with his observations that previous authors, influenced by Vitruvius, had been mistaken in their claims that such universal norms existed in ancient buildings. Indeed, there was no mention of the Greeks in this record. The evidence supplied, however, was thought to be sufficient to support theories, such as those by Claude Perrault (1613–1688)[29]. Perrault had already pointed out in his comments on Vitruvius that the proportions of the Corinthian capital considered beautiful by the

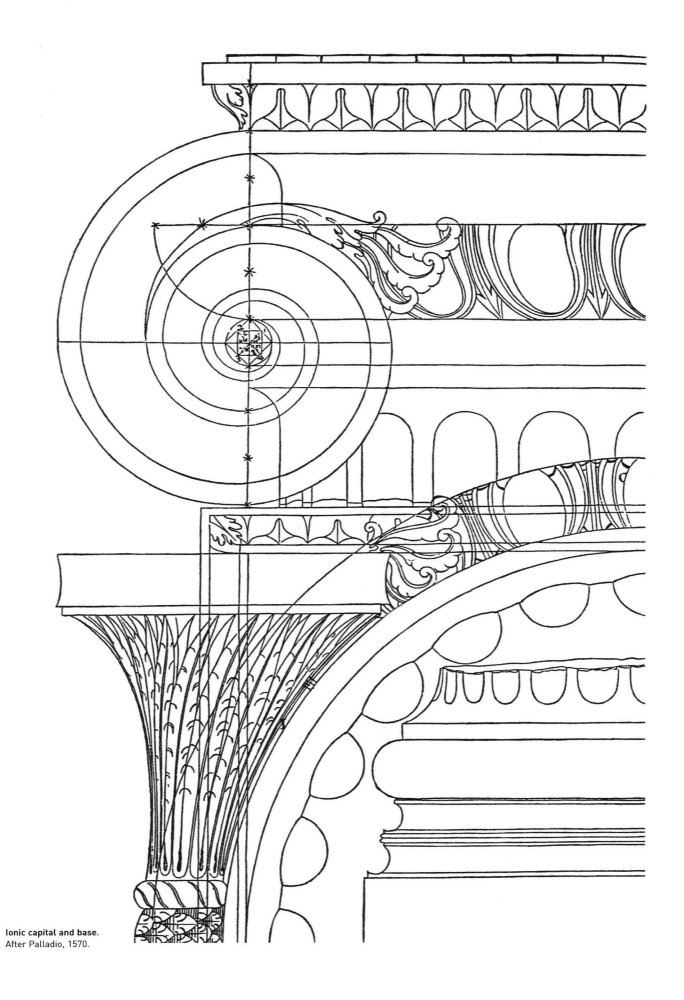

Ionic capital and base.
After Palladio, 1570.

Greeks (the height being equivalent to the diameter of one column), was not approved by the Romans, who increased the column diameter by one-sixth. He could now assert with confidence that there were no universal rules of architecture based on nature, namely the human body as Vitruvius suggested, or, Villalpando's belief that it was God who instructed the architects of Solomon's Temple in the proportions to be used, which were then passed on to the Greeks, who are credited with this invention.

The "new humanism"

The Colbert-Desgodetz-Perrault program shifting the focus from literary sources to material evidence and empirical data, and distinguishing between first and secondary sources marked the beginning of a period of rogorous studies of antiquity that Armaldo Momigliano called "the new humanism," as opposed to the traditional ideas of the Renaissance. A campaign to carry out a similar study of ancient Greek architecture was to follow about a century later. This was initiated by a young French architect, Julien David Le Roy (1724–1803) in 1755.[30] Following similar methods to those of Desgodetz in Rome, he completed his documentation in Athens in less than three months and was back in Paris to present the results to the Académie Royale d'Architecture and prepare his publication by 1758, revised 1770. His rivals, Nicholas Revett (1720–1804), and James Stuart (1713–1788), who had started their research earlier and had more stringent standards of exactitude, though less enthusiastic supporters than Le Roy, published their results four years after him.[31]

Like Desgodetz in Rome, when confronted with the richness of the actual buildings in Greece, Le Roy had become critical of the normative, rationalist approach of Vitruvius.[32] "Vitruvius determines on the basis of truth the number of columns that each type of temple must bear on its façade"— in other words, by reasoning only—"but one still finds in Greece a great number of examples that prove that the architects of this nation did not subject themselves to it in a servile way . . . this prodigious difference in proportions . . . produced very striking varieties in the massing of the buildings and in the character of the façades." Stressing the variety of the temples that the Greeks designed he added: "If one considers the temples that still stand in Greece and in different parts of Asia, one will recognize that in each kind of temple . . . the masses vary significantly."

Gradually, from being classified under the general label of "ancients," the architecture of ancient Greece began to distinguish itself from that of Rome. This was the result not only of the accumulation of more exact data about Greek buildings, but also of emerging desires to criticize the political and cultural situation of absolutist Europe, with architecture serving once again as a kind of metaphor. By the end of the seventeenth century, the critical spirit of *renovatio* had returned, with the uncorrupted ideal being this time the architecture of early ancient Greece. Yet again the act of remembering a moment in history involved its reinterpretation, reconstruction, and alteration.

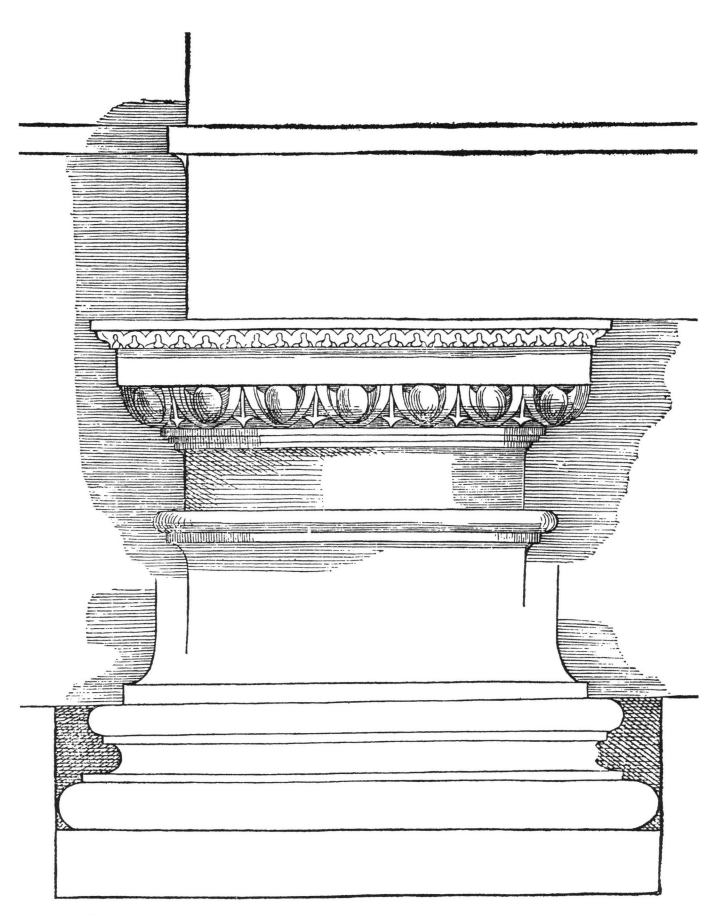

Doric capital and base.
After Martin, 1547.

The ancient Greek "ideal" was defined as true, natural, and pure, as opposed to the prevailing dishonesty, artifice and corruption of the time. The movement first appeared in literature around the year 1700. François de Salignac de la Mothe Fénelon (1651–1715), in his *Adventures de Télémaque* (1699),[33] represented "Calypso's grotto" as "a scene of rustic simplicity... where there was no gold, nor silver, nor marble, nor columns, nor paintings, nor statues to be seen." thereby censuring the absolutist practices of Louis XIV, in particular as apparent in his court in Versailles. Telemachus, the honest hero in search of justice and retribution in a corrupt environment enters the ideal city of Mentor, where "Mentor... prohibited... luxury and sloth.... [and] restricted the use of architectural ornament... to temples;... prescrib[ing] models for a simple and gracious architecture... [whereby] every house... should have a small peristyle, ... severely prohibiting superfluous ornament and magnificence in these dwellings."

Fénelon's Homer is referred to as a contemporary, remembered and revised to fit the aspirations of a renewal through *renovatio.* The same is true of Alexander Pope (1731) and Shaftesbury (1731), who, in a similar way, chose architecture as a metaphor for their vision of a new culture and morals. Like Fénelon's Homeric "rustic simplicity," they suggested an extreme situation within which buildings were absent and only the *Genious of the Place* (1711)[34] "at last prevailed... things of a natural kind, where neither art nor the conceit or caprice of man... has spoiled their genuine order... the horrid graces of the wilderness itself... more engaging... [than] the formal mockery of princely gardens." In fact, even the "primitivism" of the "apostle" of nature, Jean-Jacques Rousseau, owes as much to Homer and ancient Greek tragedy, as it does to accounts about newly discovered "savages."[35]

In the same vein of *renovatio,* Homeric primitivism combined with Vitruvius' account of the development of architecture passing from the discovery of the cave as shelter to finding "some fallen branches... raising, and... arranging them in a square," as Marc-Antoine Laugier (1713–1769) wrote in his *Essai* (1753)[36]. Thus Laugier concluded, "man is housed... Such is the course of simple nature... All splendors of architecture (including the ancient temples)... have been modeled on the little rustic hut." Francesco Milizia (1725–1798) identified even more directly "the only architecture which is true and reasoned with simplicity and prudence" with "Greek architecture, for the Greeks only imitated the *hut.*"[37]

Johann Winckelmann also shared the vision of Greek architecture as natural, simple, and honest. Winckelmann devoted his life to Classical antiquity and, being the first historian to draw a sharp distinction between Greek art and its Roman copies, contributed much to the rise of Greek revival architecture. Winckelmann's distinction was based on what he thought to be the Greek preference for "noble simplicity and quiet grandeur," in contrast to the "degenerate Roman versions."[38] He believed that after ancient Greece everything "went into decline," because "appearance was put before substance" and the "architects who could neither equal nor surpass their predecessors in beauty, tried to look richer . . . by applying decoration." By this, he meant not only a vague expression of cultural degeneration, but also purely stylistic decline in a technically definable sense.

A strong preference for ancient Greek architectural style isolated from social criticism and reformist ideals prevailed before the end of the *ancien régime*. A generation before the French revolution, ancient Greek architecture swept over Paris as pure *fashion*, in a way similar to the triumph of the counterculture during the end of the 1960s in the United States and Western Europe. To quote Jean-François Blondel[39] (1705–1774), "square forms whose corners are so offensive . . . and impede the movements of persons . . . in our places of residence . . . the excuse is used that these shapes are in imitation . . . of the Greeks, without reflecting that they employed them only in their Temples or in the exterior decoration." Even more critical was Baron Friedrich Melchior Grimm (1723–1859)[40] in his observations that "for some years now . . . everything is made in the Greek manner . . . the exterior and interior . . . of buildings, furniture, materials, jewels . . . there is nothing in Paris at the moment that is not in the Greek style. Taste has gone from architecture to the shops of our vendors of fashions; our ladies all have hair styled in the Greek way, our dandies would think it disgraceful if the snuff box they carried were not after the Greek manner." It was indeed a "revolution" to quote again the baron, leading to "corruption and fall."

Reacting against this trend, the eminent British architect William Chambers questioned the wisdom of spending money on expeditions to document Greek architecture, warning that this emphasis on studying sources while neglecting more sophisticated forms of art and products of a more advanced and richer nation—namely, those of the Romans—could be even dangerous, with the "deformities" of "Greek buildings" penetrating English architecture. An even more outspoken opponent of the Greek *renovatio* movement was Giovanni Battista Piranesi (1720–1778)[41] who, anticipating the nineteenth-century romantics, declared, "the law . . . imposed of doing nothing but what is Grecian, is indeed very unjust. Must the Genius of our artists be so basely enslaved to the Grecian manners, as not to dare to take what is beautiful elsewhere, if it be not of Grecian manners, not of Grecian origin?"

Others like Laugier,[42] twelve years after the publication of his *Essai* in 1765, tried to find a way out of what was increasingly perceived as a "tyranny," with unforeseen consequences suggesting "the possibility of a New Order of Architecture" and declaring that "it would be humiliating to think that the Greeks have the exclusive privilege of inventing the orders of architecture. Why other nations would be forbidden to get involved in the quarry that the Greeks first exploited."

Perhaps, the most passionate and extreme attack on the movement of Greek *renovatio* came from young Goethe (1749–1832), when he was just nineteen years old.[43] Contrary to Chambers and Piranesi, Goethe's reaction was not about style. Moreover, Goethe wholeheartedly supported the aspirations of his time to renew culture by returning to the honesty and simplicity of the dawn of history; however, he refused the myth that had become history identifying the Greek temple with the primitive hut and turning it into a prototype for a new architecture. "The primitive hut is not Greek," he affirmed, "the world's first-born . . . is an invention much more primeval." Indeed, a century earlier, Sir Christopher Wren (1632–1723) in his *Tracts on Architecture* (1670s) had already argued that "the Orders are not only Roman and Greek, but Phoenician, Hebrew, and Assyrian."

In this debate, both friends and foes of ancient Greek architecture approached it as a collection of end products, and not as a historical phenomenon. However, this was not the case of Goethe fourteen years after the publication of his early text. Goethe regretted his youthful emotional outburst, but retained the idea of a "primeval" original work from the earlier essay. Expanding on this thought, he began to inquire into the problem of genesis of form in nature and culture prefiguring later theories of natural evolution. In pursuit of this idea, in 1786 he traveled to Southern Italy, searching "in the gardens of Sicily" for "insight into botanical matters" to discover the "primal vegetable," as he reported in his *Letters from Italy,* characteristically subtitled *Auch in Arcadien.* We do not know if it was the quest for "primeval" form in architecture that prompted him to visit the ancient Greek temples of southern Italy, but he recorded that the view of the gardens of Sicily reminded him of "the happy island of the Phaecians" and made him "rush out to buy a copy of Homer."

Furthermore, Francesco Milizia, in one of his last and most polemical texts, *The Art of Seeing in the Fine Arts* (c. 1810), written to point out the potential failures and open possibilities in art to the people of the young French republic, warned of the dangers in taking ancient Greece as a model based on false history, such as in the "enthusiastic effusions" by writers like Winckelmann and Mengs. These writers, he wrote, imagined the Greeks as "a people favored by . . . climate and the beauty of its individuals . . . exposed to so many nudes . . . their artists became expert at recalling and recreating beautiful forms. The truth is far from these exaggerated opinions. The maidens of Lacedemonia danced . . . in the public squares. But were these ever a meeting place for Greek artists?" Milizia considered equally fabricated the claims that the Venus de Milo was "modeled . . . on the [Greek] wives," while these women actually "lived in retreat-like conditions" similar to "a Turkish harem," or the ideas, in vogue during the end of the eighteenth century, that "the Spartans, [a] nation of soldiers laboring under the thumb of an austere and almost monastic regime . . . produced the great Greek artists."

Winckelmann never traveled to Greece and his passion for Greek culture, like many of his contemporary philhellenes, had more to do with the repulsion he felt for his contemporary world, which, to paraphrase Heine, "had exiled its Gods," or which, according to an apocryphal story, caused Hölderlin to perceive being Greek as the opposite of being Germans.[44] Winckelmann would have expanded this to include the eighteenth-century French along with the German.[45] Others, however, closer to our time, have added the African, the Semitic, and the Oriental. Today given the rigor of archaeological and historical research, it

Erectheion, Acropolis, Athens. Detail, west elevation.

is harder than ever before to propose and perpetuate such forged reconstructions of the past—even if they are driven by the noblest spiritual aspirations.

Worldmaking

Has there been any progress? Do we know the Greeks any better now than at the time of Vitruvius, Fénelon, or Winckelmann? Are we any better at handling Greek architectural heritage than the previous generations of *renovatio*?

We probably do know more about the Greeks today than in the past. This is not merely because we have more data and are better able to analyze them, but because we care more about who they were and how they lived their lives than at any other time in the past. We come closer to them as we recognize the distance that lies between us.

Furthermore, we know that this distance will never be fully bridged—not because we are destined to be different, but because some fragments of what it meant to be an ancient Greek have been lost irrevocably. The process of erasing is irreversible. No scientific reconstruction will ever provide a contemporary audience with the sense of political passion evoked by the Parthenon, the fear of *miasma* born of the idea of a criminal trespassing a *temenos*, or the exhilaration brought about "from a minute calculation," the smallest detail, *to para micron*, of the profile of the capital of the temple of Athena at Tegea by Skopas.

Why should it matter that the inability to recall such experiences authentically will always make us removed from the ancient Greeks in some respects, when there is so much that can be recovered in concrete reality rather than abstract identity to unite us?

Perhaps more valuable than the shapes and

Erectheion, Acropolis, Athen. Detail, west elevation.

patterns of the cornucopia of ancient Greek buildings is the process of cognitive "*co-revolution*"—the new ways of parallel crossover, recombination, and adaptation of architectural knowledge from Greek and non-Greek regions that brought about a new system of spatial intelligence. This was a creative process, similar to the systematization that took place in Greek music, poetry, and religion, where Pandemonium was transformed into the twelve gods of Olympus, as the research of Jean Pierre Vernan and his collaborators has shown. Common to all these cases was the construction of striking new conceptual tools for, what Nelson Goodman called, "world making," or what Bruno Snell referred to as the "the discovery of mind."[46] This may then explain why ancient Greek structures—even in scattered fragmentary form—remain so very moving and exciting, thereby implying the system of spatial intelligence that itself gave rise to them.

Approaching ancient Greek architecture as a process of emergence and an outcome of a network of interactions has immediate implications for how to begin and end the inquiry. At what point does Greek architecture start to be Greek? Where does it stop? Rather than becoming entangled in intractable problems of criteria and endless regress, our approach will be to commence in the middle of the story: the moment when ancient Greek architecture emerged as "Classical," and when the relations between the different kinds of architecture—rather than the identity of individual kinds—came to dominate architectural thinking.

Temple of Apollo at Phigaly-Bassai.
Photograph by Walter Hege.

"If one does not expect the unexpected, one will not discover it."
Heraclitus, fragment 18

"Trial is the beginning of wisdom."
Alcman

CHAPTER I

THE TEMPLE OF APOLLO AT BASSAI

On April 22, 1811, a farewell party took place aboard the ship *Hydra* harbored in Piraeus. The ship belonged to Lord Elgin, whose name has been notoriously linked with the removal of the Parthenon sculptures and their acquisition by the British Museum in 1816. The host was the renowned poet, revolutionary, and adventurer Lord Byron. The guests were a mixed group of artists and architects from Northern Europe, all sharing a common passion for the world of ancient Greece, its ideals, history, and culture. However, as with Cyriaco D'Ancona, as we saw earlier, this desire for knowledge was combined with pecuniary motivation, in the discovery, extraction, and selling of Greek antiquities. The day after the party, Byron's guests were due to continue their voyage to the island of Aigina. Their intention was to study the temple of Aphaia, as well as to take away and sell its sculptures and decorations. Three months later, having succeeded in this task, almost the same group turned its attention to another monument of Greek antiquity: Apollo's temple located in a remote part of legendary Arcadia, Bassai.

Surrounded by mountains, the temple of Apollo Epikourios stands at a height of 3,711 feet (1,131 meters), at a place called Bassai, facing north on one of the western terraces of the Arcadian Mount Cotilion, part of the larger Lykaion mountain. Most of the information we have about the temple has come down to us from Pausanias who visited it in the second century; unfortunately, this information raises more questions than it gives answers. Pausanias mentions that the temple was dedicated to Apollo the Helper, because the god "turned away a pestilence there" as he did "in Athens during the Peloponnesian War," thereby saving the local community. This is, however, a dubious explanation for some contemporary scholars and provides no information as to why this particular location was chosen, "five miles away from the city" of Phygalia.

While Pausanias informs us that the architect of the temple was Iktinos, he fails to tell us why and how Phygalia—only a small town in Arcadia—was able to commission this most prestigious man, "contemporary of Perikles and architect

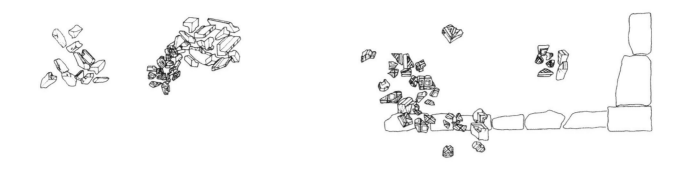

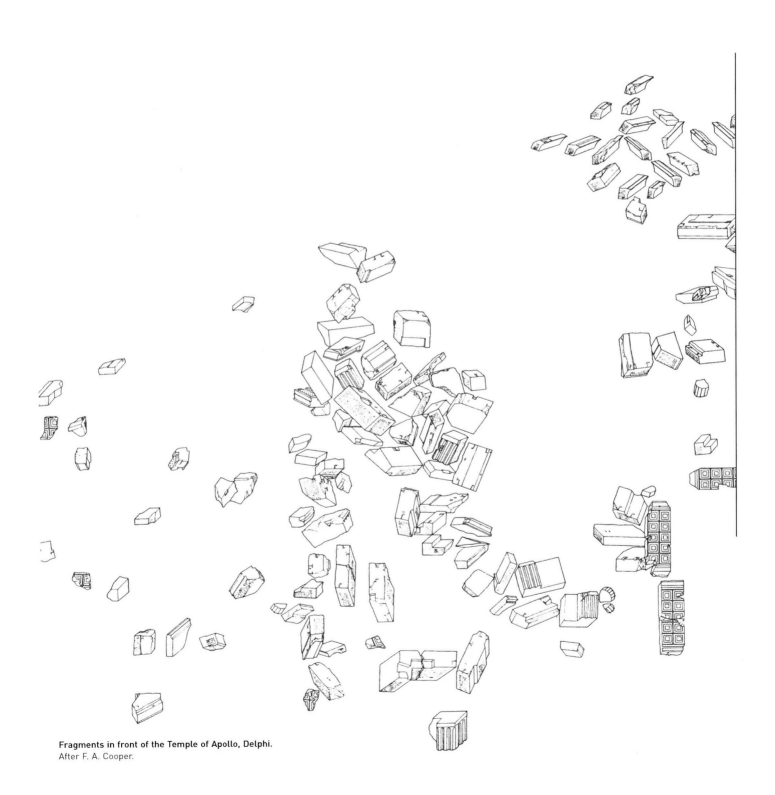

Fragments in front of the Temple of Apollo, Delphi.
After F. A. Cooper.

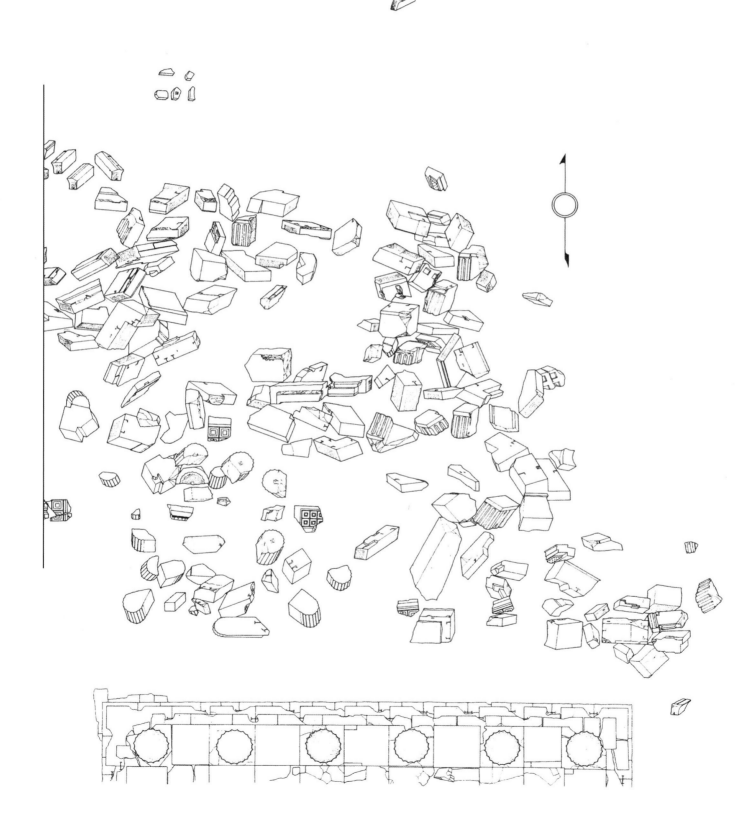

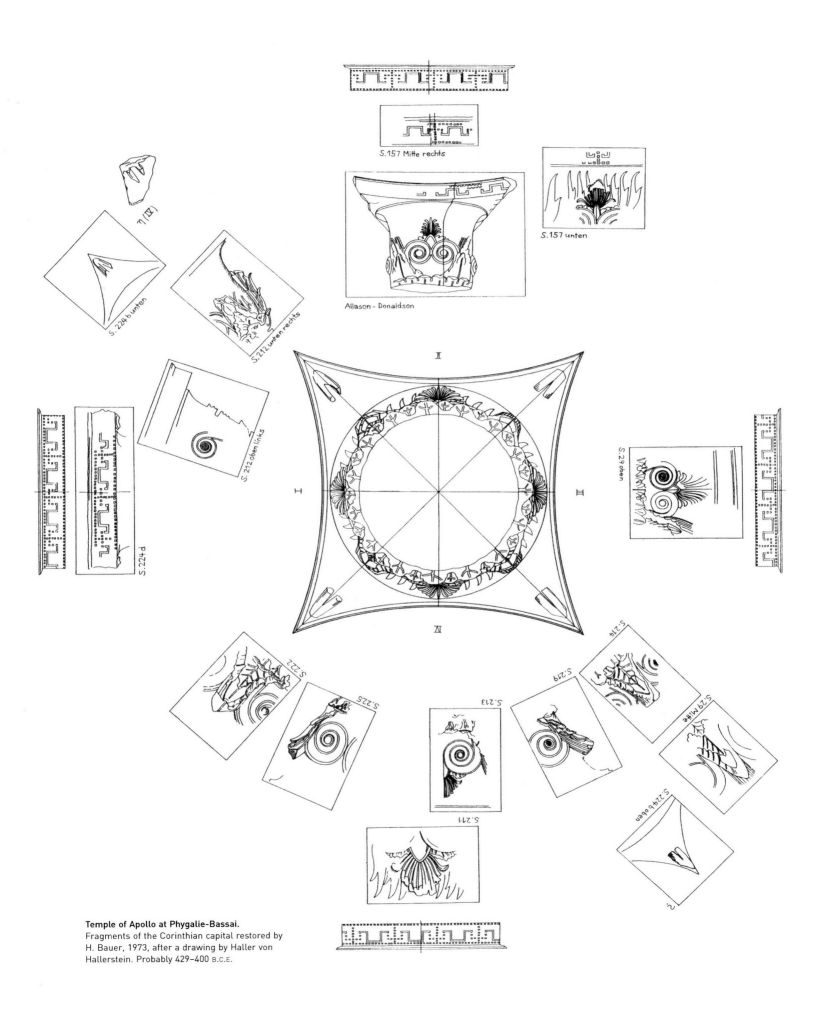

Temple of Apollo at Phygalie-Bassai.
Fragments of the Corinthian capital restored by
H. Bauer, 1973, after a drawing by Haller von
Hallerstein. Probably 429–400 B.C.E.

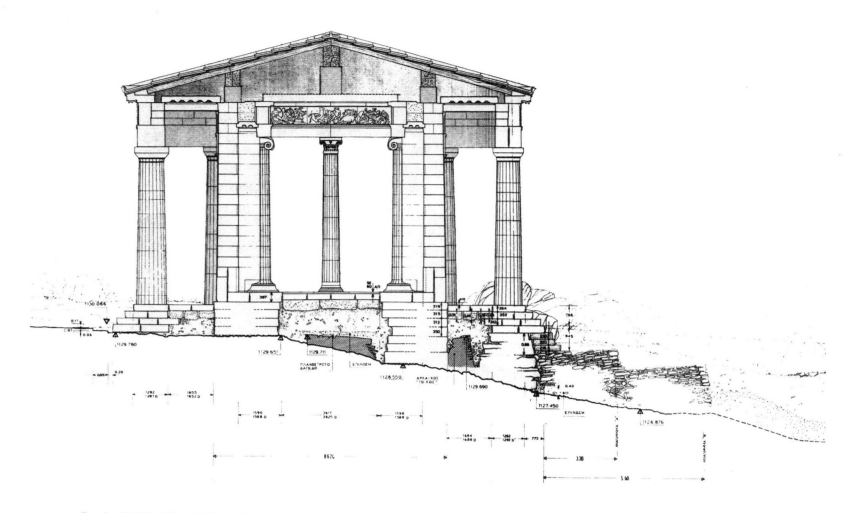

Temple of Apollo at Phygalie-Bassai. Restored cross-section with foundation looking towards the Adyton and the Corinthian column.
Studied by D. Svolopoulos, drawn by D. Koliadis.

of the Parthenon of Athens" and of the Telesterion at Eleusis. Pausanias' claim about the involvement of Iktinos implies that the building dated from the Periklean period, but he provides no evidence to support this. Thus the puzzle for contemporary scholars: Did the building that ingeniously fuses architectural archaisms with unprecedented innovations in its design, thereby giving it a strange dual conservative-revolutionary identity, have two different architects—one for the early part and another for the later? Did Iktinos start his career with the Parthenon, 447–438 b.c.e., and end it in Arcadia with the temple at Bassai 429–c. 400 b.c.e.? We know next to nothing about Iktinos.[47] His name—amusingly like Le Corbusier's—meant in Greek "kite," a bird of the hawk family. Was he perhaps a born a slave? In ancient Greece, slaves could be architects, and typical slave names were nouns for animals, birds, placenames, heroes, or adjectives denoting human traits. Was it a nickname? Was Callimachus, the man Vitruvius credited in a quasi-anecdotic way as the inventor of the Corinthian capital, and Pausanias as the designer of a golden lamp for the Erechtheion, involved in the design of a unique Corinthian capital in this temple?

Pausanias pays tribute to the temple's exceptional roof "made out of stone" exclusively; in fact, the ceiling employed wooden beams. Furthermore, he praises it as being "of all the temples in Peloponnesus, next to the one at Tegea . . . first for the beauty of its stone and the harmony of its proportions."[48] Yet he remains silent about the pioneering combination of columns—Doric outside, Ionic inside—and the appearance of this Corinthian column in the middle of the interior of the temple as a historical breakthrough that was to have an enormous worldwide impact on architecture for centuries to come.

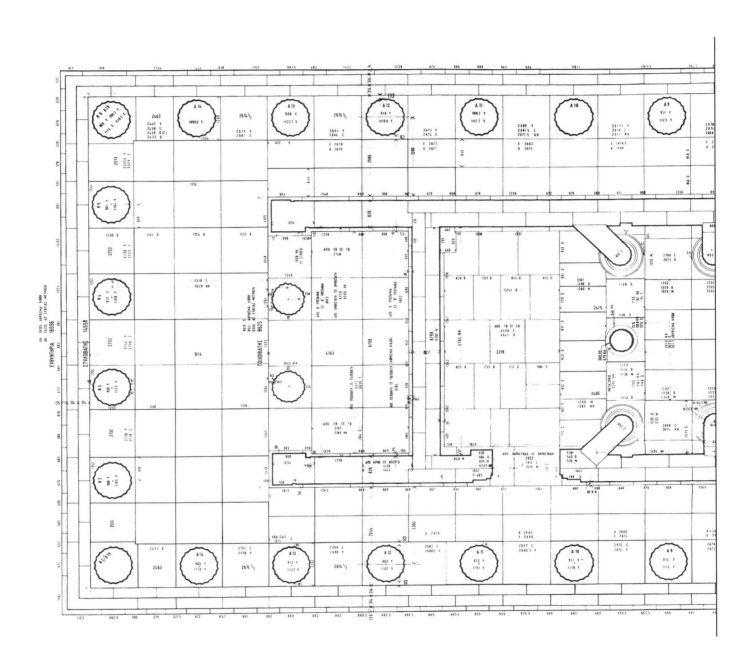

Temple of Apollo at Phygalie-Bassai. Restored plan.
Studied by D. Svolopoulos, drawn by B. Trizonis.

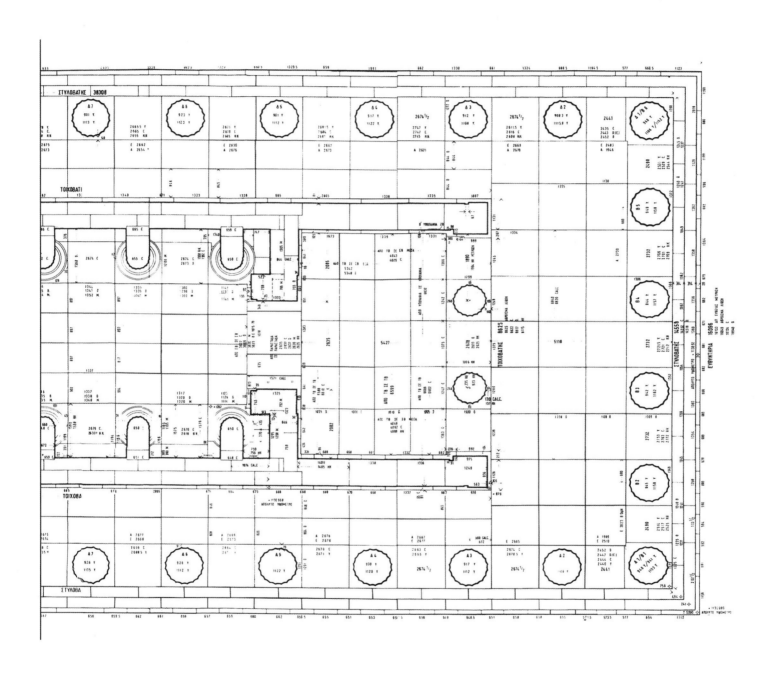

The temple remained forgotten for centuries, and it was not until November 1765 that the French architect Joachim Bocher, traveling around the Peloponnesus, reached this isolated mountainous area to discover the ruins. Bocher, apparently fascinated with his find, returned to the spot to study the monument in more detail—only to be murdered by robbers. Half a century after this tragic event, Byron's friends were more fortunate when they visited the temple. The group included Charles Robert Cockerell (1788–1863), Carl Haller von Hallerstein (1774–1817), John Foster (1787–1846), and Jacob Lynckh (1787–1841). They knew that the temple was fairly intact, with thirty-six of its thirty-eight columns still standing, which offered the opportunity to examine one more specimen of the legendary Greek Doric architecture, so different from the architecture of the Romans and about which Western Europeans still knew very little at the time. However, apart from the opportunities for study the temple offered, they were also attracted by the opportunities for profit offered by the sculptures of its frieze buried under the ruins of the collapsed roof. With the exception of Cockerell, and accompanied by other Northern Europeans, Byron's guests returned the following year to carry out the excavations and remove the frieze.

The work began on July 9, 1812, with approximately sixty Arcadian shepherds hired to assist in the manual work. Many areas of the temple had been dismantled, as the locals had helped themselves, removing the metallic clamps that held together the stones and putting them to new uses, such as making pots and pans. Moreover, there were many such joints—perhaps because of the desire of

the architect to secure the building against earthquakes that are frequent in that region. The columns had been spared because the peasants had apparently found that the drums contained only wooden joints and no iron. The experience of the Northerners was not unpleasant. They lived in huts surrounding a communal tent and used blocks of stone from the temple for their needs. On days of celebration, dances took place inside the temple and a fire was lighted—the climate can be chilly at night even in summer in this part of Arcadia—and the hired peasants played music.[49]

With the help of Georg Christian Gropius, an experienced German polyglot who had spent several years in the Eastern Mediterranean, Cockerell, Haller, Foster, Lynckh, and T. Legh had signed a contract with Veli Pasha at Tripolitsa on June 1, 1812, dividing the booty of the excavations in half for their sale that was planned together with the marbles they had already obtained from Aigina the previous year. The Europeans were fortunate because in the end the Pasha was displeased with the finds and sold his share to them.[50] Two auctions were held at Zakynthos.[51] On November 1, 1812, the Aigina marbles were sold to Crown Prince Ludwig of Bavaria. They were later restored by the Danish sculptor Thorvaldsen and displayed in the Glyptothek, a museum designed by the Neoclassical architect Leo von Klenze in Munich. The Bassai marbles were sold to the British Museum on May 1, 1814. One piece remained unsold: an architectural fragment—a Corinthian capital—that was a germinal object in the history of world architecture, probably the first capital of its kind.[52] It seems the piece remained on the island of Zakynthos, rather

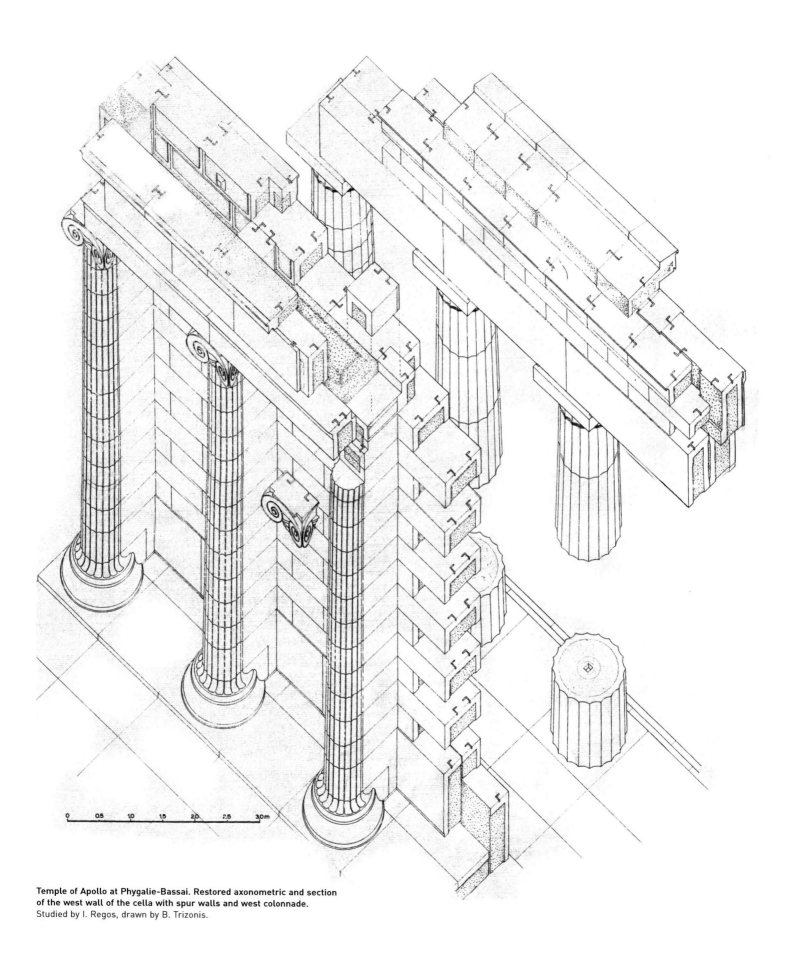

**Temple of Apollo at Phygalie-Bassai. Restored axonometric and section
of the west wall of the cella with spur walls and west colonnade.**
Studied by I. Regos, drawn by B. Trizonis.

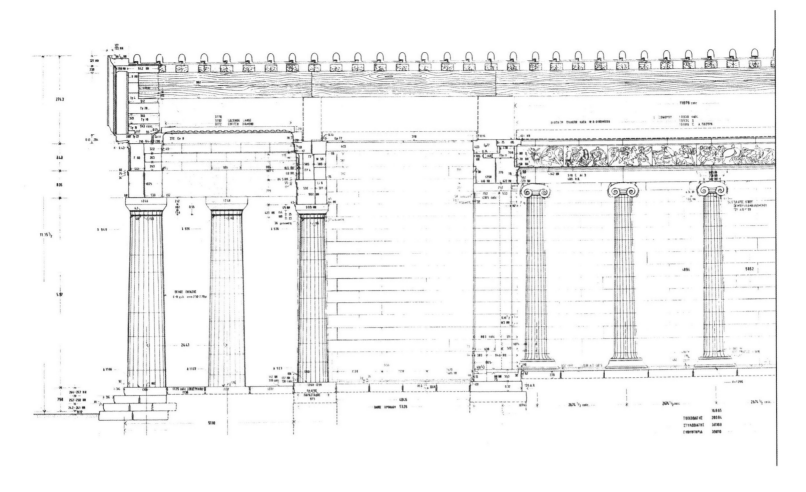

Temple of Apollo at Phygalie-Bassai.
Restored longitudinal section end elevation towards the east.
Studied by D. Svolopoulos, drawn by B. Trizonis.

forgotten and never further documented until the devastating earthquake that razed the city in 1953. Its unique form would have vanished altogether from world memory were it not for the set of drawings made by archaeologist and artist Haller von Hallerstein who, together with Otto Magnus von Stackelberg and J. Foster, carried out detailed documentation of the whole ruin.[53] Indeed, Haller von Hallerstein's notebook remains the most useful source of information about the genesis of the Corinthian capital.[54]

In the autumn of 1815 the marbles purchased by the British Museum arrived in London, celebrated by the influential aesthete Payne White as the "the only examples extant of the . . . admirable school of Phidias, exhibit[ing] the sublimity of poetic imagination."[55] White's lavish praise, which was not entirely factually correct, was motivated by personal feuds with Elgin and the desire to belittle the

importance of the marbles of the Parthenon. The fact is that neither he nor any of the members of the group that had carried out the excavation and studied the Bassai temple realized the architectural significance of the building and its pivotal position in the history of ancient Greek architecture—perhaps the most creative moment of its evolution.[56]

The temple stands on a platform 131 × 246 feet (40 × 75 meters), partially cutting into the underlying rock and partially resting on earth fillings. The arrangement of the foundations in many respects resembles that of the Athenian Acropolis, thereby strengthening the claim about Iktinos' association with the project. The foundations are laid out according to a rectangular grid. The temple's stepped platform base, *krepidoma,* measures 2.44 feet (0.745 meters), one-eighth of the height of its column. In other contemporary temples—the Hephaisteion in Athens or the Temple of Poseidon

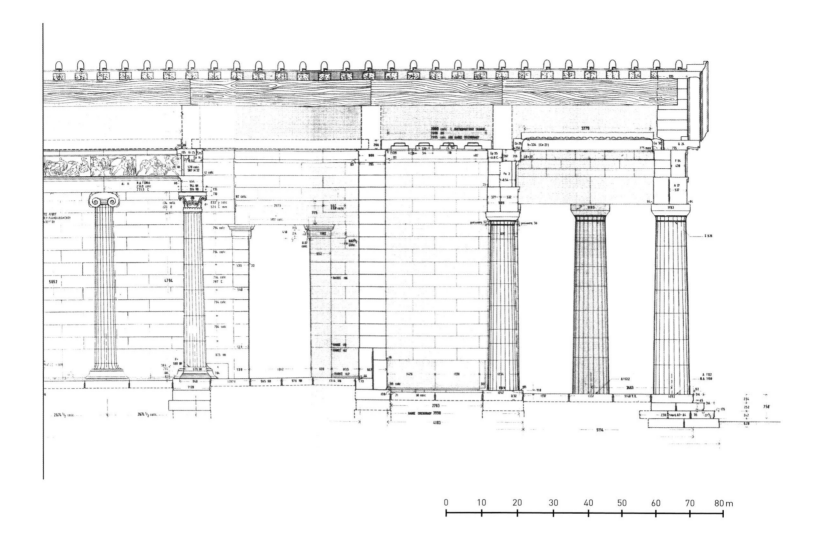

```
0    10   20   30   40   50   60   70   80 m
├────┼────┼────┼────┼────┼────┼────┼────┤
```

at Sounion—the relation of the *krepidoma* to the height of the column ranges from one-fifth to one-sixth. The blocks of the stylobate, the last step of the *krepidoma* on which the columns rest directly, were laid out from the opposite corners toward the center—a building technique that required precise dimensioning of the interior elements.[57]

The plan of the Apollo temple, like almost all ancient Greek temples, consists of a space formed by walls, posts, beams, roof, and, contained within it, sculptures. The basic structural component is the post-and-beam or post-and-wall frame—that is, horizontal beam members resting on vertical supports. The temple is of the peripteral kind. It consists of a narrow space surrounded by a single row of columns—a *pteron*—forming a ring, which has been called a *peristasis* (*peristylion* being a more general term meaning a colonnade surrounding the exterior of a building or circumscribing an interior court). The

central part of the plan is divided into three parts: a central hall, *sekos* (*naos*, or cella); a front porch, *pronaos*; and a back one, *opisthodomos* (or *posticum*). The *naos* has an *adyton*, an inner, probably more restricted room, cut off from the rest of the space for cultic reasons. The arrangement possibly imitated an older temple of Apollo in Delphi.[58] No door divided the *naos* and *adyton*. Instead, the architect used an unprecedented device: a central column—the Corinthian capital, the first of its kind—that stood for an implicit divide.

As with all ancient Greek buildings, next to the basic divisions of space, what characterizes the Apollo temple in Bassai is the number of members that constitute its body, their relative size, and the interval distances (intercolumniation) between them. The number of columns, six by fifteen, gives the temple an unusually long plan of archaic proportions since in most classical temples the

Temple of Apollo at Phygalie-Bassai. Ionic base.

immediately on the stylobate, and they have a top-most member—a capital—composed of a square slab—an abacus—supported by an echinus (a convex parabolic curved cushion cut in one block). Together with the capital, the height of the column is 19.55 feet (5.959 meters).[59] The column shafts are divided into twenty flutes and, being Doric, they meet at a sharp angle. The shaft is divided into five to nine drums. The horizontal joints of the drums are pierced by cuttings to receive the *empolia*, wooden joints that allow the drums to resist horizontal forces. Necking grooves are cut at the top of the shafts and a chamfer around the bottom of the capital joins two half-grooves in the top drum to form a set of three incisions (*hypotrachelia*).

Upon the capitals rests the entablature, a highly articulated beam member comprising the architrave, the frieze and the horizontal cornice *projected* outward to protect the frieze from rainwater. Along the soffit of the horizontal *geison* and over each triglyph and metope was placed a mutule, a slab with rows of guttae (drops). The pediment, a triangular termination of a ridge roof, stood atop the entablature. The frieze itself consisted of vertical grooves—the triglyphs—alternating with *metopai*, plain or sculptured slabs. The roof of the temple is typical: double-pitched, with a ridge pole and beams going lengthwise and rafters placed at right angles above them, above which were placed the tiles, plain and cover, each row ending at the sides in an antefix. The triangular space at each end of the roof was called *aetos* ("eagle" pediment) and was closed by a *tympanon* and protected by a cornice. The pediment usually contained sculptures, fastened with dowels, and its three edges were decorated by

number of columns at the long side is given by the formula 2 x +1. From a distance, the design appears standard and informal. However, the relative size of the members and their spacing varies significantly. Equally archaic is the thicker size of the columns of the north side, where the entrance is located. Furthermore, the depth of the north and south passageways, the *pteron,* is bigger than that of the sides, as is the intercolumniation distance.

The columns of the *peristylion* are made out of local gray limestone. They are in the Doric style: that is to say, they have no bases, being placed *akroteria.* An effort was made to minimize the number of joints by using larger pieces of this material that had to be brought from afar. The roof was decorated along the gables with a *sima* and, at the eaves and along the peak, with palmette antefixes. In contrast with the local stone used for the rest of the building, the roof covering was entirely of marble. For the pavement of the temple, the architect employed an orthogonal grid system whose dimensions varied for each major part of the building.

In contrast to the *pteron,* the porches had sculptured metopes. The interior of the *sekos,* as in most Greek temples, had no windows, and contained a horseshoe colonnade. As opposed to the interior colonnades in earlier temples such as the fifth-century Temple of Aphaia in Aigina, the Temple of Neptune at Paestum or the Temple of Zeus at Olympia, the interior colonnade was made out of two parallel flanks and the columns were different to those of the exterior. They were Ionic, attached to the wall with projecting buttress-like spurs of masonry. They seemed to support the frieze—the first to appear in a temple's interior running around the cella—but the support is only suggested. The real impact of the columns was to generate a sequence of divisions of space articulating niches, which might have had a ritual function. The scheme is unprecedented but has strong affinities with the Iktinian Parthenon in two respects: the horseshoe colonnade and the Ionic columns, which in the case of the Parthenon are hidden in the back *adyton* portion.

In contrast to the Doric, Ionic columns have a base with layered divisions. The base of the Ionic columns here is rather unusual, with a concave sweep resembling an exaggerated apophyge. Their capital is also more elaborate than that of the Doric. Instead of an echinus, it has an ornamented necking, above which is a pair of volutes joined by an arched curve continuing that of the volutes. This stands in contrast to the type of connection where the two volutes are joined by a straight line parallel to the top line of the abacus. A variant of this capital made of lime was found in the site of the Apollo temple, revealing the element of experimentation in the design of the project. A narrow flat band separates the flutings of one shaft from another. The Ionic architrave is usually subdivided into three projected bands. These are not present in the Apollo temple. On the top of the architrave is a frieze that, instead of Doric triglyphs and metopes, has a row of dentils or a continuous sculptured frieze as in our temple here. An Ionic *geison* crowns the entablature of the interior, cut in steel-gray local limestone and contrasts with the marble of the frieze beneath.[60] An additional "idiosyncrasy" of this temple lies in the diagonal spurs, which terminate the row of Ionic columns. Dinsmoor suggested that the diagonal spur walls had Corinthian capitals, but Cooper believes them to have been Ionic, of blond limestone.[61] In contrast to other innovations of the temple, this diagonal arrangement was not found in Classical Greek architecture.

Without doubt, the most novel feature of the temple is the central column with a Corinthian capital, part of the interior colonnade facing the axis of the door. As mentioned above, this capital, considered to be the first of its kind in history, no longer exists. The only documentation we have is the sketches Haller von Hallerstein made during the excavations. If we attempt to piece together the information from these sketches, the capital would appear to have contained almost all the standard attributes of the so-called Corinthian kind: its shape was that of an inverted bell-like four-sided volume, topped by a concave-convex abacus. Although the elements on which the abacus rested are missing, from the remaining sketch fragments one can infer that some kind of plant-shaped spire volutes would have supported it. The space left between them was taken up by two well-documented inward curling fatter volutes, out of which emerged a large *antheme* palmette. A double ring of low curving acanthus leaves occupies the bottom part of the capital. The drums, diameter, taper, the number and shape of the flute channels of the Corinthian column are the same as those of the Ionic ones, as is the base.

In simplistic terms, one may say that the ancient Greek temple existed only for two reasons: to house the single image of the god, and to frame a series of sculptures narrating a relevant mythological story or stories. Consequently, the shape, dimensions, and location of the framing architectural elements—the pediments, metopes, and friezes—constrained the organization of the plot and episodes—units, divisions, and succession—of such a narration.[62]

In contrast to other Greek temples, the temple at Bassai did not have sculptures placed on its two pediments or on the metopes of the *peristasis*. On the other hand, following the Peloponnesian tradition, it had sculptured metopes on the Doric *pronaos*, *opisthodomos* frieze and the Ionic frieze of the *naos*.

The *pronaos* metopes show Apollo returning from the land of the Hyperboreans. The god occupies the front of his temple facing north, the direction from which he is believed to have arrived. The remaining figures and actions are embedded in relation to the spatial organization of the temple.

The metopes of the *opisthodomos* show the rape of Leukipiddai, with similar correspondence between the centrality of locations in the composition and significance of characters and actions in the plot of the myth. Greeks fighting Centaurs, Herakles fighting Amazons, and Greeks fighting Amazons are the stories shown in the Ionic frieze of the cella. The episodes run without architectural interruption, the beginning and end of the two subjects coming together in the northwest corner. The reading of the frieze follows a direction that begins to the right of the viewer upon entering the cella, continues around the cella from right to left, and ends at the entrance. The progression of the narration corresponds to the movement of the viewer, and concludes facing Apollo, with Herakles occupying the central position on the other side facing the entrance, just above the Corinthian column.[63]

The intention behind both the choice of the resident god, Apollo Epikourios, and of the embedded narrative sculptures remains obscure to us today. Even the name Epikourios is an enigma. Pausanias reported that it meant "Succorer" at the time of the plague, though contemporary scholars doubt this. They are more inclined to think that it related to the support they believed Apollo gave in recapturing the city from the Spartans. Even the choice of the Athenian architect, his willingness to be involved in such a "side–line" sanctuary, and

Temple of Apollo at Phygalie-Bassai.
Photograph by Serge Moulinier.

indeed in the architectural affinities of this temple with the Parthenon, may partly account for their opposition to the adversary of the Athenians.

Because the Temple of Apollo Epikourios is in very bad condition today, it is difficult to assert with certainty that the current shapes and dimensions correspond to the original ones. The question is important if we hope to examine whether the temple's lack of common measures or geometry is the result of damage, or of an intentional avoidance of regularity—what has been called "refinements." Refinements are computed deviations from a rule objectively stated to correct errors resulting from the subjective perception of a building. Corrections of this kind are identified as having originated in the sixth century. They have been considered an indication of architectural achievement and their disappearance has been interpreted as an indication of decline. In general, this is a much disputed problem in Greek architecture, but

one that is rather important for the Apollo temple because the application of refinements is thought to have reached its peak in the buildings of the Acropolis of Athens, especially in the Parthenon, during the period when the temple of Apollo was built. For this reason, their presence in the Temple of Apollo is important evidence of the presence of Iktinos in Bassai, and of the centrality of the project as an architectural avant-garde experiment, despite the peripheral nature of the location.

Archaeologists have discovered masons' marks on the hidden sides of some of the stone blocks used in the construction of the temple. In general, these signs indicate the place of origin of the inscriber, the realization/completion, and, in the case of large sanctuaries, provide information on the organization of the construction, the name of the monument, and of the contractor or supplier of the materials. Such marks are to be found at Bassai inscribed on the rooftiles, from which we can infer that two contractors were employed in the building: one for supplying the materials and the other for organizing the construction. They also indicate the position of the specific piece in the overall structure.

The data provided through these inscriptions suggests that rough stones were brought to the construction site and put in a particular place to be cut and carved according to the specifications of the architect.[64] From the character of the letters of these inscriptions at Bassai we can infer the date to be c. 427–400 B.C.E. and determine the composition and origins of the crew; more specifically, we learn that the craftsmen were not Arcadians, but migrant specialists, Doric Peloponnesians, working alongside Islanders and Athenians.[65] Another source of data used by researchers to identify the date, the network of contacts, and knowledge flow that led to the design and construction of the project comes from the use of architectural details: the crowning hawksbeak, the *geison*, and the Ionic moldings. Likewise the result of a widespread network of interactions was the choice of materials used in the construction, ranging from local stone to marble, the latter originating from Naxos, Paros, Delos, and Cape Tainaron. It is clear that the construction of this temple was a highly complex process. A large number of pieces were prepared separately according to a highly coordinated scheme that enabled them to be assembled into a single structure. In addition, the process of acquisition of the materials from different areas and their transportation to and within the construction site required a very sophisticated plan of concurrence. Further complications came from the fact that the means of transporting the stone building blocks—wheeled cars—were in very limited number, with the contractors being obliged to share them with farmers who used them for harvesting, threshing, and ploughing. Additional care had to be taken in scheduling construction to adapt to frequent warfare and to the regular religious festivities.[66]

The divinity worshipped at Bassai—Apollo—was one of the most important gods of the Greeks, whose major places of worship were the Ionic island of Delos and the oracular sanctuary at Delphi. Strangely, no altar—a major feature of Greek sanctuaries—has been found in connection with the temple at Bassai. Equally strange is the fact that no statue of the deity has been unearthed for us to discuss here. The uncanny aura of the temple, its ambiguous identity between archaic and modern, cosmopolitan and regional status, the enigmatic inscrutability of the Corinthian capital, its design, designer, position in the plan of the temple, its meaning for the Arcadians, and—the climax of the mystery—its disappearance in our time make the building one of the most inscrutable of ancient Greece.

Concerning the Corinthian column, N. Yalouris[67] suggested that it might have stood in the position usually occupied by the cult statue in Greek temples. In fact, there was a tradition of representing deities in the form of a column, pillar, or tree. In addition, this might help us explain the absence of the cult statue. Indeed, according to Clement of Alexandria, citing the seventh-century poet Eumelos, "the statue of Apollo at Delphi was a column."[68] Hence, we may deduce that the Corinthian column *was* the cult statue.

If this theory is true, it would further suggest that, as much of the design of the temple was innovative, its newness was derived from recruiting and recombining preceding elements irrespective of whether these elements were far removed or very close in time and space. Furthermore, recent studies have brought forth more evidence that the design of the Classical temple was derived in many respects by recombining elements from the sixth and early fifth-century B.C.E. temple of Apollo at Delphi with elements recruited and preserved from earlier structures that had stood on that site. In fact, one might say that, quoting Cooper, the "sequence of the temples of Apollo I to IV" on the site that preceded the Iktinian temple represented in a concise manner the "development of Greek temple architecture." Furthermore, the temple also encapsulated the way that creative design was emerging in the Greek world of that time. It demonstrated how the existence of a unique network of diverse, distributed experts bringing together their knowledge for one project as and when needed made possible—even in a geographically outlying area—the creation of a new idea that was to be diffused globally.

Temple of Concorde, Akragas, Sicily.
Photograph by Serge Moulinier.

"First emerged Chaos . . . then broad-bosomed Gaia . . .
misty Tartaros . . . and Eros."
Hesiod, *Theogony*, 116

"Black Earth whose boundary stones fixed in many places I once removed:
formerly was she enslaved, now she is free."
Solon, fragment 24

CHAPTER II

SPATIAL ARRANGEMENT AND THE "KINDS" OF ARCHITECTURE

The Temple of Apollo Epikourios today stands in fragments surrounded by various devices that seek to protect and restore it. Nevertheless, the image that emerges out of the chaos of these ruins and equipment is one of a well-partitioned, articulated, and harmonized world within a world in the heart of Arcadia. The work of scholars in recovering, recognizing, and identifying the different pieces found in the Bassai site has enabled us to reconstruct not only most of the temple's structure, but also to some extent the complex network of human intelligence involved in the recruitment of workers, the use of materials, and the underlying knowledge that gave rise to this.

However, to answer the questions of how the temple of Apollo could ever have evolved as a mental construct, how the interior space was differentiated from the exterior, how it was divided—into *pronaos, opisthodomos,* and *adyton*—and how the kinds of columns became specialized given the location and nature of these divisions—Doric for the exterior colonnade, Ionic for the interior, and the newly invented Corinthian to introduce the innermost *adyton*—one needs to probe more deeply into timescales, and investigate case by case the temple's "descent with modification."[69]

Probably the outcome of material and functional needs, the emergence of the external colonnade that surrounds the core building—the *peristasis*—would also seem to have been a key precondition for the conceptual development of ancient Greek architecture. Indeed many scholars believe that it was the feature that distinguished the path of Greek architecture, as a way of thinking and style, from the other architectures of the Eastern Mediterranean, including the Mycenaean, the earliest architecture to be found in that region. It was the invention of the *peristasis* that enabled the identification of the building as a distinct, spatial object—an autonomous entity in space—that was to pave the way for the development of the great invention of Greek culture: the system of Classical architectural composition the Canon, and the discovery of spatial intelligence.

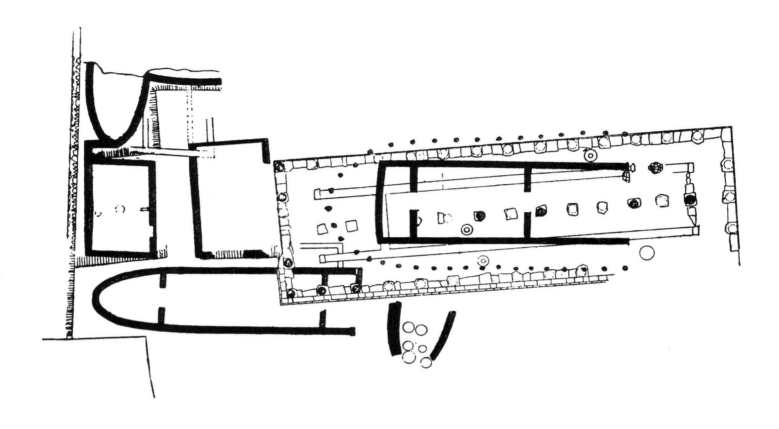

Megaron A and B at Thermon.
Tenth to eighth centuries B.C.E.
After W.B. Dinsmoor, 1950.

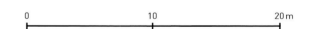

0   10   20 m

The initial intention to surround the building with columns had very little to do with its later conceptual uses. In all probability, the objective of the first colonnades was technological and functional: to protect the walls of the building that in earlier times were not made of durable stone, and to offer shelter to people gathering during communal events around a central place. However, although the colonnade has become almost synonymous with Greek architecture, its emergence was deeply rooted in local conditions, and its development very much interlinked with the technological and intellectual events in other regions that were communicated through the "cosmopolitan" Mediterranean web of contacts.

Years before the first attempts at peripteral colonnades, the palatial "Mycenaean" complexes of Mycenae, Tiryns, Pylos and other less significant structures dominated Greece. The question of why these splendid high-density centers of collective life ended around 1100 B.C.E., to be followed by centuries of poverty and meager construction remains unanswered. Information on the disappearance of the Mycenaean civilization is in short supply and obscure, given the absence of written records and scarcity of material remains. In an analogy to a similar period in Western European history—the early Middle Ages—this period has been called the "Dark Ages" of ancient Greek history which, even if recent research has argued was not as "dark" and backward as previously thought, still presented a great contrast with the palatial culture that preceded it. It is still not known how and why this process of deprivation, depopulation, and distraction occurred, bringing about the collapse of the palatial system of government and the whole economic, social, and

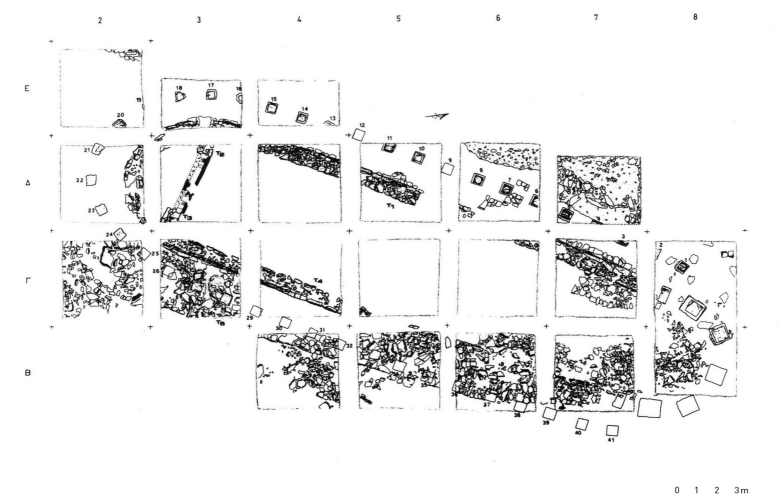

Plan of the Hekatompedon at Ano Mazaraki (Rakita).
After M. Petropoulos (1996–97).

0 1 2 3m

cultural organization that surrounded it. One possibility is excluded: the early theory that speaks of a blitz invasion by the Herakleids, the descendants of the mythical Herakles who, together with the Dorians, a northern people—rough, tough, and vital—conquered a Greece of Southern, sophisticated, and mild-mannered people after the Trojan War or the "People of the Sea" that put an end to the old order. In all probability, as with the "decline and fall" of the Roman empire, a combination of many factors—natural causes, earthquakes, climatic changes, famines, social unrest, sea raiders, and the introduction of a new military technology—contributed to this extraordinary change.[70] The reconstruction that followed this devastation—even if adjacent to older Mycenaean sites—used poor materials, a lower level of technology, and was on a reduced scale, being spatially dispersed.

The oldest and most important architectural example of the so-called Geometric period that marked the beginning of a renaissance is the Heroon of Lefkandi, situated on the west coast of Euboea.[71] From the remains, archaeologists have come to the conclusion that it was an elongated hairpin-shaped building.[72] The interior comprised a shallow porch connected by a wide opening to a squarish room, which in turn led into the main space that contained the burial shafts, presumably of *heroes*—ancestors—hence the name of the building. There was also a second direct access to the main space.

The dating of the Heroon is complex. It appears that, since the beginning of the second millennium B.C.E., the site saw periods of use, followed by periods of desertion. The objects found in the burial area are estimated to date from the thirteenth or

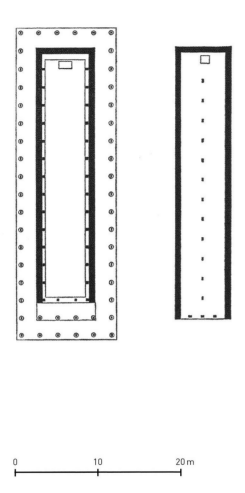

Temple of Hera, Samos 700–650 B.C.E.
Hekatompedon I and Hekatompedon II. The reconstruction is disputed.
H. Berve and G. Gottfried, 1961.

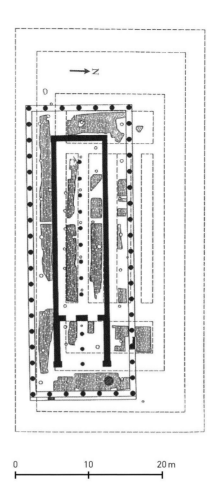

Temple of Poseidon at Isthmia, plan.
After W.B. Dinsmoor Jr.
O. Broneer, 1971.

twelfth centuries B.C.E., but the building is believed to be from the tenth century B.C.E. A colonnade surrounded the three sides of the building, leaving open the entrance, which was protected by a porch. An axial wooden colonnade supported the pitched roof with a continuous slope from the eaves to the ridge.[73]

The scale of the Heroon is small and the materials poor, if compared with the Mycenaean stone complexes. In contrast to the compactness of these complexes, the Heroon is a freestanding structure. Yet even this primitive building existed amid an intricate network of exchanges, revealing the dawn of Greek cosmopolitan intelligence. Pottery from Euboea has been discovered on the coast of the Levant. Euboeans were among the earliest "colonizers" of Greece trading with the Levantine coast

and Cyprus. Conversely, Cypriot and Near Eastern metal objects have been found at Lefkandi. It is highly probable that the Northern Canaanite alphabet was one of their imports, or imported by the Phoenicians to Lefkandi. Indeed, some of the earliest examples of Greek writing scratched onto pots are to be found here.[74]

Some evidence of the evolution in question, concerning wall construction, openings, columnar, and roof elements, can be drawn from the votive architectural clay models found in sanctuaries, such as the models of the Heraion at Perachora or the Heraion at Argos (first half of the eighth century B.C.E., 800–750 B.C.E.). There is no indication of an external surrounding colonnade in these models. Instead, the columns stood in the form of a porch, *in antis*, in front of a single room,

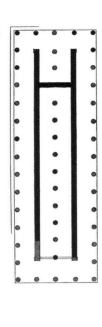

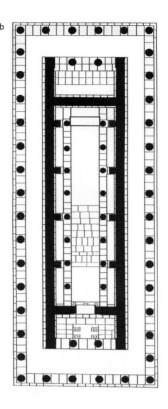

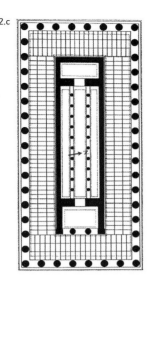

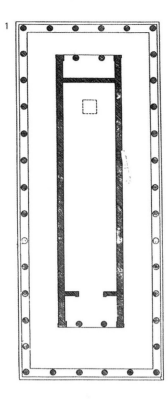

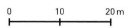

1- Old Temple at the Argive Heraion at Argash. 650–625 B.C.E.
After E.I. Tilton, 1902.

2.a- Archaic Temple of Apollo at Thermon. 630–620 B.C.E.
After W.B. Dinsmoor.

2.b- Temple of Hera at Olympia. 600–590 B.C.E.
After A. Mallwitz, 1966.

2.c- Temple of Artemis at Kerkyra (Corfu). 580–570 B.C.E.
After H. Schleif.
H. Schleif, Korkyra I, 1940.

which very often had an apsidal horseshoe shape at the far end. This conforms to the structures of Gonnos in Thessaly and Apollo Daphnephoros in Eretria.

These porch temples seem to have been conceived in "reminiscence" of the *megaron,* suggesting that the new temple recalled local precedents, rather than recruiting examples from overseas. Were elliptic or apsidal geometric houses the results of such reminiscence? "Reminiscence" is a term frequently used; however, it is merely a metaphor of ambiguous meaning. People remember. Societies have collective "memories" through written documents or stories transmitted orally from one generation to the next. Yet how does a community remember a building technique or form? It is clear that in such circumstances, remembering

the form of a complex artifact like the *megaron* would have been rather difficult—especially in a society that had forgotten how to write its own language, and was in the process of importing a new system of notating vocal sounds. Furthermore, the repertory of plans of the Mycenaean palaces did not contain any apsidal and elliptic forms of the kind encountered in the Geometric period.

A unique example is the Building T at Tiryns, the only structure that suggests continuity with the Mycenaean precedent in terms of location and plan configuration. The plan bears strong similarities to the former *megaron* in its floor level, two column bases, and the old throne base. The two steps leading to the porch of the old *megaron* are also reused.[75] Drawing an analogy with the poetry of the period, in which great efforts were made to construct a new

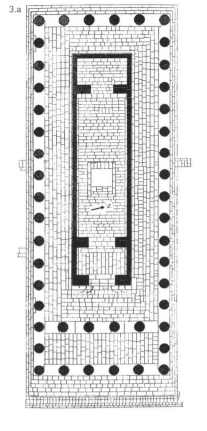

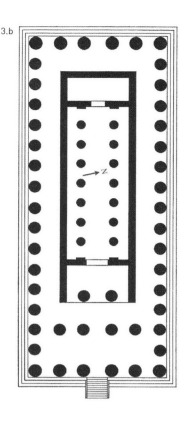

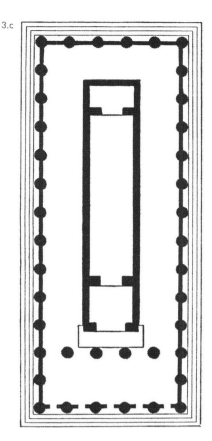

0   10   20 m

3.a- Temple C at Selinous, Sicily.
570 or 550 B.C.E.
After Gruben.
H. Berve, G. Gruben, and O.Puchstein, 1899.

3.b- Temple of Apollo at Syracuse.
Early sixth century or
570–550 B.C.E.
After Gruben, 1978.

3.c- Temple of Athena (F) at Selinous.
560–540 or even 520 B.C.E.
After J. Hulot and G. Fougères.
H. Berve and G. Gruben, 1978.

identity for the Greeks by returning to the myths and stories of the heroic Bronze Age of the Mycenaean past, one might suggest that the resemblance is intentionally a *renovatio*.

The Mycenaean example still leaves unanswered, however, the question of the origin of the peristyle and the addition of a *pteron* to a simple box-like building. The example of the temple B of Thermon shows that it was part of a building complex and not a freestanding structure. Moreover, it has now been proven that the eighteen paving stones formerly believed to constitute the bases of a *peristasis* added later to the main building were installed after the destruction of Megaron B.[76] After excluding other propositions that temple B of Thermon (eighth century B.C.E.), the temple of Hera (Hekatompedon IA) at Samos (eighth

century B.C.E.), and the Hekatompedon of Apollo at Eretria (c. 660 B.C.E.) were surrounded by columns, scholars have retained only two candidates in their most recent conclusions about the oldest Greek peristyles. The first is the temple at Ano Mazaraki (Rakita) constructed around 750–650 B.C.E. on Mount Panachaiko in Achaia, at an altitude of 3,707 feet (1,130 meters)—which, together with the temple of Apollo Epikourios in Bassai, is the tallest for a temple. This would appear to be the only genuine case of an eighth-century B.C.E. peripteral building. The hypothesis of a colonnade surrounding a core is supported by the discovery of rough sandstone and poros stone bases. The floor was also made out of stone. The core structure was apsidal with an *adyton* division. The surrounding columns were wooden and their

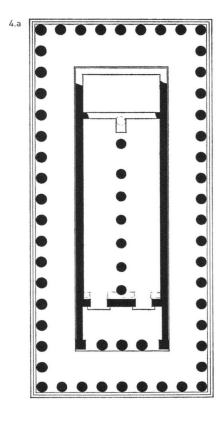

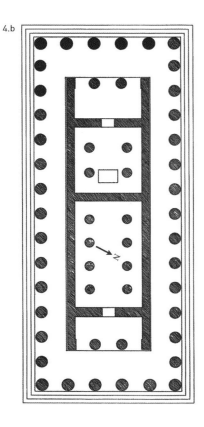

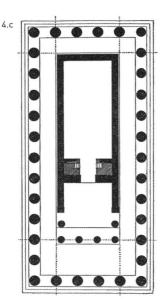

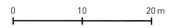

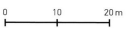

4.a- Hera-Temple I (Basilica) at Paestum. Plan of the original design.
575 or 550 B.C.E.
After F. Krauss. H. Berve and G. Gruben, 1978.

4.b- Temple of Apollo at Corinth. 540 B.C.E.
After Gruben.
H. Berve and G. Gruben, 1978.

4.c- Temple of Athena (previously called Ceres) at Paestum. 530 or 510 B.C.E.
After Koldewey and Puchstein.
Robertson, Donald Struan, 1969.

spacing irregular. Wattle and daub composed the roof and the rest of the structure. Corinthian tiles have been found at the site, but these date from a later renovation of the roof.[77]

The second case is the mid-eighth-century B.C.E. temple B of Artemis at Ephesus.[78] The plan of the cella is rectangular and, in contrast to the temple at Ano Mazaraki, its walls are built entirely of stone. The surrounding colonnade of four by eight columns was made out of wood. In the middle of the cella there are traces of four columns, between which probably stood the cult statue.[79] The roof was made out of thatch or clay.

A most important technological innovation in construction appeared in Corinth around the middle of the seventh century B.C.E. in the predecessor to the existing Temple of Apollo and in the Isthmia

Poseidon temple, 690–650 B.C.E., located on a low-lying plateau overlooking the Lechaion Valley, near Corinth. In both structures, terra-cotta tiles were used for the first time to cover the roof—a most advanced material for the time. This is a fascinating example of innovation through "technology transfer," as well as a model "win-win" situation due to open channels of communication between diverse regions and people. Initially Corinth had been a major importer of pots, vases, and clay figures using fired-clay technology. Soon after, by the middle of the seventh century B.C.E., the process was reversed. Having mastered the techniques themselves, or having imported foreign craftsmen from the Levant together with the objects themselves, the Corinthians started the local production of superior-quality artifacts. They went on to export these all over the world,

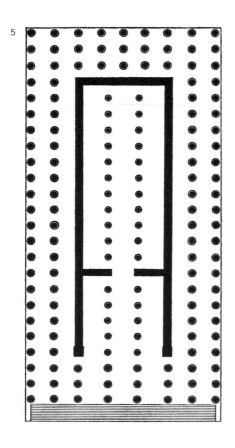

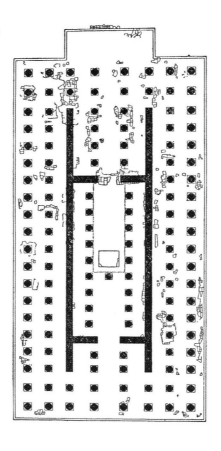

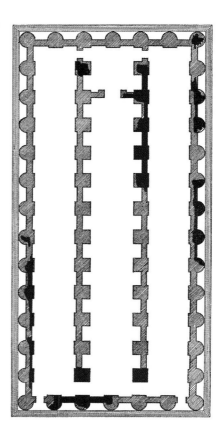

0   10   20   30   40 m

5- Temple of Hera IV (by Polycrates) at Samos.
525 B.C.E.
After Gruben.
H. Berve and G. Gruben, 1955.

6- Temple of Artemis at Ephesus.
Sixth century B.C.E.
After D.G. Hogarth.
Robertson, 1969.

7- Temple of Zeus Olympion (temple B) at
Akragas. C. 500–460 B.C.E.
After Lawrence. H. Berve and G. Gruben, 1978.

using channels similar to those for importation. Of even greater significance was the fact that the Corinthians appear to have been the first to envisage an original use for the newly acquired and mastered technology of terra-cotta. In analogy to pottery, they saw the possibility of transforming the technology of sun-dried bricks into kiln-fired tiles, and indeed the potential of this new product when applied to roof covering to channel and carry off rainwater and withstand fire.[80]

In addition to the technical improvement it brought to covering roofs—a technology that remains in use today[81]—the terra-cotta innovation had consequences for the overall conception of the structural organization, promoting the differentiation and specialization of the elements of the building, as well as their normalization.

The Isthmia temple is equally important as an early example of the evolution of stone masonry in ancient Greek architecture. Due to its monumental size, the structure is considered a forerunner of the surviving Temple of Apollo.[82] Moreover, its use of hewn stone blocks of ashlar masonry for its walls made it a key work in the evolution of the technology of ancient Greek building. The standard-sized ashlar blocks were laid in the rigorous isodomic manner—that is, set so that each vertical joint is over the center of the block beneath it and, together with its molded tiles, dimensioned to fit the spacing of columns and timber framing—and manifest an important step in the "modular prefabrication" and technological thinking in the temple's construction.[83] Another important feature was the leveling of the sanctuary plateau as a

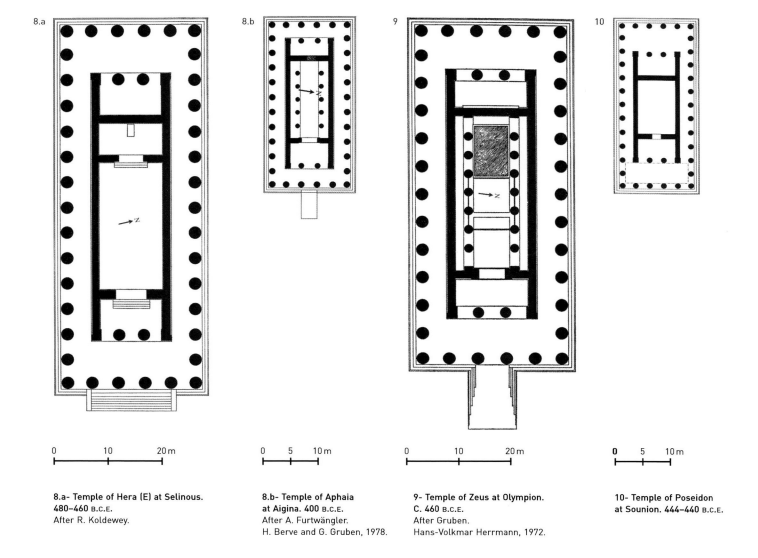

8.a- Temple of Hera (E) at Selinous.
480–460 B.C.E.
After R. Koldewey.

8.b- Temple of Aphaia
at Aigina. 400 B.C.E.
After A. Furtwängler.
H. Berve and G. Gruben, 1978.

9- Temple of Zeus at Olympion.
C. 460 B.C.E.
After Gruben.
Hans-Volkmar Herrmann, 1972.

10- Temple of Poseidon
at Sounion. 444–440 B.C.E.

preliminary step in the construction of the building. In addition, the building possessed a *geison* in stone for protection from rain. Internally it contained decorated panels. The use of both small-sized square stone blocks and terracotta tiles were original features and not an import from other regions within or outside of Greece. The innovation moved in the reverse direction: the new technological ideas applied in the Isthmia temple were later diffused to other structures around the Greek world.[84]

There has been debate as to whether, in addition to its pioneering construction method, the temple was surrounded by a colonnade. This hypothesis was finally confirmed. However, it is doubtful that the columns were Doric, as has been claimed.[85] What is apparent here is that the evo-

lution of the plan of the building involving the introduction of new and more specialized structural and spatial elements went hand in hand with the introduction of new construction technologies, thus making it difficult to identify the actual underlying force.

One thing is certain: the application of more sophisticated and costly technology implied a more wealthy economy and, by moving to the terracotta tile and then to blocks of stone extracted by advanced quarrying techniques and hewn to uniform dimensions, constituted a real jump from the subsistence economy of the Dark Ages. Moreover, given the speed at which these techniques were introduced, it also suggested the introduction of some aspects of these techniques from other more technically advanced regions.

Parthenon, Athens.
Photograph by Serge Moulinier.

Indeed, there are many indications that Greek quarrying very likely followed a method already used in Egypt and other areas of the Near East.[86] Similarly, there are indications that technology related to ashlar masonry may have been transported from monumental structures in Palestine,[87] while technology related to wood may have had its origin in the Canaanite territory to the east of the Greek cities of Ionia and Aeolia through Syria or as far as Phoenicia.[88]

While some of the above-mentioned temples have been referred to in the past as having Doric columns, the evidence to support this claim is very weak. The only conclusion we can draw from it concerns the evolution of the plan of the buildings. Even here, there has been criticism of the hasty characterization of many of these early temples as peripteral, without real evidence.[89] The result is a general lowering of dates for the first peripteral temples (650 B.C.E.), and also for the first stone columns and generalized use of stone. However, one should bear in mind that these corrections concern the timing rather than the pattern of evolution of Greek architecture during these Dark Ages. They do not disturb the basic hypothesis that the structures evolved by adding a colonnade to a hall, thereby differentiating it as an object detached from the surrounding objects, and dividing the space of this initial hall into specialized parts. Once more there is strong evidence that these developments did not occur in isolation, but as a dialogue between various Greek and non-Greek regions by means of a cosmopolitan network of traveling mercenaries, merchants, and craftsmen.

The introduction of a colonnade, a *pteron,* to surround temples, thus seems to have played an important role in the conceptual development of

Greek architecture by enabling the identification of a building as an entity. This in turn supported the development of the system of rules of classical composition, forming a canon.

However, important morphological experimentations that contributed equally to the formation of the classical canon of ancient Greek architecture, also occurred in the design of porch temples *in antis*. Early examples of the type encountered above and later developments will be examined in the context of the pioneering treasuries of Delphi and in Athens of the classical period.

Neither is the *pteron* merely an encircling row of columns. It is to be found in the stoae as a single row of columns defining spaces that serve everyday commercial and other public non-ritualistic functions. A stoa was a long covered space, whose roof was supported by one or several rows of columns parallel to a rear wall. An early building of this type is the Stoa Basileios in Athens dating from the sixth century B.C.E. The Egyptians had designed and built such stone colonnades for monumental complexes since the beginning of the second millennium B.C.E. Later, clay models representing everyday scenes showed their use in ordinary, everyday public activities.

Given the abundance of Egyptian-style scarabs and other artifacts of Egyptian appearance found in Greece around the seventh century B.C.E., it would be unlikely that the striking similarities between the early Greek *pteron* and the Egyptian stoae were mere coincidence. We lack details about these contacts as discussed by various ancient Greek authors, including Herodotus. However, we do have evidence that c. 660 B.C.E., Pharaoh Psamtik I (Psammetichos) fought the Assyrians

with the help of Ionian and Carian mercenaries, expressing his gratitude to the Greeks by according them special privileges that led to the founding of the trading town of Naukratis (in Western Egypt). Therefore the Greeks may have brought back knowledge of building design from Egypt; we do know that Egyptian methods of graphic representation of buildings at that time were very advanced. Another possibility is that Egyptian masons, who arrived using a similar network to that of numerous other traveling technicians at that time, transmitted knowledge. The significance of such contacts with Egypt, as well as with other Eastern Mediterranean regions, becomes even more evident in the evolution of the post and beam structure of the *pteron* as an articulated architectural "kind" as Greek architecture itself evolved. This will be discussed in the following section.

Conversely, the unique contribution of the Greeks becomes clear in the Greek reconceptualization of these kinds in the form of a system, the canon. The idea seems to have been nascent around 465–460 B.C.E., in a stoa structure rather than a temple—the Poikile Stoa in Athens—which was to become legendary as a "house" of philosophers who took advantage of its long shaded shape as a place where they could walk up and down discussing their problems. Architecturally this was a most significant step: it was here that saw the first attempt at combining the Doric kind of column with the Ionic, more than a decade before Iktinos sought to do so in the Parthenon and the temple of Apollo at Bassai.

Above: **Basilica or Temple of Hera, Paestum.** Photograph by Erich Lessing / AKG-images.
Below: **View of temples, Paestum.** Photograph by Erich Lessing / AKG-images.

Emergence of the Ionic and Doric "kinds"

The new architecture emerged in ancient Greece around 800 B.C.E. In contrast to the legendary Mycenaean palatial complexes, deserted by that time, these fresh structures were unattached volumes consisting mainly of one long room with an entrance on the narrow side. Within the building, an important development was the introduction of a double row of columns in the cella replacing the axial colonnade found in temples such as those of Apollo at Thermon, Hera at Samos, and Poseidon at Isthmia. This new arrangement allowed a better view of and access to the statue of the resident god, as well as unobstructed space for circulation. The entrance was placed on the narrow side and the rounded ending of the opposite side disappeared. From the outside, the building was defined as a freestanding entity through the application of columns. Columns were placed at the entrance between the ends of the side walls of the volume (*in antis*), or arranged outside the entrance in the form of a porch, or again applied around the hall as a colonnade (*pteron*). On top of these columns rested a beam element, the entablature. As far as archaeologists are able to conclude from existing findings, neither the columns nor entablatures initially bore any distinctive marks. Such characteristic elements seem to have emerged at a later stage, progressively becoming standardized. This is a very significant occurrence because it indicates that columns and entablatures, and by extension the building itself, were gradually categorized, in that they were recognized as belonging to a "kind"—the "Doric" or "Ionic" *genera* that Vitruvius discusses.

A Doric capital dated around 600 B.C.E., the Capital C, was found at the site of the Argive Heraion in Peloponnesus.[90] Many consider it to be the first of its kind, though it is uncertain whether it belonged to the temple or to the North Stoa of the sanctuary. Vitruvius wrote of the Argive Heraion that it was the earliest Doric-style temple, which—he also claimed—preceded the Ionic. Yet, at around the same time, a different kind of column was used in Asia Minor. It belonged to the temple of Athena at Smyrna[91] and shared many of the characteristics of the Ionic kind.

Capitals sharing key attributes with the canonical Ionic, contemporary with the Old Smyrna capital, have been found not only around the area of northwest Asia Minor and Lesbos, but also in Cyprus, the Middle East, and especially Palestine.[92] Their dates range mostly from the seventh to the end of the sixth centuries B.C.E. The ancient Greeks did not use "Aeolic" in reference to an architectural type of capital or column. The term was introduced by nineteenth-century scholars[93] to name a class of capitals and columns that seemed to conform neither to the Doric nor Ionic concept of "style." Other scholars have preferred to name them "proto-Ionic"—implying their possible ancestry to the Ionic.[94] However, use of the term Aeolic restricted their geographical location to the region colonized by the Aeolians, despite their appearance elsewhere. This also reduced the range of regional interaction out of which this new kind of architectural element may possibly have emerged.

Proto-Ionic capital.

Proto-Aeolic capital, Hazor.
Israel Museum, Jerusalem.

Temple of Athena (IIIA-B) at Smyrna, restored column elevation.
c. 610–600 B.C.E.
After Cook and Nicholls. Restored by J.M. Cook and R.V. Nicholls, 1998.

Aeolic capitals possess strong similarities to their Ionic counterparts, though they do differ in some basic aspects. In the Aeolic style, two volutes that spring upwards and curl outwards, split by a prominent axial plant motif—a palmette—surmount a ring or rings of overlapping leaves. This is quite the opposite of the Ionic volutes that curl downwards and inwards and are joined at the top. However, they do share with the Ionic the use of motifs resembling the palm, lotus, and lily in symmetrical arrangements.

One of the most frequently reproduced Aeolic capitals in our time comes from the temple at Neandria, built around the middle of the sixth century B.C.E. It was reconstructed from three different fragments by the archaeologist Koldewey in an imaginative, but highly controversial way. The Aeolic capital should not be confused with the Asia Minor palm capital. In contrast to the Aeolic, the palm capital has no axial element or volutes, and consists exclusively of upwardly springing palm leaves. Motifs of the Aeolic capital and supporting columns, also shared by the Ionic, have been found applied in small—ivory and bronze—and medium-sized artifacts and statuettes, as well as in capitals of votive columns[95] in several regions in northern Syria, Mesopotamia, Levant, Palestine, and in eighteenth-dynasty Egypt. In Greece, they have been located in Naxos, Delos, Oropos, and Delphi. Two votive capitals found in the Acropolis of Athens represent a remarkable intersection of Aeolic and Ionic capital characteristics. However, no use of the Aeolic capital has been found in a building in mainland Greece.

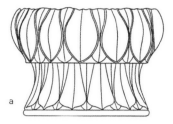

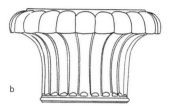

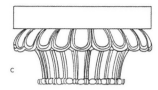

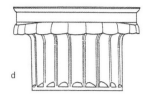

a- Capital from Temple of Athena at Smyrna. C. 610–600 B.C.E. After Coulton.

b- Capital from Northeast Stoa, Temple of Athena at Pergamon. First half of the second century B.C.E. After Coulton.

c- Capital from Massaliot Treasury at Delphi. 540–500 B.C.E. After Coulton.

d- Capital from Stoa of Attalos at Athens. 159–138 B.C.E. After Coulton.

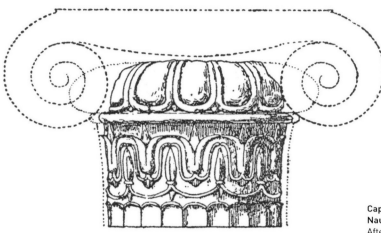

Capital from the Temple of Apollo, Naukratis. c. 565 B.C.E. After Dinsmoor, 1950.

In mainland Greece, it was the Doric that dominated. One of the first buildings with a *peristasis* with Doric columns is the temple of Hera at Olympia c. 600–590 B.C.E. Little is left of the original structure, and the Doric hypothesis is inferred from the space between the two columns, which is smaller than the space between the others—a feature called "angle contraction" that was later to characterize canonical Doric buildings. The cella of the later temple whose Doric columns have survived had two entrances with two columns *in antis,* but its most innovative feature—anticipating the column arrangement of the interior of the temple of Apollo at Bassai—was that every alternate column was replaced by a spur wall projected into the cella. Pausanias, who visited the temple in the second century C.E., spoke of a wooden column

that was still standing.[96] This suggests that the initial temple was wooden. The stone replacement happened around the middle of the sixth century B.C.E., which in turn suggests that the transformation of timber construction technology coincided with the development of the identifiable classification of architectural elements, and of the creation of features for marking and distinguishing them. As we have already mentioned, the new stone Doric elements appeared to have imitated many—but not all—details of the older wooden structure.

The chronicle of evolution that led to the plateau of the Doric "canon" shows that it was not confined to the single operation of picturing a specific technology of construction, or to any single region. Indeed, many of its features appear to have been drawn from other subjects or artifacts. It also shows

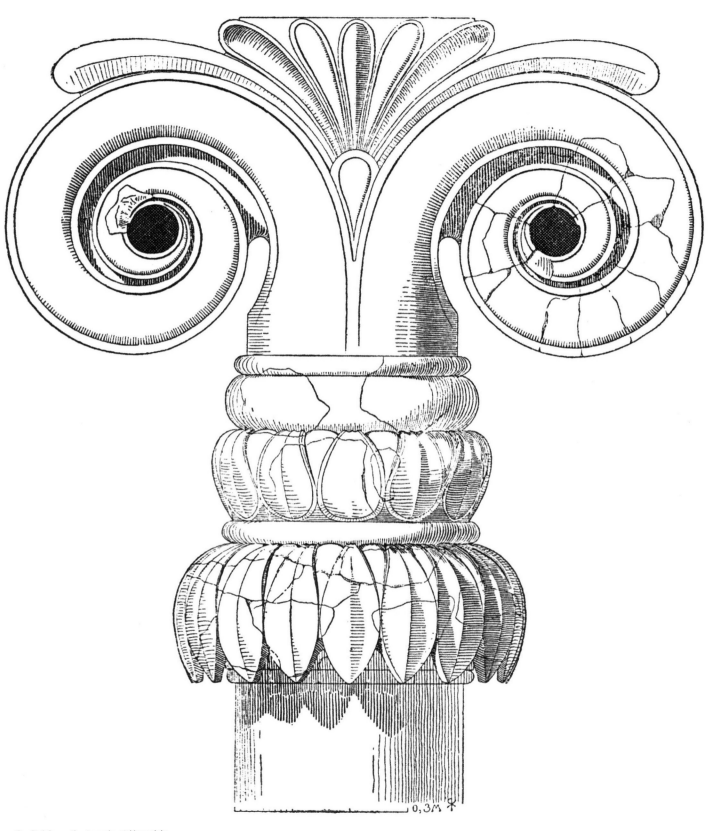

Capital from the temple at Neandria.
Middle of sixth century B.C.E.
After Koldewey 1891.

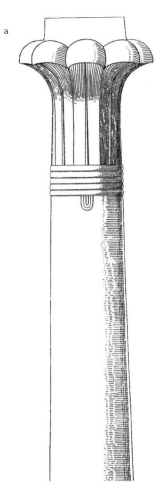
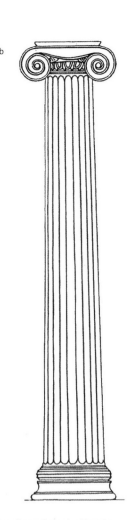
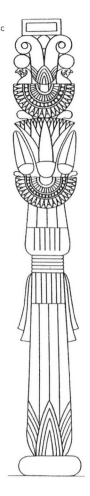

a- Palm capital and column, Egypt.
O. Puchstein, 1907.

b- Ionic marble column from the Temple
of Athena Nike at Athens. C. 429 B.C.E.
O. Puchstein, 1907.

c- Painted column with composite floral capital, Egypt.
Late eighteenth to nineteenth dynasty.
O. Puchstein, 1907.

that it emerged in interaction with many regions, including Egypt. The Doric capital was crowned with a square abacus and carried a smooth architrave whose shape and proportions bore a strong resemblance to many Egyptian ones. Again, as in Egypt, the first Doric flutes were very flat, and the preferred number was sixteen—a number also frequently used in Egypt. Later on, concave grooves were made to meet at sharp edges and their number was to rise to twenty. As in Egypt, in early Greek Doric temples, columns were often monolithic with similar proportions, the height being about six times the diameter. Such affinities are evident in the example—one of many—of the fifteenth-century B.C.E. porch of the shrine of Anubis, at Dair al Bahri. Similarly, Ionic bases and tori have been found in Syria, but using different materials.

Given the intense interaction between Greece and the southern and eastern Mediterranean regions during this period of demanding change, it is only natural that the Greeks turned to morphologies and technologies that had been already developed "overseas" in their effort to replace their temporary wooden structures by more permanent ones, rather than contemplating merely their own local wooden structures. By the middle of the sixth century B.C.E., Greek artifacts, merchants, and mercenaries were to be found in the Near East and Egypt. Naukratis—a dynamic Greek trading colony—was established in Egypt around 500 B.C.E.[97] Fragments of the limestone Ionic columns of its temple of Apollo have been found. These include the base and shaft of a column, and a capital with horizontally sprung volutes connected by

Temple of Artemis at Corfu.
Limestone pediment, figure.

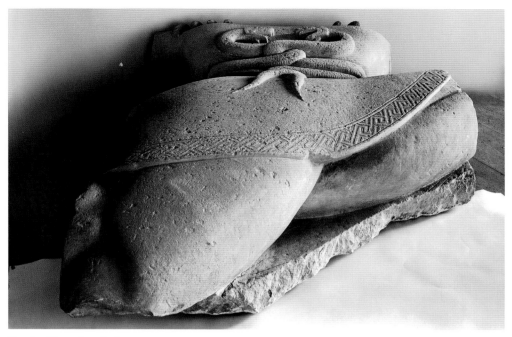

Temple of Artemis at Corfu.
Photograph by Wagner.

**Temple of Artemis at Corfu. Limestone pediment
with gorgon figure.**
Photograph by Wagner.

Temple of Artemis at Corfu. 580–570 B.C.E.
Restoration of pediment and sculptures by Buschor, 1934.

Gela Treasury, Olympia.
Photograph by Wagner.

a cushion. Below this, there was an echinus with an egg-and-dart pattern—attributes nearing those of the Greek Ionic canonic capital.

Almost contemporary with the temple of Hera at Olympia was the Temple of Artemis at Corfu (580–570 or even 560 B.C.E.).[98] Also a peripteral temple *in antis,* it had an eight-by-seventeen column *peristasis,* thus nearing the canonical proportion of 2x+1. It was divided into a front porch, main and back room, and had a double row of columns in the interior. The building is considered to be the first example of a Doric temple of full stone construction, comprising all the recognizable Doric-type features. Its stone capitals bore a herringbone pattern and had a frieze of plain metopes and grooved triglyphs. A very important architectural aspect is the sculptured pediment—perhaps the earliest of its kind—and certainly one

that was to be adopted and perpetuated for centuries to come. It contained as a central figure a gorgon flanked by leopards, and at the sides a battle between giants and gods—a representation of the new world versus the old.

From the scant evidence archaeologists have, it can be suggested that at around the beginning of the sixth century B.C.E., a great number of design innovations were distributed regionally and occurred in parallel. Some of these new designs were attempted, but did not achieve a following and subsequently disappeared. Some survived and were merged with other changes to become part of the Doric canon. The initial "post-and-beam" archaic structure evolved through the "differentiation and specialization" of components. It would seem that first came the capital, then the metope, triglyph, anta capital, followed by the *geison* and

Gela Treasury, Olympia.
Photograph by Wagner.

mutule.[99] There was certain regularity within the line of development. If we compare the Doric shaft of the Apollo temple of Syracuse with the shaft of the Apollo of Bassai—or even the Aphaia of Aigina— it looks heavy and bulky. Similarly, the echinus of the Doric capital appears flat, spreading outwards as it rises in the Syracuse Apollo or in its contemporary, the temple of Athena Pronaia at Delphi c. 570 B.C.E. Yet over a period of a hundred years, it was to achieve increasingly more upright proportions and a sharper angled profile, as in the capital of the Temple of Aphaia, or the Temple of Zeus in Olympia—a building belonging to the Classical canon. It is now believed, however, that this evolution was neither as continuous nor as smooth as entertained earlier.[100]

In addition to the evolution of each constituent element of the "kinds," one can observe the evolution of

relations between them that were gradually to coordinate and fuse them into a whole. As we have seen, the triglyphs of the Doric colonnade of the temple of Apollo in Bassai, or of the temple of Zeus in Olympia, coincide with the axis of the columns. This did not occur in earlier times. Looking at the *tholos*—a circular building surrounded by a Doric colonnade, and the first of this type to be known in Greece—constructed by Sicyon in Delphi in 580 B.C.E., we see that the system rule had yet to be conceived.

Small in scale but very significant in the development of the Ionic kind are the buildings constructed in marble in the Cyclades. Early examples are the Temple of Dionysos in Iria in Naxos, (c. 680 and 580–570 B.C.E.) and the "Oikos" of the Naxians (c. 600–560 B.C.E.) of Apollo in Delos. As with Doric structures, the earlier wooden

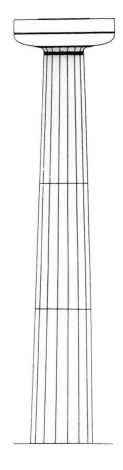 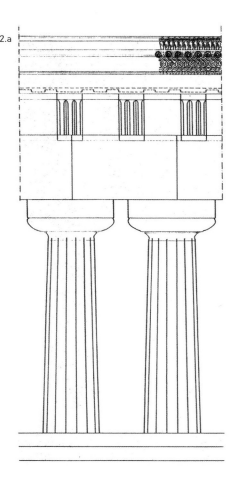 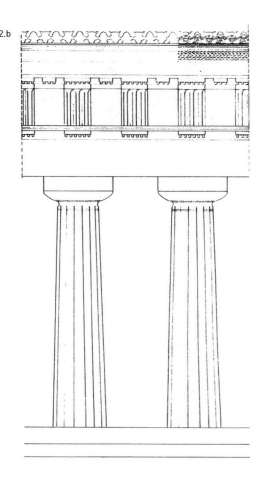

1- Column from Temple of Athena
Pronaia at Delphi, c. 570 B.C.E.
After P. de la Coste-Messelière,
1963.

2.a- Part of the elevation of
the Temple of Apollo at Syracuse.
570-560 B.C.E.

2.b- Part of the elevation of
the Temple of Aphaia I at Aigina.
570 B.C.E.
After Mertens.
Schwandner, 1996.

columns of the Oikos were replaced by marble ones. It is believed that a poorly preserved capital, probably the earliest Ionic one belonging to an architectural—as distinct from the votive—column, was from the Oikos. The low-pitched roof of the building was the first in Greece to be made out of Naxian marble, and had a simple Ionic cornice, again believed to be the earliest.[101] The third phase of construction of the building, c. 550 B.C.E., had a porch with Ionic columns with bases of the Samian kind. They consisted of a *trochilos* (scotia) and torus (a semicircular element). This base, which combined a convex torus, usually fluted, and a concave scotia, also fluted, was finally to evolve into the so-called "Attic base" in fifth-century B.C.E. Athens. As we will see, there was also a second

kind of Ionic base, originating in Asia Minor, which consisted of a torus and two large concave scotiae separated and enclosed at top and bottom with astragals.[102] Also in Delos, there was a pioneering marble structure, the first known example of an L-shaped stoa. Again this was a Naxian building (550–540 B.C.E.) with a colonnade whose columns stood on a cylindrical base.[103]

In contrast to these small prostyle Ionic structures from the islands, the eastern Ionic temples were big and possessed at least two rows of columns (*dipteroi*). The first to be attested were the Rhoikos Temple of Hera at Samos, dated 570–560 B.C.E., and the Temple of Artemis at Ephesus, dated 560–550 B.C.E. The Samian Theodoros is thought to be the architect of both temples, collaborating

Ionic votive and architectural columns, elevations:
a- Oikos of the Naxians, Delos, early sixth century B.C.E.
b- Aigina votive column, c. 580-570 B.C.E.
c- Naxian votive column, Delphi, c. 570 B.C.E.
d- Fourth Temple of Dionysos at Iria, Naxos, c. 580-570 B.C.E.

e- Naxian Stoa at Delos, 540 B.C.E.
f- Temple A at Paros, 530–520 B.C.E.
g- Old Temple of Artemis at Ephesus, 560–550 B.C.E.
h- Old Temple of Apollo at Didyma, c. 550 B.C.E.
i- Temple of Hera (Polykrateian), Samos, c. 530 B.C.E.

with Rhoecus from Samos for the Hera temple, and the Cretan Chersiphron of Knossos and his son Metagenes, for the Artemis temple.[104] The "Samos labyrinth," as Pliny called it,[105] comprised a front of two rows of eight columns, with a wider intercolumniation at the center, as in temples in Egypt. A similarly grandiose entrance was applied to the Temple of Artemis. A large number of columns were employed inside, strongly suggesting the use of design precedents from Egypt. The number of the side columns of the Hera temple is uncertain—probably twenty-one—with each *pteron* comprising at least hundred columns. Although no capitals have survived from the Temple of Hera at Samos, from the fragments discovered it has been suggested that the temple may have had wooden capitals with volute members.[106] The column had a two-part base: a torus above and a fluted *speira*. The columns of the new temple of Artemis were entirely of marble. Dedications made by the legendary Lydian king Croesus were inscribed on the base moldings of four or five of the sculpted marble column drums. The Ionic base is a very early example of the Asiatic variety. A mixture of Doric, Ionic, and Aeolian characteristics has been found in the design of both temples, thereby suggesting a moment of exploration and experimentation with assemblage and combination of elements from different regions.[107]

Equally experimental was the temple of Apollo at Didyma, thought to date from to 540–530 B.C.E. It had a double *pteron* of eight by twenty-one

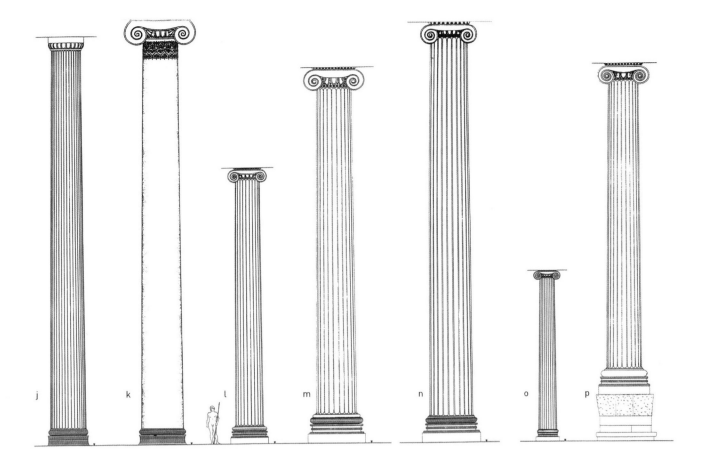

j- Temple of Hera (Polykrateian) at Samos, c. 530 B.C.E.
k- Temple of Hera at Priene, after 350 B.C.E.
l- Temple of Artemis at Ephesus, c. 356 B.C.E.
m- Temple of Apollo at Didyma, late fourth century B.C.E.

n- Naiskos of the Temple of Apollo at Didyma, third century B.C.E.
o- Temple of Artemis at Sardes, late third century B.C.E.
P- Temple of Artemis at sardes, late third century b.c.e.
After Gruben.
Ernst-Ludwig Schwandner, 1996.

columns, and a deep porch with two rows of columns. Its roofless interior contained a smaller temple building—a feature replicated when the old structure was rebuilt in the Hellenistic period. As in the temple at Ephesus, Apollo had sculpted drums, with frontally facing female figures, on the lower part of the column. With the exception of the *korai* of the Treasury of Siphnos in Delphi, this feature was not followed up later.[108] On the other hand, the triple-fasciae Ionic architrave that was to become a key characteristic of the Ionic canon was attempted here for the first time. Contemporary is the temple of Athena (c. 550 B.C.E.) at Assos, a Lesbian colony near the city of Neandria, in Asia Minor. It is a peripteral temple of six by thirteen columns, with a porch and without *opisthodomos,* or

interior columns. This is a unique example of Doric temple in Asia Minor, in the sense that it had Doric columns and triglyphs. However, the presence of what are considered Ionic elements is very significant. The dimensions of the columns and their intervals are those assigned at that time to Ionic columns, and on them rested a continuous sculpted frieze over a single fascia. The pediments of the temple were left empty.

In comparison to these daring trials, with the exception of developments in Delphi, architecture in mainland Greece was rather conservative. The remaining fragments of an important temple of Apollo dated at 540 B.C.E., at a major center of the time—Corinth—show Doric monolithic columns standing without *entasis* and tapering

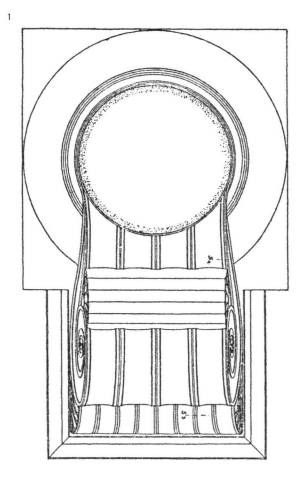

1

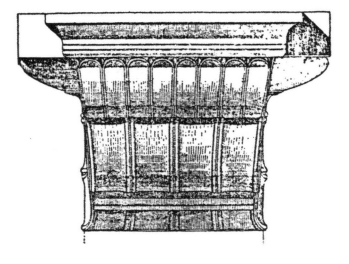

2

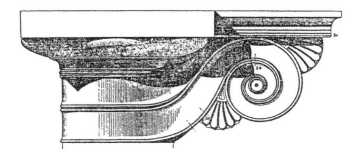

3

Facing page (top): Temple of Apollo, Corinth.
Photograph by Erich Lessing / AKG-images.
Facing page (bottom): Temple of Apollo, Corinth.

1, 2, 3- Capital from Throne of Apollo at Amyclai (restored).
530–525 B.C.E.
After Robertson, 1943.

upwards on a curved platform devoid of any adventurous design of major future consequence. However, another structure, the Throne of Apollo, Amyclai, of 530–525 B.C.E.,in an area outside of Sparta, manifests an intriguing cohabitation of Doric and Ionic elements—yet the architect of the building, Bathykles, was from Magnesia, a Greek colony in Asia Minor. Here we have a singular experiment that literally fused the Doric and Ionic capitals into a single double-faced structure. It was a daring trial, and one that—if followed—would probably have changed the course of architectural development in Greece. However, it was to have no subsequent visible impact.[109]

Equally exploratory was the character of the extensive building work that took place in the eastern colonies of Greece. Elements that would later be specialized into the two major kinds—Doric and Ionic—were tried out here in several combinations. These illustrate not only the process of searching, but also the presence of a network of interactions that made regional architectural findings available globally. The Apollo of Syracuse (570–560 B.C.E.)—a Corinthian colony in Sicily—comprises elements that probably originated from different regions and which were recombined in a fresh way. The temple was peripteros, six by seventeen, with a Doric *perstylion*. On the east stylobate there was an inscription pronouncing that Kleomenes dedicated the temple, and that Epikles had made its columns. The columns were bulky Doric, with a flat echinus, and monolithic shafts: they were not divided into

Treasury of Massalia, Delphi.
Photograph by Georges de Miré.

Treasury of Siphnos, Delphi.
Photograph by Georges de Miré.

drums. The end columns were thicker, as befitted the Doric canon still in development at that time; however, following of Eastern Aegean practice for Ionic temple colonnades, the angle intercolumniation was not contracted and the central space between the columns was wider.[110] The cella walls terminated in a spur with no anta facing—again, an Ionic element.

Similarly, Doric and Ionic elements mix in the sixth-century B.C.E. Temple of Hera, known by the name "Basilica": the flutes of its Doric columns terminate in moldings and a necking with narrow leaves resembling the Ionic variety. The Temple of "Ceres" of 530–510 B.C.E. appears to have combined a Doric peripteral colonnade of six by thirteen columns, circumscribing a cella that was entered through a four-column Ionic portico forming an extension of the antae—as if there was

The Athenian Stoa, Delphi.
Photograph by Georges de Miré.

a temple within the temple. The inclusion within the same building of Doric and Ionic elements preceded by a century the combination carried out in the Temple of Apollo of Bassai and in the Acropolis of Athens. Furthermore, the temples of the Greek colonies contained elements of Egyptian origin, as in the Temple of Apollo at Krimisa. A concentration of temples has also been found at Selinous, a colony of Megara Hyblaea. These are known by the letters A, B, C, D, O (the Acropolis), and GT, FS and ER (the lower terrace). Like the Syracuse Temple of Apollo, temple C (peripteral, six by seventeen columns) on the Acropolis (c. mid-sixth century) has a second inner colonnade in the front behind the *pteron*, with possible affinities to the deep porch entrance of the temples of Asia Minor. The temple FS of Athena dating from 560–540 B.C.E. has a unique Egyptian feature on its *pteron*: stone

screens half the height of the columns are placed between columns to block the passage.

This mixing of Doric and Ionic—not to mention Egyptian—elements in southern Italy has been referred to as "odd" or "free" from convention. Yet, since architectural conventions had yet to be established, such characterizations as deviating from them or being freed from them are anachronistic. In addition, these remarks miss what is perhaps the most important attribute of the period and place: the intense experimentation and dialogue involving "fusion and fission" of heterogeneous elements from regions occupied by Greeks or non-Greeks—a process that contributed to the emergence of the different kinds of architectural compsition, as well as to a canon or *koine*.

Marble was introduced to Delphi during the first third of the sixth century B.C.E. with the Naxian votive sphinx column. The treasuries of Massalia, Clazomenai, the Cnidos, and the Siphnos followed. Treasuries were small buildings often dedicated after a victory. Between the seventh and fourth centuries, twenty-three such treasuries were constructed in Delphi alone. Similar treasuries—also referred to as *oikos*—were to be found in Olympia, and in each place were generally placed one next to the other, almost in row. Their builders were tyrants, Greek cities, and colonies, the most prominent being those of the cities of the Cyclades and Asia Minor. Their plan resembled that of a small temple: a volume with a porch, with two columns *in antis*. At Delphi many of them were Doric. However, some showed great experimentation with the new elements they employed: their sponsors evidently had the means, as well as the ambition, to innovate and distinguish themselves from others.

The introduction of marble—a very expensive material—helped experimentation with moldings and sculpture to be suitable for the fine carving of the treasuries of Delphi, becoming forerunners of later developments of the Periklean Classical period. The continuous sculpted frieze, rather than the earlier Ionic dentils, was first introduced here. The Cnidian treasury introduced a torus with horizontal fluting, as well as a bead-and-reel astragal of exaggerated size and articulated in detail; while in the Siphnian treasury—apparently in competition[111]—an immense bead was used to take the place of a less flamboyant fluted torus. The same building also initiated a doorway frame using Ionic details as a tag, which was to be taken up by the designer of the door of Erechtheion. Two of the treasuries had columns with palm capitals—sometimes referred to as Aeolic—clearly showing their Egyptian origin. The Treasury of Massalia (540–500 B.C.E.), a colony of Phocaia from Asia Minor, and later the city of Marseille, combined this capital with an Asiatic base and Doric fluting shaft. The treasuries of Cnidos, Siphnos, and a third treasury were the first to use young female figures, *korai*, as columns. The Treasury of Siphnos was constructed in 525 B.C.E. out of marble and, as Herodotus reports,[112] the Siphnians, "were richer than any other of the osland peoples, having gold and silver mines so productive that a tenth part of their output was enough to furnish a treasury at Delphi" to finance their lavish building. The *korai* stood on square pedestals and had as echinus an inverted bell sculpted with a scene of two lions killing a bull and, on the very top, a square abacus. They were to become the prototype of the so-called "Maidens of the Erechtheion."[113] Many of these novelties, together with the continuous sculpted frieze, were to become elements of the future Ionic canon.

Located at a very prominent position on the Sacred Way, the Athenian treasury at Delphi dated 490 B.C.E., was also entirely of marble. Its two columns were Doric, holding a frieze with thirty sculpted metopes representing the Labors of Herakles and Theseus. The treasury—not very adventurous in its design in comparison to its Asia Minor counterparts—received over one hundred fifty inscriptions on its walls, the most significant being the Hymn to Apollo with musical notation. On the terrace at the southern side of the treasury, an inscription declared that the Athenians dedicated this building to Apollo after the battle of Marathon.

Ionic column of the Naxian votive Sphinx column, Delphi.

The Stoa of the Athenians at Delphi, c. 479–470 B.C.E., was narrow—only ten feet (3.1 meters) wide. It had a wooden entablature and columns entirely of marble, with bases that were a first attempt at the Attic Ionian variant. The shafts were monolithic, with sixteen flutes, and the Ionic capitals had an echinus without eggs. The stylobate bears the earliest surviving occurrence of the word "stoa", stating that the Athenians dedicated the arms and ornaments of the ship's prows from the enemy's booty.[114]

As with Aeolic motifs first executed experimentally in artifacts and subsequently introduced into architecture, one cannot exclude a similar transfer of elements of the Ionic capital from the votive stele. Among the first Ionic capitals there are four votive examples: the Sangri capital (625 B.C.E., the

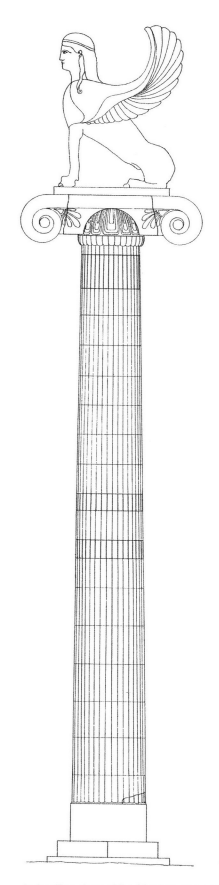

Ionic votive column with sphinx from Aigina, elevation.
c. 580–570 B.C.E.
After Furtwängler, 1906.

Temple of Aphaia, Aigina.
Photographer unknown.

Temple of Aphaia, Aigina. South view.
Photograph by Hellner.

earliest surviving example of a canonic Ionic capi-tal without an abacus); the Aigina Sphinx column (600–575 B.C.E.); the forty foot (12.1 meter) high Naxian Sphinx column at Delphi (570 B.C.E.); and the Sphinx column at Delos, (560 B.C.E.) per-haps also a Naxian gift.[115] The Delian and possibly the Delphi capitals possessed an upward floral cen-tral element between the volutes, resembling the configuration of the Aeolic capitals and thereby suggesting generic affinities between the two.[116] All these votive Ionic capitals are crowned by the statue of a sphinx—a mythical creature, with the wings of an eagle, the body of a lion, and the head and breasts of a woman.

Sphinxes, together with other imaginary winged creatures—such as the winged Gorgon—migrated from the Middle East and Egypt, together with a large number of deities and cults.[117] Their meaning

is obscure. Sphinxes are well known, however, for asking riddles. There is an inscription on the base of an archaic stele from Thessaly that reads: "O sphinx, dog of Hades, whom do you watch over, sitting . . . over the dead?"[118] This might explain why sphinxes are associated with the memory of the dead. Equally puzzling is the way in which the com-plex counterfactual configuration of the artifact was created, making associations between distant objects by extracting, transferring, and recombin-ing pieces from factual creatures. Interestingly, the construction of the sphinx was contemporary to that of the Ionic capitals. There is a correspon-dence between the shape of the wings of the sphinxes and the spirals of the voluted capitals, as well as between the formal structural treatment of the sculpture and the architectural form that may reveal the common roots of the training of sculptors and architects. Yet even more intriguing might be the analogy between the conception of the sphinx and the creation of the Ionic capital.

The period of very intense exploration appears to have reached a plateau towards the end of the fifth century B.C.E. A number of buildings dating from this time manifest a process of consolidation of what had already been achieved: namely, a remarkable repertory of elements that clearly identified two distinct kinds of architecture—the Doric and the Ionic—and a method of coordinating both of these kinds of elements into spatial compositions. A perfect example of this achievement was the small limestone temple of Aphaia in Aigina. Situated on a ridge in a pine grove with panoramic views of the sea, the Peloponnesus, and Attica, this temple was built towards the end of the fifth century B.C.E. An older building on the same site was non-peripteral, *in antis* with narrow metopes. As in the case of Bassai discussed earlier, whenever a community replaced a non-peripteral with a peripteral temple, it was common to construct a new building rather than to modify the existing edifice. The new temple of Aphaia was *in antis* with porch and *opisthodomus.* The *pteron* had six by twelve monolithic Doric columns sloping sharply inwards and, except for the corner increase, constant diameter and intercolumniation. Black and red were used to enhance the stonework. In the cella, a double Doric colonnade supported an architrave that bore a second story of smaller columns, again Doric, supporting the roof. Later, a wooden floor was inserted at the level of the architraves to create a second level. Only the acroteria were made out of marble. The building had terra-cotta tiles, with

the exception of those of the ridge of the roof that were of marble. The very high quality pedimental sculpture of this edifice is today at the Glyptothek of Munich; it was sold by the same team of Europeans who attended Lord Byron's party in Lord Elgin's boat at the beginning of the nineteenth century, then continuing on to Bassai.

Around 470–460 B.C.E. began the construction of one of the biggest Greek temples, the temple of Olympian Zeus at Akragas of Sicily, which was left unfinished in 406 B.C.E. The most impressive feature of this temple is its pseudo-*pteron*: seven by fourteen half-columns, with Doric capitals built in two courses, and backed by rectangular pilasters, were engaged in a continuous wall with Ionic moldings on the base. Small blocks were thus used in rows rather than shafts and, instead of single architrave blocks covering the gap between columns, three blocks (from axis to axis of the columns) reinforced with iron bars and dowelled together were used. Male figures with lowered heads and raised arms so as to support the architrave have been restored between the columns.

At Paestum, the Doric temple of Hera—often referred to as the "Neptune" temple—bears some similarities with the Aphaia temple. Built c. 474–460 B.C.E., it is a peripteral building with six by fourteen columns and two *in antis* porches (*prodomos* and *opisthodomos*). The external columns taper upwards. In the interior, a double row of columns supports an architrave and a second story of smaller columns, as in Aphaia.

On the top of the hill of Kolonos Agoraios over the Agora of Athens facing the Acropolis stands the

Temple of Zeus at Olympia, section. c. 460
After Herrmann, 1972.

white marble temple of Hephaistos, one of the best-preserved and most canonical Doric buildings of ancient Greece. Its construction started before Parthenon, in 449 B.C.E. and was completed in 444 B.C.E.[119] The temple has a six by thirteen Doric *pteron*, a deep porch with a smaller *opisthodomus*, and an internal U-shaped Doric colonnade on two levels. The building possessed pedimental sculpture, with the apotheosis of Herakles on the East pediment and the Labors of Herakles on the ten Eastern metopes. The Doric purity is broken only in a few places. Over its porch runs a continuous Ionic frieze framed with Ionic moldings depicting Theseus in a battle. Theseus is the subject of eight other metopes, and for this reason the temple is commonly called the "Theseion." Square pits dug out of the rock and containing vessels for flowers have been found around the temple, indicating a garden—the first discovery of its kind in a Greek temple; the first planting is thought to date from the third century B.C.E.

The marble Temple of Poseidon (about 440 B.C.E.) at Sounion, dedicated to the god of the sea, is situated on the top of a promontory and could therefore be seen by seamen from far away. Because of strong similarities, it has been argued that both the Temple of Poseidon at Sounion and the Hephaisteion were the work of the same architect. The Doric columns of the temple have sixteen flutes and no entasis. The temple had no pedimental sculpture. As in the case of the temple of Hephaistos, the design of the Temple of Sounion achieved an exact alignment of the porch façade columns with the third columns of the *pteron*, and in general of all its major constituent elements.

Temple of Poseidon, Sounion.
Photograph by Kleemann.

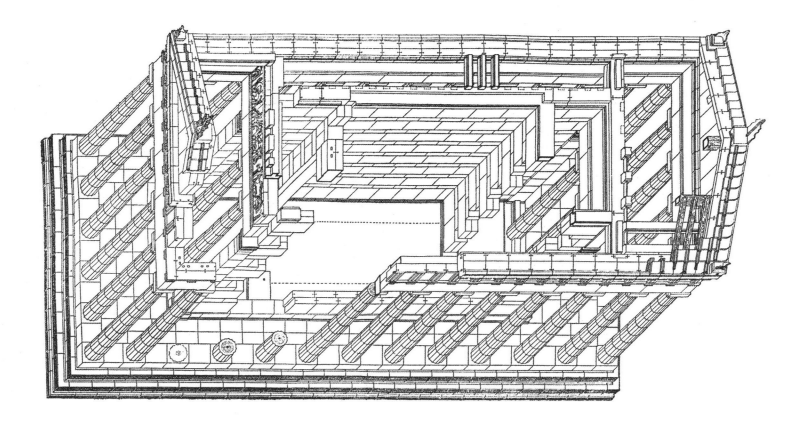

Temple of Poseidon, Sounion. Axonometric view after restoration.
After M. L. Bowen, 1950.

The early fifth-century B.C.E. also saw the beginnings of the construction of the limestone Temple of Zeus at Olympia. The architect was Libon of Elis and the temple bears the same characteristics as that at Aphaia and of Zeus at Akragas, but with the canonical number of six by thirteen columns. The lower architrave for the superimposed interior columns supported a level over the aisles, thus creating galleries that could be visited by means of winding staircases that continued to the roof, from which the visitors could admire the colossal statue of Zeus sculpted by Phidias. As in the Temple of Apollo at Bassai, there were sculptured metopes above the architrave of the porch and *opisthodomus*, a practice that continued to be used in the Peloponnesus. The temple must have been completed in 457 B.C.E.; in 432 B.C.E., Phidias began work on the gold and ivory-seated statue of Zeus, replacing the old one at the end of the cella. The Zeus temple is a typical example of the evolution of Doric architectural elements, in their more canonical form.

Neither the Doric nor the Ionic were kinds in the sense of "natural kinds." They were constructed by people who worked over a specific period and who came into contact with each other through an extensive network that enabled the flow of knowledge. The last group of buildings under discussion here shows that this exploration yielded results that reached a certain stage of completion almost concurrently in mainland Greece and southern Italy. However, around the same time, little building occurred in Asia Minor. The Greek communities entered into a series of skirmishes that would escalate to a major war between several Greek cities and the Persian Empire. It is difficult

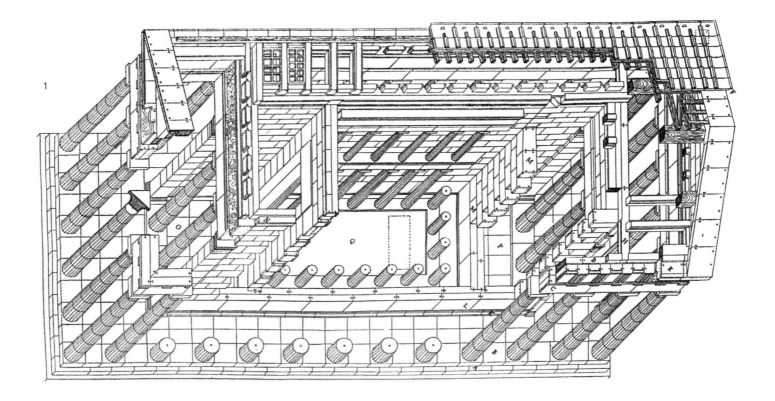

1

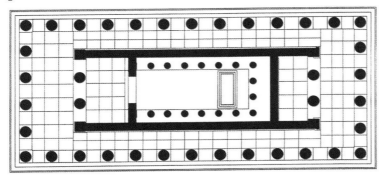

2

3

1- **Temple of Hephaistos, Athens.**
Axonometric view after restoration.
After M. L. Bowen.

2- **Temple of Hephaistos, Athens.**
Plan of the ceiling.
After Baumeister.

3- **Temple of Hephaistos, Athens.**
Plan after restoration.

Temple of Hephaistos, Athens.
Photograph by Waldemar Deonna.

to say to what degree this colossal conflict—that was to conclude with the military triumph of the Greeks over the Persians—created a new era in the evolution of architecture. The fact remains that, just as Greek architecture appeared to have resolved all the problems it had set up as targets, a new set of problems emerged that was to retrigger the process of exploration. These problems demanded a more precise differentiation between the interior and exterior of a building. It also asked for buildings that responded to more complex programmatic needs, and to more constrained site circumstances. By that time, the Greeks—or rather the Athenians—were richer, more knowledgeable, and more confident about pursuing this new phase of exploration.

Parthenon, Acropolis, Athens.
Photograph by Frédéric Boissonas.

*"Nothing comes into being nor perishes, but is rather compounded or dissolved
from things that are; so it is right to call coming into being composition
and perishing dissolution."*
Anaxagoras, fragment 17

*"Gods have not revealed all things to men from the beginning;
by searching in time, men invent better things."*
Xenophanes, fragment 18

CHAPTER III

CANON AND *KOINE*

The Acropolis of Athens

On the southwest side of the Acropolis of Athens, the Mycenaeans built a rampart atop the Pelasgian wall of defense at the end of the thirteenth century B.C.E. More than half a millennium after this construction took place, in c. 550 B.C.E., under Pisistratos, the Athenians dedicated a *temenos*, or small sanctuary, to Athena Nike, the goddess of victory. It comprised a small temple, and an altar. War was one of the many things the goddess specialized in, and the inhabitants of ancient Athens—always a mixed population—boasted that victory would never abandon them and that they would never come under foreign rule. Such is the alleged explanation for the lack of wings on the ancient *xoanon* in this temple, although Nike is usually depicted with wings: the Athenians cut them off to prevent victory from ever flying away from their city. However, it is much more likely that the ancient idol did not have wings because Athena Nike, like many rudiments of Greek culture, was a composite construct combining an Eastern winged goddess, Nike, with a local wingless one, Athena.

Almost every ancient Greek city had its *acropolis*—a highly fortified place. The rock of the Acropolis of Athens remained for centuries the city's unique citadel because of its impregnability, and with its added advantage of the legendary Klepsidra Spring, the extant water resources. During the Mycenaean period, Athenians constructed a principal gate to control access to the Acropolis; this opened on the west side and possessed an adjacent a rampart for its defense. During the Archaic period, construction on the Acropolis increased and at least two major limestone peripteral temples were added. After Pisistratos, in 527 B.C.E., a second peripteral temple of Athena was built which, with the establishment of democracy by Kleisthenes in 508 B.C.E., was once more to be replaced with a new one. However, this temple was never completed. Instead, in 490 B.C.E., after the victory at Marathon over the Persians, construction started on the first marble Parthenon only to be stopped shortly thereafter—with the imminence of a new Persian invasion, funds were redirected to defense tasks.

Parthenon, Acropolis, Athens.
Photograph by Mark Edward Smith.

Parthenon. Doric capital.

In 480 B.C.E., the Persians invaded Attica and wrecked "the whole Acropolis" including the major Temple of Athena Polias that, as Herodotus wrote,[120] "they stripped of its treasures and destroyed by fire." The consequences of the war were grave not only for Attica and the Acropolis, but also for the whole Greek world. For almost thirty-five years there was very little building activity, with the exception of the colonies in Italy. The Parthenon on the Acropolis remained unfinished to remind Athenians of the war with the barbarians, as the oath of Plataea prescribed. The situation changed by 447 B.C.E. when Perikles initiated a new era by launching a major reconstruction program for the whole Acropolis. Whatever the visions of Perikles, who was in many respects allied with innovators and modernizers (the philosopher Anaxagoras being one of his friends), the site was not a tabula rasa—even if the Acropolis was virtually a pile of ruins. The building process had to cope with numerous constraints imposed by preexisting structures—both physical and institutional—as well as conflicting vested interests. The confrontation between these restrictions and the forces of innovation brought about a fascinating architectural result.

The Temple of Athena Nike

Soon after Perikles' decision to commence his construction program, in 447 B.C.E., preparations for rebuilding the sanctuary of Athena on the southwest side of the Acropolis began. However, not much was done until c. 448 when Kallicrates was selected as the architect of a new temple of Athena Nike. There were still further delays and his work only actually

Temple of Athena Nike, Acropolis, Athens.
Photograph by Erich Lessing / AKG-images.

began in 427 B.C.E. It is possible that this setback was due to the construction next to the future Athena temple of the new gate, replacing that of Pisistratos that had also been destroyed by the Persians. Furthermore, it was claimed that a dispute arose between Kallicrates and Mnesikles, the architect of the Propylaia, as the new gate was called. The quarrel, which was supposed to have also involved the priests of the temple of Nike, was about the height of the temple's platform. Lowering the level was finally agreed upon and building commenced in 427 B.C.E. In contrast with all preliminary delays, the edifice was completed very quickly during the Peloponnesian War, around 425 B.C.E.

The temple is very small and resembles the Delphic treasuries discussed earlier. Fashioned entirely from Pentelic marble, it exhibits the same excellence in design and execution as the treasuries. The building

has an amphiprostyle tetrastyle plan—a portico with four columns on both ends and no columns on the sides—with an unusual cella of square proportions *in antis* that contained a reproduction of the old wooden *xoanon* of the goddess. The two porches have Ionic columns with monolithic shafts. They carry a sculpted Ionic frieze running above a three-fasciae architrave. A parapet running along the edge of the Acropolis wall, and around the sides and the back of the temple enclosed the site. The friezes depict battles between Greeks and Persians, Greeks and Boeotians (who allied with the Persians), as well as Athena among the gods pleading for the Greek cause. The parapet was also carved with winged figures of Nike and Athena.

There is nothing in the architectural arrangement to reflect the conflicts that preceded the planning of the temple. As with the early and mid-fifth-century

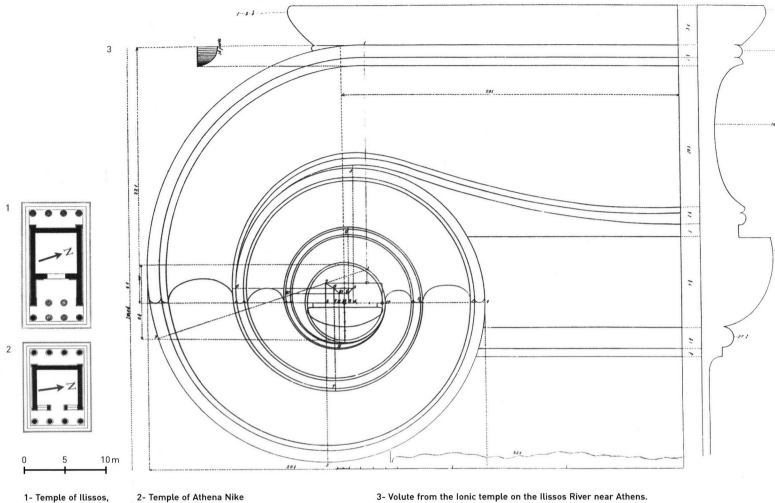

1- Temple of Ilissos,
Athens. 440 B.C.E.

2- Temple of Athena Nike
at the Acropolis.

3- Volute from the Ionic temple on the Ilissos River near Athens.
After M. Lafever, 1883.

B.C.E. Doric buildings discussed earlier, the Ionic Temple of Nike appears as a self-contained object—a composition that, after a period of exploration, has finally achieved a certain stage of satisfaction. The same may be said of another Ionic temple erected near the Ilissos River, at around the time the Temple of Nike was planned. Our knowledge about this temple derives from the meticulous documentation by Stuart and Revett, published in 1762—unfortunately, however, the building was demolished in 1778. Both the Nike and Ilissos temples were Ionic tetrastyle buildings, and both exploited the possibility that the Ionic capital offers to form a corner version of it by bending the volute. The Ionic base of the Nike column harmonized with the profile of the molding at the bottom of the cella wall, establishing a regularity of detail throughout the whole building that was to become part of the Classical canon.

The Ilissos Ionic base had an Attic arrangement: two convex tori with a single concave molding between them formed a pattern that would be applied in the Erechtheion, and that was to become part of the Classical canon. Both buildings appear to have resolved almost all problems related to the alignment of their elements via the modular coordination of their dimensions, taking no notice of complex programmatic needs and site circumstances.

The Parthenon

Built between 447 and 438 B.C.E. from the best quality white Pentelic marble, the Parthenon appears to have achieved an even greater harmonization of members and details. Like the Temple of Nike, it would seem that the plan of the building reflected no

Parthenon, view from the Propylaia.
Photograph by Émile.

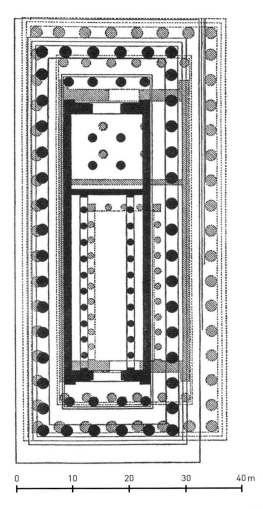

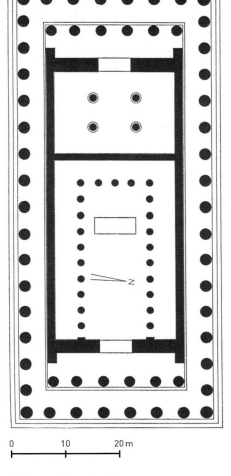

Subsequent layers of the Temple of Athena, Acropolis, Athens.
Older and Periklean Parthenon. 447–432 B.C.E.
After B.H. Hill, 1912.

Parthenon, Acropolis, Athens.
After Gruben, 1978.

site constraints and, relatively speaking, its program was rather straightforward. The architects of the building included Iktinos, architect of the Apollo temple at Bassai, and Kallicrates, who, with Iktinos, coauthored a book on the Parthenon. Phidias was responsible for statue of Athena inside the cella and the rest of the architectural sculptures. He may have had additional larger responsibilities as a kind of overall director of the project.

The temple is a peripteral amphiprostyle building with a peristylion of eight by seventeen Doric columns and two prostyle, hexastyle (six-column) porches. These six columns carry an Ionic frieze that continues around the hall. The front room of the hall had a U-shaped interior colonnade, which, like the interior colonnades of previous fifth-century B.C.E. Doric temples such as Aphaia or the temple of Zeus at Olympia, had a two level superimposed five-by-ten column, Doric colonnade surrounding the chryselephantine statue of Athena by Phidias. Bronze barriers were fixed between the columns to make it possible to walk around the statue of Athena. The statue was illuminated by two high windows placed just beneath the architrave in the wall of the east porch to either side of the entrance. A staircase was enclosed inside the wall leading to the interior of the roof. The back room—the *adyton*, the original *parthenon*, or "room of the virgin"—contained four columns, forty-one feet (12.5 meters) high, which were Ionic. No fragments of the Parthenon Ionic capitals exist, although there is enough evidence about this feature, regarded as an important innovation. The importance of this decision—already attempted, as we have seen in the Paestum temple of

Parthenon, Acropolis, Athens.
Photographer unknown.

Parthenon, Acropolis, Athens. South corner of west frieze.
Photograph by Walter Hege.

"Ceres" and the Athenian Poikele Stoa—was more than a mere mixing of the Doric with the Ionic.[122] Its significance lay in the canonization of a new design rule. In addition to construction benefits,[123] the rule made it possible to differentiate architecturally the various zones of the building, by assigning to each a specialized kind of architectural element. This new rule was applied soon after, probably by the same architect, Iktinos, in the interior colonnades of the Apollo at Bassai and by Mnesikles in the Propylaia. It was gradually to become part of the Classical canon.

The metopes of the Doric entablature, carved in high relief, represent on the west side the Greeks fighting the Amazons, on the south the Centaurs and on the north the Trojans. The battle between gods and giants is the theme of the east side metopes. The fasciae above the triglyphs and metopes have a crowning beaded astragal, and a row of marble antefixes was assigned to run along each side of the building. Once more, Nike was celebrated in the form of enormous acroteria. Athena was honored in the two pediments, the eastern representing the birth of Athena, and the western the contest of Athena and Poseidon for the possession of Athens. By 432 B.C.E., on the eve of the Peloponnesian war, the pediment sculpture was in place. The long continuous Ionic frieze resting on the Doric columns of the porches and the walls of the cella—a unique feature not to be found in previous Doric temples—represented a procession, with clear references to the real-life ritual procession of the Great Panathenaia. On the other hand, contemporary scholars have suggested that it alludes to the Athenians who died in the battle of Marathon. Interestingly, the procession that starts from the same spot, the southwest corner, splits into two processions moving in the opposite

Parthenon, Acropolis, Athens. Northwest corner.
Photograph by Freiler.

Parthenon, Acropolis, Athens.

direction meeting over the main entrance, at the center of the east frieze.

One of the most important qualities for which the Parthenon is known is the abundance of its architectural refinements—intentional deviations from regularity. Refinements were to be found in Greek architecture from the sixth century B.C.E. and much earlier in Egypt. They disappeared by the end of the fifth century B.C.E.—a fact that many scholars consider as an indication of decline.[123] Their absence in modern imitations of ancient Greek buildings was regarded by Penrose, the person who first publicized them, as the reason for their perceived "hardness and dryness."[124] Equally important was the role of its alleged proportions in contributing to the reputation of the temple. The great archaeologist Dinsmoor observed that there was a consistency in proportions of 9:4 and 4:9 in the design of the Parthenon.[125] Both qualities,

however, are hard to establish and as we will discuss later in the chapter on the poetics of ancient Greek architecture, they may be influenced by anachronistic biases.

Similar biases have influenced our view of the role Perikles played in the construction of the Parthenon, his first building commission. Plutarch, in his *Life of Pericles,* written more than five hundred years after Perikles' death, gave an account of his involvement with the Parthenon. Plutarch heroizes Phidias as the sole director of the whole building program, while he might only have been responsible for the statue of Athena. Dates indicate that he probably left the city in 438 B.C.E., before the carving of the Parthenon pediments. Plutarch simplified the complexity of the project. Surviving records of the money spent on construction during an entire year of work suggest that about two hundred craftsmen and fifty sculptors

Parthenon, Acropolis, Athens.
Photograph by Kleemann.

Parthenon, Acropolis, Athens.
Photograph by Serge Moulinier.

worked at the Parthenon. These included Athenians, citizens from the islands, and even slaves, all of whom were paid the same amount of money.[126] In the context of the Athenian democracy it is doubtful that a central authority would have managed this, in the manner of projects at the time of Plutarch's writing. Plutarch also implied that the projects were built with the money of the Delian League, transferred to the Acropolis in 454 B.C.E. However, after centuries of accusations, recent studies show that this was not the case. Most of the costs were covered by the *tamiai*—the treasurers of the goddess—and from Athenian reserves coming from spoils of war, harbor fees, court fines, silver mines, renting houses belonging to Athena, and private contributions.[127] Plutarch even goes as far as to suggest that Perikles started the Peloponnesian War to avoid being brought to court in relation to Phidias' actions and the building of the Parthenon.

The Propylaia

The construction of the Propylaia, the west entrance to the Acropolis in place of the sixth-century Pisistratid gate, began in 437 B.C.E., immediately after the completion of the Parthenon. The architect was Mnesikles and like the Parthenon, the building was of marble. In contrast to the Parthenon and the Temple of Nike that appear to have been unaffected by the distinctiveness of their context, the now much stronger site and programmatic constraints generated the scheme of the building. The result was not only an unprecedented product, but also the creation of a new set of design rules that would become part of the nascent classical canon.

Essentially, a *propylon* was a roofed gate-passage, as illustrated by the sixth-century B.C.E. Pisistratid Propylaia. On the other hand, the new gate was

Propylaia, Acropolis, Athens.
Photograph by Frédéric Boissonas.

required to include new functions, in addition to respecting those in existence. An additional difficulty faced by Mnesikles was the steep angle of the site and the level differences between the adjacent structures. Mnesikles retained the central part of the *propylon*, but extended its length, adding two hexastyle Doric porches to both exterior sides, and Ionic columns on the two sides of the axis of passage. In addition, he included within the same composition, attached on the sides, two volumes. The North volume accommodated a picture gallery, or *pinakotheke*— the name denotes a hall for votive plaques, but the space was also intended in banquets.[128] The south one related to the older Sanctuary of the Graces. Mnesikles brought together all three parts—the gate proper and wings conceived for the Western entrance—in the configuration of a U-shaped stoa. This was a novelty in itself, as only linear and

L-shaped stoae existed up to that moment—the first example being the Stoa of Zeus Eleutherios in the Athenian Agora, built in the last quarter of the fifth century B.C.E.[129] Next to this arrangement, the wing of *Pinakotheke* resembles the arrangement of an anta-treasury.[130] The south wing with its open porch was intended to make the shrine of Athena Nike accessible.

There are affinities between the Propylaia and the Parthenon. The dimensions of the central west part of the Propylaia resemble those of the west room of the Parthenon in the ratio of the height of the column to the lower diameter of the column. Similarities also exist in the optical refinements, the entasis and inward inclination of the columns, as well as the curvature of the architrave. The fact is that the Propylaia followed the Parthenon chronologically, and several technicians of the Parthenon

Propylaia, Acropolis, Athens.

were even transferred in 438 B.C.E. to the workshop of Mnesikles.[131]

The building may be seen as the intriguing outcome of a chance collision between the preexisting constraints of the site, the new programmatic requirements and traditional design rules, to which Mnesikles passively responded by bringing into the heart of the scheme a central section hall, to which he added two fronts and two wings.[132] Bundgaard, in his monograph on Mnesikles, suggested that the design was determined by the archaic Propylon and the structure that preceded the Pinakotheke. Thus, the main building was nothing more than a central section with two added fronts that followed the proportions applied to the peristasis of the Parthenon.

Yet, this was more easily said than done. A major new problem that Mnesikles faced was to create a single composition, his obvious strategy being to apply bilateral symmetry of the façade. However, he did not apply this strategy to the individual spaces of the plan. Dörpfeld assumed that the building was to become symmetrical in the end, but the northeast and southeast sides were never completed due to the Peloponnesian War. Indeed, the Propylaia remained unfinished, thus making the building a typical case of *hymiteles*, or a permanently incomplete work—a notion we will discuss later. As Hurwit remarks, "protective, working surfaces on the steps and floor of the building were never removed . . . scores of lifting bosses . . . were never chiseled off . . . on the East walls of the Northwest and Southwest wings and on the North and South walls of the central gatehouse."[133]

On the other hand, there were many objections to Dörpfeld's idea. Obviously, a symmetrical design would have required the dismantling of the Cyclopean wall south of the Propylaia. Furthermore, recent research shows that the construction of the Propylaia progressed systematically in accordance with strict time and material limits, and not in any improvised way. It is suggested, therefore, that the interruption of the building of the Propylaia was neither sudden nor unforeseen.[134]

Dörpfeld's design represents, perhaps, a reconstruction of the original initial concept behind the adopted plan—a concept that was never actually built by Mnesikles. Mnesikles appears to have been a pragmatic yet revolutionary architect as far as design methodology goes. His design strategy would seem to be the inclusion of all programmatic and site aspects, rather than the reduction of a project to its minimal essentials that would guarantee a harmonious scheme, as was the case of the temple of Olympia or of Ilissos. His design tactics, on the other hand,

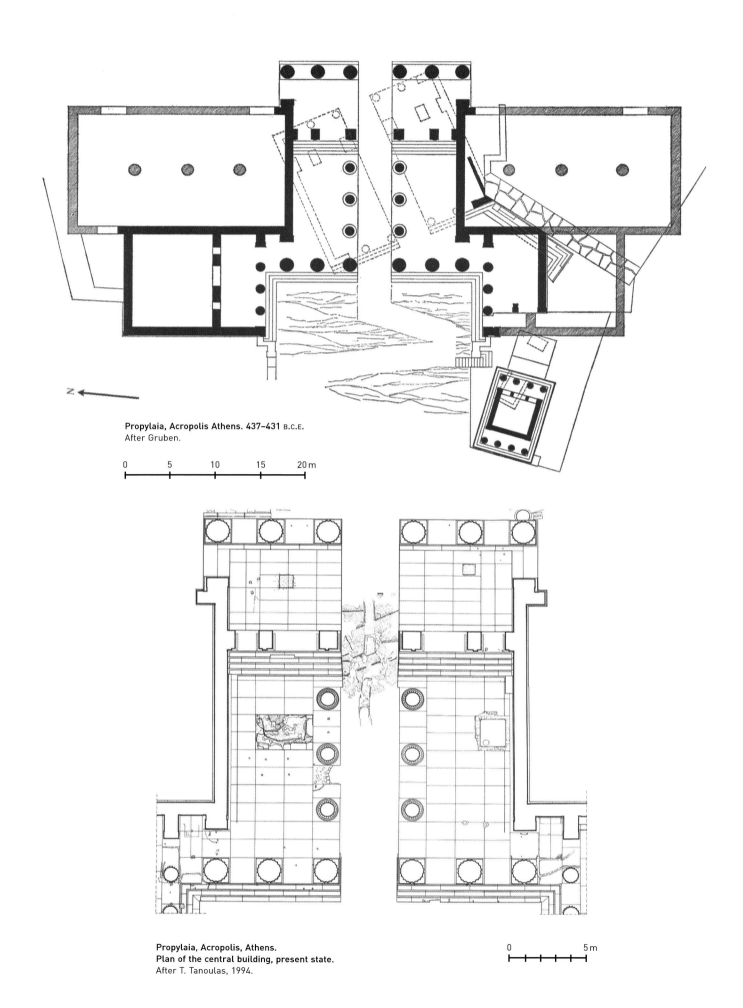

Propylaia, Acropolis Athens. 437–431 B.C.E.
After Gruben.

0   5   10   15   20 m

Propylaia, Acropolis, Athens.
Plan of the central building, present state.
After T. Tanoulas, 1994.

0   5 m

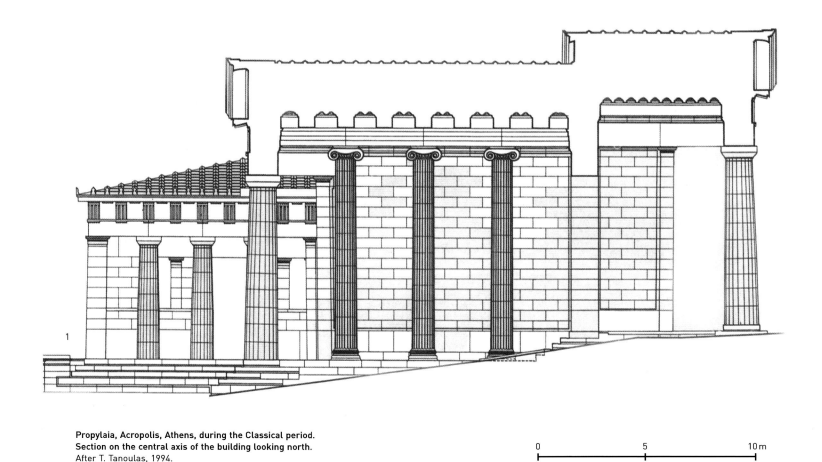

Propylaia, Acropolis, Athens, during the Classical period.
Section on the central axis of the building looking north.
After T. Tanoulas, 1994.

0　　　　　　5　　　　　　10 m

Propylaia, Acropolis, Athens.
South elevation of the north wall of the central building.
After T. Tanoulas, 1994.

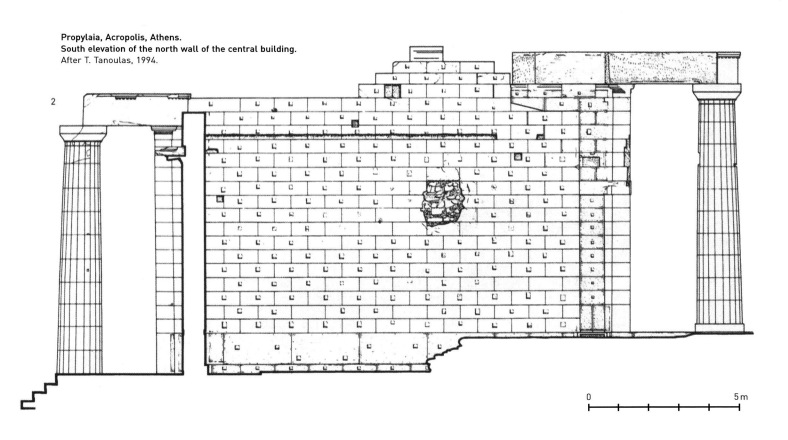

0　　　　　　　　　5 m

Propylaia, Acropolis, Athens.
Photograph by Walter Hege.

Propylaia, Acropolis, Athens.
Photograph by Walter Hege.

Erechtheion, Acropolis, Athens.
In the background, the Parthenon.
Photograph by Frédéric Boissonas.

Erechtheion, Acropolis, Athens.
View of east elevation.
Photograph by Frédéric Boissonas.

appeared to combine already achieved precedents into an unprecedented new building. In addition, like Iktinos, one of his devices was to make use of the potential inherent in the combination of both Doric and Ionic kinds of architecture: the Doric in the exterior façades, and the Ionic in the interior of the passage. Coordinating all these components was a most difficult task: one of the techniques for this being to use two different types of units of measure—one for the design of the ground plan, and the second for the elevations.[135]

The Propylaia as a prototype of innovateness and ingenuity impressed not only architects only. Like the Parthenon, it was admired by the public at large. Characteristically, it is alleged that Epaminondas, who also admired the Parthenon, declared that if Thebes were to be as great as Athens, it would have to transport the Propylaia from the Acropolis to the Kadmeia.

Erechtheion

Perhaps no other building on the Acropolis better demonstrates the degree of complexity and sophistication that ancient Greek architecture achieved at that time than the Erechtheion. The building is paradoxical. While in its detail it has been considered an exemplar of the Classical canon, bringing together the successful results of regional explorations, in the arrangement of its plan it has been recognized as one of the most daring experimental schemes. Its lack of bilateral symmetry and its "pinwheel" form made it the darling of avant-garde architects at the dawn of the twentieth century of our era.

Like the Propylaia, its innovative features resulted from the acceptance of the complex constraints of the site and program as determinants of the scheme. The building was basically intended to replace the

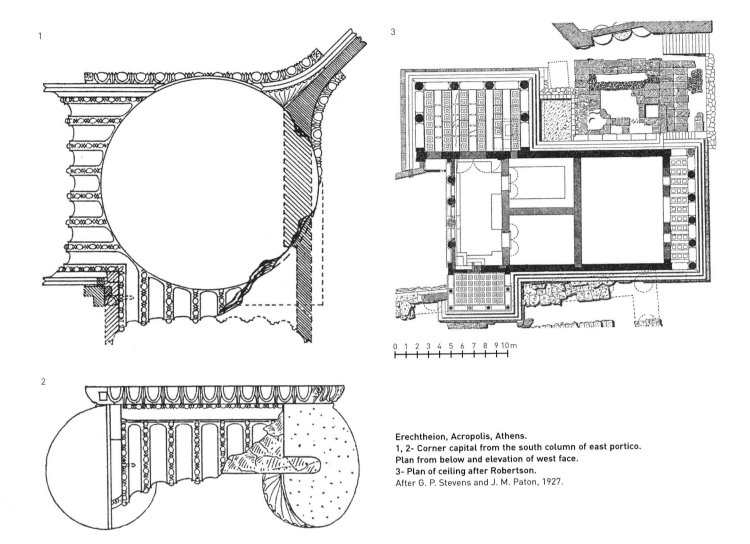

Erechtheion, Acropolis, Athens.
1, 2- Corner capital from the south column of east portico.
Plan from below and elevation of west face.
3- Plan of ceiling after Robertson.
After G. P. Stevens and J. M. Paton, 1927.

Temple of Athena Polias, destroyed by the Persians in 480 B.C.E. But other functions had to be housed too. Partially a tomb, a center of mysteries, and a temple, the basic decisions about the project—which in the end amounted to a cluster of facilities—had to be made by a committee, with numerous priests insisting that their sacred ground had to be respected.

It has been conjectured, thought not without opposition, that the main east cella was for Athena, and the west for Poseidon and Erechtheus, with the sacred olive tree of Athena outside.[136] The east room contained the wooden *xoanon* of Athena that was believed to have fallen from the sky as a present to the mythical serpent-king and founder of Athens, Kekrpos—his sanctuary was on the southwest side of the complex. During the invasion of Attica and the destruction of the Acropolis, the statue was rescued by the Athenians and hidden away in the island of Salamis. The north porch contains marks on the ground believed to be the traces of Poseidon's trident or Zeus's thunderbolt—an opening in the roof indicated the point. Through the north porch one entered the *prostomiaion.* The rear of the building housed an altar to Hephaistos.

These are only some of the elements that the plan of the building was to accommodate. The scheme was unprecedented: the east side employed engaged columns, while those on the west side were free-standing. On the north side, there was an Ionic porch, and on the south a most rare type of porch employing "Caryatid" maidens as columns, raised on a parapet. The east porch used Ionic columns with a braided Attic tripartite base, consisting of a

1- Erechtheion, Acropolis, Athens. North portico, view of ceiling.

2- North portico, view of ceiling and door.

3- East and north porch.

4- North porch.

projecting base torus, an almost vertical scotia, and an upper non-fluted torus. This arrangement was to be canonical for centuries to come. The Ionic capital included a palmette anthemion carved beneath the capitals. It was repeated, in a most consistent manner, onto the anta capital and cella wall. This motif strongly resembled that of the Ionic capital of the fifth-century B.C.E. Locri Maraza temple in Italy. There are also strong affinities between many of the motifs of this temple and those employed in several of the treasuries of Delphi. The complex included many openings, two doors in the back of the north porch, two windows and a door in the east porch. What is significant about these openings is that, following the example of the treasury of Siphnos at Delphi, all these openings are framed by ornamental carved profiles and are thus categorized

as belonging to the Ionic kind—a further contribution of the building to the construction of the Classical canon.

The choice of materials for the Erechtheion was highly selective: the foundations were of Piraeus poros stone. The background of the frieze was of blue Eleusinian limestone, with delicate white marble figures. Colored stones and gilt bronze were also used. There was also a lamp made of gold by one Callimachus, and a bronze chimney in the shape of a palm tree, perhaps by the same designer. There have been speculations that this was one of the precedents of the Corinthian capital, but the dates do not seem to confirm the claim. The rest of the structure was of white Pentelic marble of the finest quality.

Puzzled by the unprecedented character and complexity of the scheme of the Erechtheion, as well as by

Erechtheion, Acropolis, Athens. Anthemio and egg-and-dart *cymatia*.
Photograph by Walter Hege.

its acceptance, Vitruvius rationalized it epigrammat-ically as one of those buildings that "transfer to the sides all that we find in the front in other temples." There is some truth in this, the plan being the result of the recombination of prior elements—but the intentions and the process were much more complex than Vitruvius implied. The scope of the innovations also included in the project surpassed Vitruvius' view, allocating as he did the building almost to the mar-gins of his *Books*.

Erechtheion, Acropolis, Athens. Caryatid.
Photograph by Walter Hege.

Erechtheion, Acropolis, Athens. Caryatid.
Photograph by Walter Hege.

Erechtheion, Acropolis, Athens. Caryatids.
Photograph by Walter Hege.

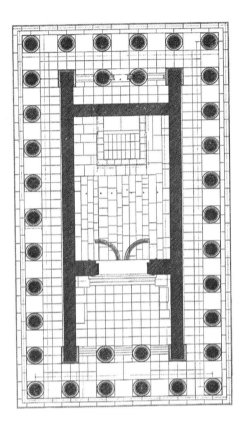

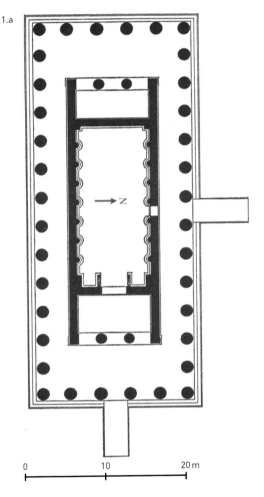

Temple of Athena Polias at Priene.
H. Berve and G. Gruben, 1978.
New drawing from M. Courby, *Fouilles de Delphes*, 1927.

1a- Temple of Athena Alea at Tegea. 350 B.C.E.
After W. B. Dinsmoor, 1950.

Innovation and Diffusion

Since the middle of the fifth century B.C.E., and within a period of not more than fifty years, the architecture on the Acropolis of Athens yielded not only a number of new buildings, but also a new way of design thinking of vast historical significance —what has been called "Classical Architecture"—whose vehicle was a *canon*, or body of explicit design rules, and a *koine*, or common body of implicit design conventions.

The achievement was accomplished within a small geographical area by a handful of people. Yet it was only possible because a large number of experts, expert communities, and expert knowledge distributed over regions of Mediterranean had been brought together in Athens through an extensive network of communication, alliances, and reciprocities. There were tremendous possibilities for this recruited knowledge in the production of new artifacts and new ideas during the fifth-century B.C.E. reconstruction of the Acropolis. Finances were available and there existed "poly-archia" or opportunities for many points of view and many experiences to become public—though, certainly not democracy in the contemporary sense. The recruited knowledge was debated, recombined into new conceptual constructs, and tried out in real projects. Last but not least, with victory being celebrated at every corner of the rock of the Acropolis, there was confidence in the potential of Athens to create a new world.

On the other hand, the same time there were severe constraints. Space on the Acropolis was extremely tight and, as we have seen, traditions—rituals and taboos— and vested interests were numerous, stubborn, and powerful. It was the concurrence of the two that brought about this creative innovation in architecture.

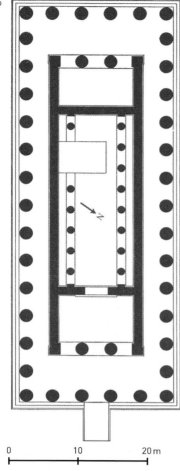

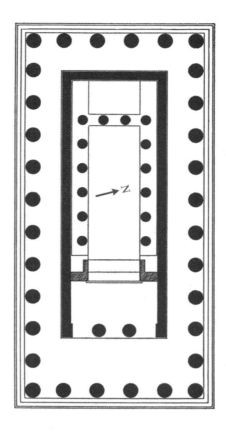

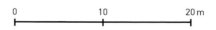

1b- Temple of Apollo VI at Delphi. 346–326 B.C.E. (Fourth century B.C.E.)
H. Berve and G. Gruben, 1978.
New drawing from M. Courby, *Fouilles de Delphes*, 1927.

Temple of Zeus at Nemea. 330 B.C.E.
After Gruben, 1978.

However, according to several scholars, the period that followed the creative reconstruction of the Acropolis was disappointing. Characteristically, Dinsmoor has commented that the great temple-building epoch on the Greek mainland had passed with the end of the fifth century B.C.E., most of the subsequent architectural activity being concerned with the further addition of ornament or the mixing of "orders".[137] Certainly, the same criticism may be directed at the architecture of the classic Acropolis itself. In many respects, this fails to match the daring groundbreaking architectural experiments of the archaic period. Indeed, most of these evaluations look at the performance of one period through the accomplishments of the other. On the other hand, if we consider these periods as a set of strata of constructions, each of which offering the grounds for the next to be erected, the period that followed the reconstruction of the Acropolis and that of the reconstruction itself, may both be recognized as pioneering in ways that were to have a lasting impact on the evolution of architecture—even down to our own time.

Innovation in the post-Acropolis era moved in two directions: on the one hand, the development of a framework integrating the different kinds of architectural elements into a new conceptual spatial system; and, on the other, the development of new types of spatial organization of buildings. The design rules contained in the emerging canon referred to above was expressed in the numerous books written by a large number of Greek architects. The conventions of the *koine* of architecture were diffused through technicians who moved around from one site to another—from region to center, and the reverse—as conditions demanded and as opportunities permitted.[138]

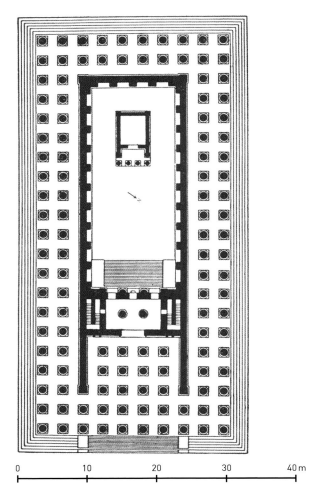

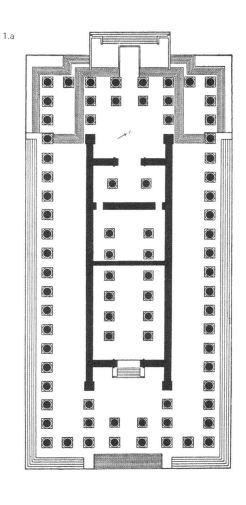

1.a

Temple of Apollo at Didyma. Third century B.C.E. and later.
W. Arnold Lawrence, (1957).

1a- Temple of Artemis Cybele at Sardeis. 300 B.C.E.
Restored by Butler. Dinsmoor, 1950.

Ionic Purity and Rigor

For the Classical canon and *koine* applied to the Ionic kind, as developed in the temples of Ilissos, Athena Nike, the Erechtheion, and Apollo of Bassai, precedent architectural knowledge was recruited from the regions of Naxos, Delos, Samos, and Delphi. Canon and *koine* were implemented and further developed in the region of Ionia. In Priene, Pythios designed the temple of Athena Polias (350–344 B.C.E.), whose use as a precedent enhanced the evolution of the *koine*. He also wrote a book about architecture that contributed to the formulation of the canon.

The temple must have been of some importance because Alexander the Great himself dedicated it. It was a six by eleven building with a cella that could be reached from the porch. Some of the elements were clearly regional. Pythios preferred the Asiatic base of

the older Artemision at Ephesus rather than the Attic for the columns of his building. Over the fasciae ran an astragal, an egg-and-dart row, the dentils and a repetition of the previous motif—astragal, and egg and dart row—on a smaller scale. A plain band, a convex cymatium, a flat fillet, and finally a pediment with flamboyant profile crowned the arrangement. Pythios' achievement—that was to be admired by Vitruvius and apparently by his contemporaries in general—lay in his coordination of all architectural elements that entered into the scheme down to the smallest detail. For this he devised a universal grid to mark the positions. He also chose the specific details that would satisfy this objective. The very choice of the kind of elements applied was made with this goal in mind. Thus he excluded the Doric: as it had been formed during almost two centuries of exploration, it was restrictive, rigid, and

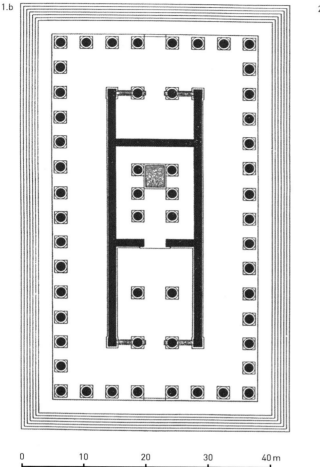

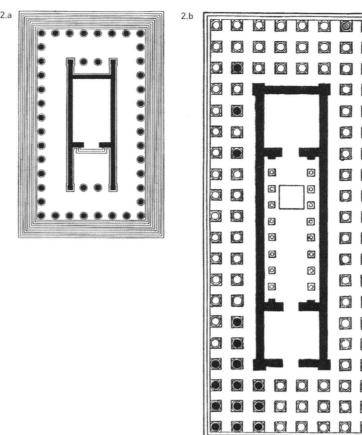

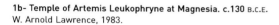

0   10   20   30   40 m

1b- Temple of Artemis Leukophryne at Magnesia. c.130 B.C.E.
W. Arnold Lawrence, 1983.

0   10   20 m

2.a- Temple of Apollo Smintheus
in the Troad. 150 B.C.E.
After Dinsmoor, 1950.

0   10   20   30   40 m

2.b- Temple of Zeus Olympios at
Athens, Hellenistic. 174 B.C.E.
After Dinsmoor, 1950.

had incompatible components. Apparently, Pythios was very conscious of this problem because, according to Vitruvius, in his book he attacked Doric temples as being faulty and incongruous due to the problem of the "arrangement of triglyphs and metopes," the triglyph not always corresponding to the center of the columns.[139] Indeed, there is only one example of scale drawing in antiquity: it is to be found on a wall block of this temple and is supposed to have been executed by the architect.[140]

Still drawing on Attic precedents, though more rigidly canonical, followed a century later, at around 150 B.C.E., the temple of Artemis Leukophryne at Magnesia. The architect was Hermogenes who, like Pythios, wrote a book about his temple. Vitruvius admired Hermogenes as practitioner and theoretician, and for his contribution to the development of the Classical canon. Hermogenes, continuing the

work of Pythios, advanced a rigorous method of achieving regularity in Ionic temples through a system of proportions that coordinated the size of the elements of the building on the basis of a common module derived from the diameter of a column.[141] According to Vitruvius, Hermogenes' choice to apply the Ionic kind to the temple was the result of purely architectural considerations. He claimed that Hermogenes had initially chosen to build a Doric temple. It was only later—at the very last minute and after he had ordered the materials for construction—that he decided to abandon the Doric and to design an Ionic building.

Vitruvius also admired Hermogenes as innovator and inventor of a new type of plan—the "pseudo-dipteral."[142] Hermogenes demonstrated this new type in the design of his temple of Artemis Leukophryne. In addition, he described its rules in

Temple of Athena Polias, Priene.
Photograph by Erich Lessing / AKG-images.

Temple of Athena Polias, Priene.

his book. Through the pseudodipteral, by "taking away the row of inner columns," Hermogenes succeeded in creating an unparalleled effect of spaciousness—a daring decision at the time, both from the morphological and the technological point of view. The temple had an eight by fifteen Ionic colonnade, with a cella equal in size to the *opisthodomus*, and a front porch. The inner columns were aligned with the *pteron*. The base of the columns was Attic, as was the frieze. The pediments of the temple were vacant and the acroteria were of virtually the same height as the pediment beneath them. This was uncommonly large—perhaps for reasons of optical correction, an issue that had started to come under discussion at that time.

There may also have been regional motivations—perhaps of local identity and pride—in the adoption of the Ionic kind of architecture by Hermogenes.[143]

However, both through his design and his writings, Hermogenes promoted the Classical canon and *koine* with a global impact that can be identified not only in Roman architecture and the text of Vitruvius, but also in the architecture and architectural treatises of the seventeenth, eighteenth and even nineteenth centuries in Europe and America.

The formation of the system of architectural kinds

When reading Vitruvius and focusing on the influential Ionic temples, one might have the impression that the Doric kind of architecture underwent a crisis and was put to one side. Yet this was far from being the case.[144] There was a parallel development in Peloponnesus related to the use of the Doric kind—one

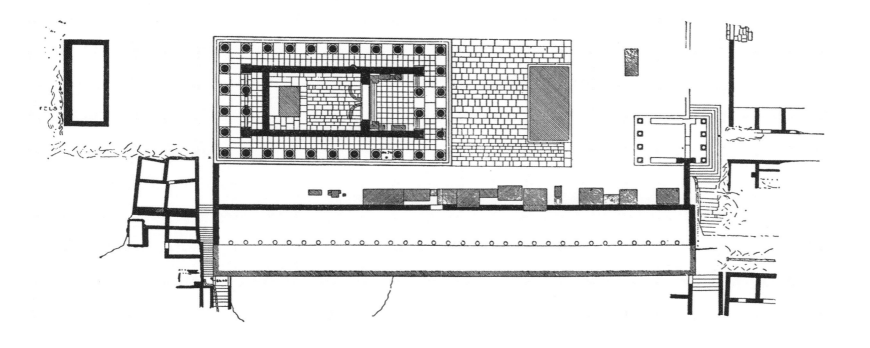

Temple of Athena Polias at Priene, plan.
Dedicated in 334 B.C.E.
After Gruben, 1978.

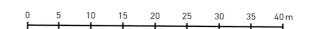

0 5 10 15 20 25 30 35 40 m

that was perhaps more innovative than the canonization of the Ionic in Asia Minor. While Pythios and Hermogenes worked towards developing an Ionic canon that opted for a reductive purity and produced a rigorous system of correspondences between elements of the same kind—the Ionic—the architects working in the Peloponnesus, drawing on the precedents of the Parthenon, the Propylaia, and the Apollo of Bassai produced a system that incorporated the Doric, Ionic, and Corinthian kinds. This system involved more than simply "mixing the orders" together. It provided a new framework for design thinking that categorized architectural elements as kinds, belonging to a ranking that corresponded to an equivalent categorization and ranking of the building in terms of spatial zones. As we will see later, further testing, adaptation, and rethinking brought together both systems into what we call "Classical Architecture."

Drawing on the precedent of Bassai, the temple of Athena Alaia—Alaia was a local deity fused with Athena—at Tegea, incorporated all three kinds of architecture. Built c. 350 B.C.E., it was the structure most admired by Pausanias, after that of Olympia. It was a peripteral six by fourteen building with a Doric peristylion. The north long side of the *pteron* accommodated an unusual second entrance in the center. Internally, the temple employed a Bassai-like colonnade of attached columns. However, unlike Bassai, and like the temple of Olympia or the Hephaisteion, this colonnade was on two levels. The innovative step was that the first level was Corinthian and the second Ionic. The designer of the Corinthian capital—with an acanthus leaf at the center—was the great sculptor Skopas, who may also have been involved in the conception of the whole building.

Tholos of Delphi.
Photograph by Waldemar Deonna.

The temple of Nemea, of c. 330 B.C.E., had many similarities with Tegea. It was a peripteral six by twelve building with a Doric exterior colonnade. Inside, like Bassai, it had a U-shaped colonnade. The internal colonnade possessed two levels, like the Tegea: the first level was Corinthian, and the second Ionic. The shaft of the Doric column of the exterior colonnade was slender, thus marking the shift of the Hellenistic period away from the bulky origins of the Doric.

The Tholos

Exterior use of the Doric was also combined with interior deployment of the Ionic and Corinthian, in a very different type of building, the Tholos,[145] a circular building. The Tholos was not a novel building to fourth-century architects. It had archaic—if

not even earlier—roots but its circular shape seems to have made it unpopular. The Delphic Tholos (c. 380–370 B.C.E.) followed a sixth-century Tholos, also in Delphi, and one that was built c. 470 B.C.E., in the Agora of Athens, a building used by the presidents, *prytaneis*. Contrary to these earlier Tholoi that employed only Doric elements, the fourth-century Tholos in Delphi combined Doric with Corinthian. Its outside peristylion had twenty slender Pentelic marble Doric columns resting on a three step *crepis* composed of forty blocks and a stylobate of forty-eight feet (14.5 meters) in diameter. Two metopes corresponded to each intercolumniation, and the cella wall with orthostates ended with a Doric frieze of forty metopes. Inside, a Corinthian colonnade was attached to the walls. The capitals resembled the Bassai capital. Marble was also the material of the roof of the building. According to Vitruvius,

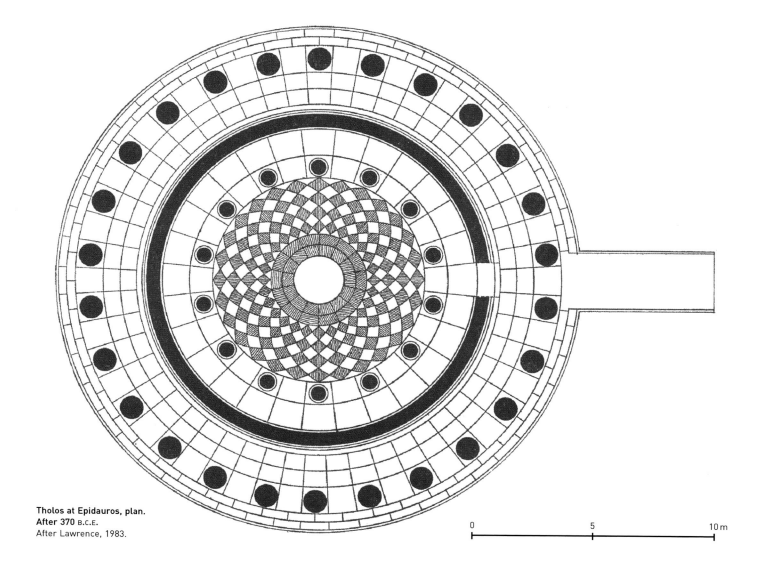

Tholos at Epidauros, plan.
After 370 B.C.E.
After Lawrence, 1983.

0   5   10 m

Theodoros Phocaeus (from Phocaea of Asia Minor) wrote a book about this building, and it is for this reason that he is considered its architect. The Tholos of Epidauros, called *Thymele*, followed that of Delphi and was built around 360 B.C.E. It was a limestone building, with a diameter of seventy-two feet (21.82 meters) and an outside colonnade of twenty-six columns. As in Delphi, this colonnade was Doric and the fourteen interior columns were Corinthian. The metopes of the exterior Doric frieze carried a large rosette carved in the middle. Under the building there was a crypt with a complicated labyrinthine arrangement of concentric circles, interlinked through an irregular pattern of accesses. The architect, according to Pausanias, was Polyclitus.

The Philippeion at Olympia was built later, around 335 B.C.E. It had an Ionic exterior colonnade, combined with Corinthian half-columns engaged in the inner face of the cella. This combination prefigured later Roman and post-Renaissance developments of the Classical architecture canon, whereby the Corinthian occupies the third place in the hierarchy of kinds of architecture, after the Doric and the Ionian.

The Stoa

Significant design innovations took place during the fourth century B.C.E. in the stoa. Like Tholos, the stoa was a building type whose roots lay in the Archaic period. Its early development also drew extensively on Egyptian precedents. During the second part of the fifth century B.C.E., the demand for stoae—very useful multifunctional buildings—grew, as did the development of the plan. Fourth-century innovations

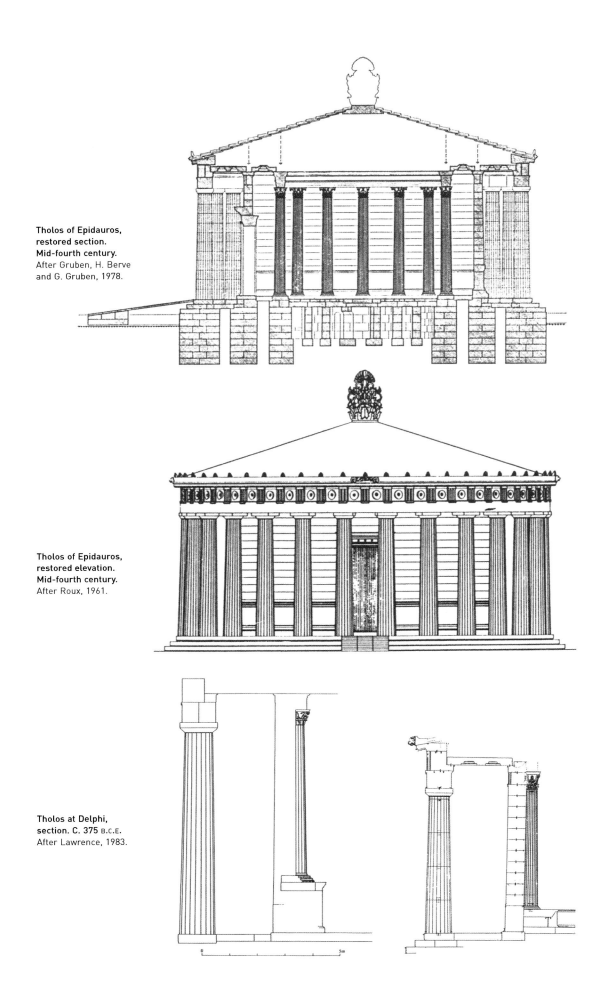

Tholos of Epidauros, restored section. Mid-fourth century. After Gruben, H. Berve and G. Gruben, 1978.

Tholos of Epidauros, restored elevation. Mid-fourth century. After Roux, 1961.

Tholos at Delphi, section. C. 375 B.C.E. After Lawrence, 1983.

Attalos, Agora of Athens.

contributed to the advancement of new L- and U-shaped plan configurations. Rooms and a second story were also added. During this time, the stoa became the first type of building in ancient Greece that was used as a means of defining an outside area, of surrounding sanctuaries or markets, and of forming places, rather than simply as an independent object inserted in space. In addition, the stoa rivaled the temple as the building type in which the "architectural kinds"—Doric, Ionic, Corinthian, and even "palm"—were systematized.

Zeus Eleutherios (c. 430-421 B.C.E.) in the Agora of Athens was the first U-shaped stoa combining a Doric exterior colonnade with an Ionic interior. In the middle of the second century, a number of stoae were added to the Athenian Agora with Doric front colonnades. Around the same time, stoae were built in other Greek cities following very similar arrangement: in c. 340 B.C.E., the Stoa of Philip in

Megalopolis had a densely spaced Doric colonnade accompanied by two rows of sparsely spaced Ionic colonnade inside. During the first half of the second century B.C.E. a stoa was built surrounding the earlier Doric Temple of Athena in Pergamon with a very experimental interrelation between the kinds of colonnades and entablatures. It had a Doric colonnade with three triglyphs per inter-columnar interval. Superposed on it was an Ionic colonnade with a frieze-like balustrade between its columns. The Ionic colonnade with a two-band entablature was combined with a Doric frieze that possessed a denser, four per inter-columnar interval number of triglyphs.

A rather consistent systematization of the different kinds of columns, in parallel to the systematization of the different kinds of zones in a building, took place in the long two-storied stoa in the Agora of Athens, built between 159-138 B.C.E., and sponsored by King Attalos II of Pergamon. The building combined

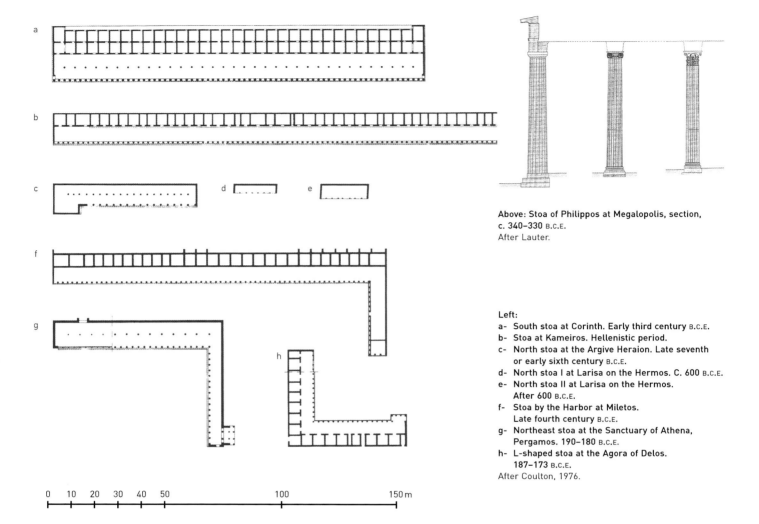

Above: Stoa of Philippos at Megalopolis, section, c. 340–330 B.C.E.
After Lauter.

Left:
a- South stoa at Corinth. Early third century B.C.E.
b- Stoa at Kameiros. Hellenistic period.
c- North stoa at the Argive Heraion. Late seventh or early sixth century B.C.E.
d- North stoa I at Larisa on the Hermos. C. 600 B.C.E.
e- North stoa II at Larisa on the Hermos. After 600 B.C.E.
f- Stoa by the Harbor at Miletos. Late fourth century B.C.E.
g- Northeast stoa at the Sanctuary of Athena, Pergamos. 190–180 B.C.E.
h- L-shaped stoa at the Agora of Delos. 187–173 B.C.E.
After Coulton, 1976.

0 10 20 30 40 50   100   150 m

a Doric colonnade, outside on the ground level, with an Ionic exterior superimposed upon it; and an Ionic colonnade, inside on the ground floor, with a superimposed colonnade comprising bell-shaped palm capitals. The choice of the palm capital is interesting. According to the canon—as it would appear to have been formed by then—it was possible to use a Corinthian capital–(see the precedent of the Tholos of Delphi). The reason for reusing this explicitly "oriental" palm capital last seen in the treasuries of Delphi where it was employed by colonies associated with Ionia—but eclipsed for almost four centuries since that time—might have been related to the sponsor, Attalos. He intended to employ the building as a political act to gain prestige and visibility, with Athens gradually replacing in that the role of Delphi.

Another development of the period concerned the fusion of two different elements, each of which belonged to a different architectural group. An example is two colonnades meeting together in one columnar corner element. However, while corner columns have been treated apart—as in the case of corner Doric columns being enlarged, or of corner Ionic capitals having a special configuration—their form was not generated by fusion. We have demonstrated earlier an extreme case of a fused element, that was never to be followed up afterwards, in the composite capital from the Throne of Apollo at Amyclai. The problem was already present in the arrangement of the plan of the Propylaia of the Acropolis and its own U-shaped plan. However, it became acute with the development of new, more complex types of buildings, such as the U- and L-shaped stoae. The corner triglyphs developed since the sixth century B.C.E. in southern Italy were such a kind of fused element that attempted a solution to

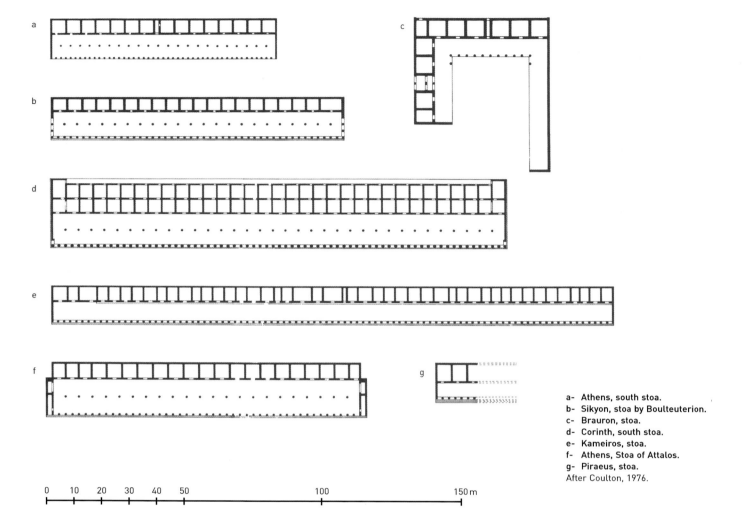

a- Athens, south stoa.
b- Sikyon, stoa by Boulteuterion.
c- Brauron, stoa.
d- Corinth, south stoa.
e- Kameiros, stoa.
f- Athens, Stoa of Attalos.
g- Piraeus, stoa.
After Coulton, 1976.

0 10 20 30 40 50   100   150 m

the problem. Likewise was the corner configuration of the plan of the north market stoa of Miletos, which raised the question of how to treat the corner column where the two colonnades came together. In the Miletos stoa, a composite cardioid column has been adopted.

Architectural records

Since the reconstruction of the Acropolis and drawing on its experience, in addition to the growth of the stoa building, there was a proliferation of new types of buildings. Iktinos worked on the Telesterion at Eleusis, adding an Ionic porch to a previously existing building that had a Doric triglyph. This was a temple dedicated to Demeter. The ritual practice that took place within it was different from that of other temples, and it was

shrouded in great secrecy. The building was a huge enclosed hall capable of holding thousands of celebrants and it was rebuilt several times throughout history. During the last years of the sixth century B.C.E., the Pisistratids contributed the first square plan building. This was destroyed by the Persians and rebuilt without a porch in the early fifth century. Iktinos' plan returned to the square configuration. The roof of the building rested on a unique—for the time—support system of cross-row columns with clear Egyptian affinities.[146] Philon of Eleusis was finally to attach a Doric porch to it.[147]

The inscriptions found in the sanctuary, as mentioned earlier, testify to the difficulty of finding resources for construction during antiquity. As many as thirty-three animals were needed to pull a single column drum from Pendeli to Eleusis: since the same animals also had to be used for plowing,

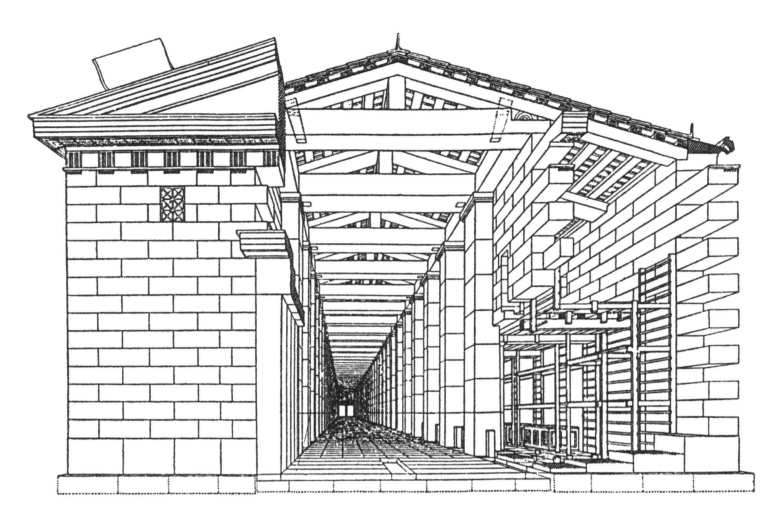

Arsenal of Philon at Piraeus, restoration.
347/6–329 B.C.E.
After Lawrence, 1983.

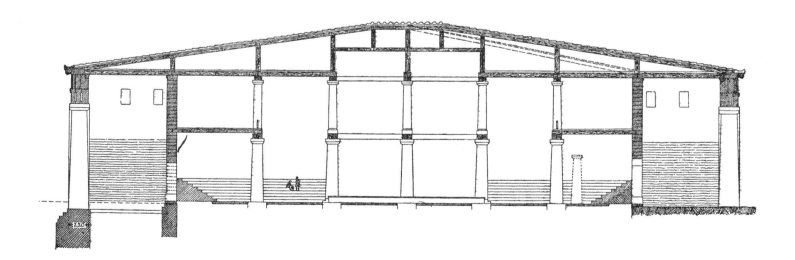

Telesterion at Eleusis by Iktinos,
south-north section. C. 440 B.C.E.
After Robertson, 1969.

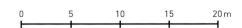

threshing, and harvesting, any major construction work that involved the transportation of heavy objects could take place only during agriculturally slack periods.[148]

Another massive building, with a new type of plan arrangement, was the naval Arsenal in Piraeus c. 340 B.C.E. An even more detailed inscription was found here containing unique information on the technical specifications, procedures and responsibilities of construction in Athens at that time. It was written by its architect Philon of Eleusis, architect of the above-mentioned porch of Eleusis, and who was also well-known—as we have already seen—as the author on a book on architecture, and an eloquent verbal promoter of his work. Like the Telesterion, the Arsenal was a large building, extremely simple and functional. The plan consisted of a double loaded passage with storerooms on both sides. Windows were placed on the ground floor, opposite the intercolumniations on the long sides. Outside, the Arsenal had a Doric frieze surmounted by triglyphs. It was argued that Philon used this, along with Ionic columns,[149] as part of the general experimentation of the period with combinations of the various kinds of architectural elements.

Curiously, the above-mentioned Arsenal inscription did not refer explicitly to any Ionic elements. It itemized two rows of thirty-five stone columns or pillars and their shapes and sizes that were to be decided upon by the architect to the contractor at a later stage. Beginning with general guidelines, it became more detailed towards the end. More specifically Philon's text referred[150] to the location of the Arsenal, the dimensions of its plan, the layout of the foundations and the main features of the ground plan. It also included the specifications of the stone construction and the main features and dimensions of the doorways, walls, windows, cornices, pediments, stylobate and columns, the architraves, roof construction and tiles, the galleries and shelves for the tackle, the chests for sails and side curtains, the ventilation and finally, various stipulations.

The inscription contained what the Athenian Assembly had approved, and sought to inform the public at large of the general nature of the project. It was a legal text binding builders and subcontractors: "All these things shall be carried out by the contractors in accordance with the specifications (*suggraphas*) and with the measurements (*metra*) and the model (*paradeigma*) indicated by the architect." The *paradeigma* was a specimen made of wood, stucco or clay, but also stone, used to supplement information about the form of more intricate details. This was all the more necessary at the time, given the innovative character of practice that rendered words insufficient—even when somebody with Philon's talents set them down. The *paradeigma* could later be placed in the actual building.

An equally unique document illustrating the degree of rigor of architectural design reached during this period was to be found in the huge new Temple of Apollo at Didyma, 360 by 170 feet (109.34 meters by 51.13 meters) designed about forty years after the Arsenal. The Persians destroyed the original Temple of Apollo, c. 494 B.C.E. The construction of the new temple began with the help of Alexander the Great and with architects Paeonios of Ephesus and Daphnis of Miletos, in around 300 B.C.E. The temple was still under construction in the second century of our era and was never really completed.

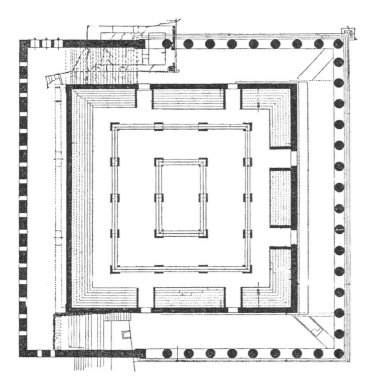

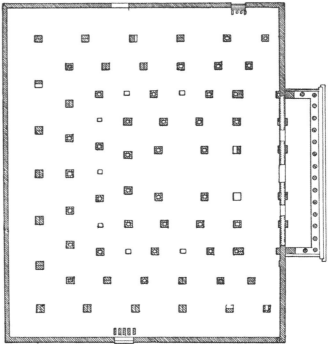

Telesterion, Eleusis.
After Robertson, 1969.

Thersilion, Megalopolis.
After Robertson, 1969.

The temple had a double *pteron* sitting on a platform of seven huge steps. It surrounded a roofless cella that contained a court, housing an Ionic shrine. The front porch was very deep, and its columns had varying bases. From there, one had access to the interior court through two small side doorways, a tunnel, and a flight of monumental steps. On the wall of the Didymean Apollo cella, in 1978, Lothar Haselberger[151] discovered the first architectural drawings to be known in Greece. The drawings cover almost six hundred sixty square feet (200 square meters) of the walls, columns and the pediment of the *naiskos*. They compute the entasis of the shaft: the upper and lower diameters are drawn in full size, the height of the column shaft is drawn to a scale of 1:16, and an arc drawn in the shortened shaft defines the entasis. Another drawing shows the division of a semicircle into twelve parts (at fifteen degree inter-

vals), representing the division of the fluting, for the drawing represents a plan of a half-column. Other representations describe the computation of the moldings of a torus for the base.

Collective places

With the intensification and increased organization of social and political public life, a new type of building was developed during the fourth century B.C.E. This was to facilitate collective gatherings or meetings that previous places, such as the Pinakotheke of the Propylaia of the Acropolis—little more than a room with seating around the walls—could not accommodate. The precedent of the Telesterion, however, must have played some role in this development. The mid-fourth-century

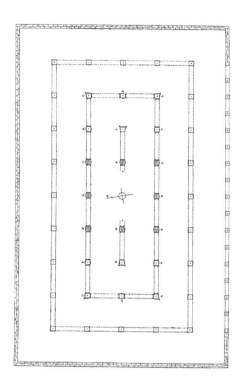

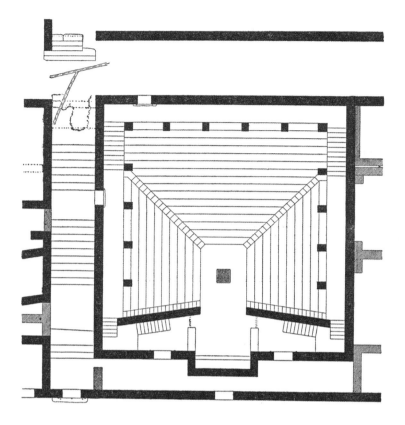

Hypostyle Hall, Delos.
After Robertson, 1969.

Ecclesiasterion, Priene.
After Robertson, 1969.

Thersilion in Megalopolis had a seating capacity of six thousand and an intricate radial arrangement of columns that could accommodate unobstructed spectacle. Both the porch and interior columns were probably Doric. The Hypostyle Hall (c. 210 B.C.E.) of Delos was used as a mercantile exchange. It was supported by a structural system of embedded rectangular frames, of which the outer was Doric and the inner Ionic. The Doric columns had Ionic fluting. The Ecclesiasterion of Priene, built c. 200 B.C.E. for the assembly of citizens, had no internal supports. It was a square building sunk into the slope as a theater, with a U-shaped seating arrangement. It could house over six hundred seated persons, and fourteen square pillars supported its roof. A similar, almost contemporary, assembly building, the Bouleuterion of Miletos, built around 170 B.C.E. by Antiochus IV could seat more than 1,200 persons.

Stadia were places where athletic contests took place. Although very significant socially—as in those at Delphi, Olympia, and Isthmia—their architectural importance was minor. Another type of collective place, with significant architectural organization that was to emerge as a major institution mainly after the invasion of the Persians, was the theater. The ancient Greek theater consisted of two main parts: the orchestra, whose circular shape is believed to have originated from the threshing floor where ritual dancing took place, and the *ikria,* seating stands. The earliest stands probably had a wooden structure, as in that built in the Agora of Athens for Thespis, during the time of Pisistratos in 534 B.C.E. The structure collapsed in 498 B.C.E. The artificial slope of the stands was replaced by the natural rise of the hillside—the first probably being on the side of the Pnyx between the Areopagus and the Acropolis.

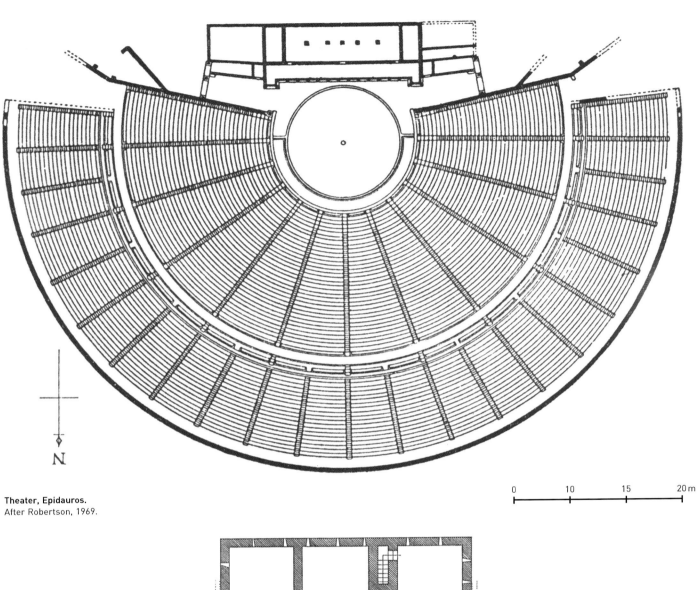

Theater, Epidauros.
After Robertson, 1969.

0   10   15   20 m

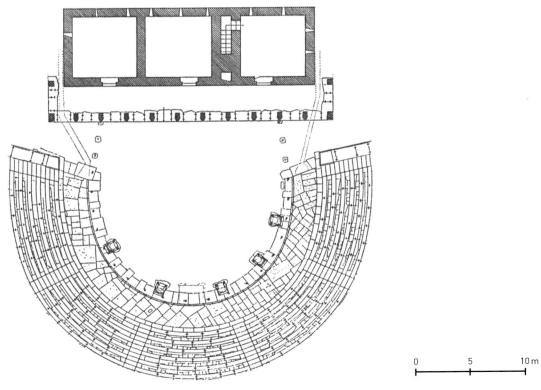

Theater, Priene.
After Lawrence, 1983.

0   5   10 m

Theater, Epidauros.
Photograph by Serge Moulinier.

About the middle of the sixth century, a sacred precinct was dedicated to Dionysos on the south slope of the Acropolis. An altar, a temple, a grove, and an orchestra were the first elements in the site, where ritual singing and dancing took place. It was here that the first tragedies by Asechylus were performed and, according to Vitruvius, Agatharchus invented *skenographia,* scene painting.[152] Gradually the site was transformed into what came to be known as the Theater of Dionysos. Around 421–415 B.C.E., the scene became a permanent building, articulated with stoae and temple colonnade architectural elements. By 330 B.C.E., the whole structure gradually came to be built of stone.

The most famous and harmonious theater of antiquity according to Pausanias was the theater of Epidauros, built in c. 365 B.C.E.[153] The same author wrote that its designer was Polyclitus, the architect of

the Tholos on the same site. As opposed to Roman theaters, the structure was minimal, with the open air seating arrangements being carved inside sloping grounds. Its auditorium was symmetrical, organized into thirteen radiating staircases, twelve sections, and a lower and upper gallery. The front row had elaborately designed seats for priests and politically important people. The orchestra was circular and contained in the center a round stone upon which stood the altar. The original *skene* was simple, but became more elaborate during the Hellenistic period, thus offering more opportunities for illusionist representations and mechanical devices.

The theater of Priene, built c. 340–300 B.C.E., followed the same principles of spatial arrangement and construction as the two earlier theaters mentioned above. Its most significant component—the two-story stone *skene*—was a permanent architectural

Theater of Dionysos, Athens.
Photograph: AKG-images.

composition. It was built around the beginning of the third century B.C.E. The first floor consisted of a row of Doric half-columns, and the second of a tripartite structure of wide openings, probably intended for changing painted panels.

Monuments

A number of large-scale buildings that were to serve only as monuments—a role confined to much more modest structures in the past—began to develop as a type in its own terms. From the architectural point of view, they were important because they provided a platform for experimentation with ideas of spatial organization. The Nereid Monument at Xanthos was built around 400 B.C.E.[154], just as the Erechtheion in Athens was completed.

There are several affinities between the two buildings in the detail, the use of an oversize base—as in the caryatid porch—and the integration of human figures as architectural elements. The base has two sculpted bands and terminates in a double egg-and-tongue molding. On the top stands a four by six colonnade and, in the inercolumnar interval, a female figure representing the Nereides (Breezes).

There is a strong affinity between the Xanthos structure and another monument of much larger scale, the Maussolleion of Halikarnassos. Commissioned by Maussolos—after whom the name of the building type, mausoleum, was derived—a non-Greek and an enemy of Athens, the building was designed by Pythios and Satyros c. 350 B.C.E. The two wrote also collaborated in the writing of a book on the work.[155] Like the Xanthos monument, the Maussolleion had an oversized tripartite base

Theater, Epidauros.
Photograph by John Hios / AKG-images.

crowned by a sculpted frieze—in this case—surmounted by a temple-like structure. On top of it stood a nine by eleven Ionic colonnade with statues between the columns.[156] Pythios was in charge of a four-horse chariot of marble resting on the top of a pyramid supported by the colonnade. The east side of the building was carved by Skopas, the north by Bryaxis, the south by Timotheus, and the west by Leochares. However, before they completed their task, the queen died. Nevertheless, being very conscious of the value of the work, they refused to abandon it unfinished. In contrast to the inside that contained a solid core of slabs of tufa, costly marbles covered the outside.[157]

On a different scale, in comparison to the cases of the two monuments referred to above, on the West side of the street of the Tripods leading to the Theater of Dionysos in Athens, stands the 335–334 B.C.E. Choragic Monument of Lysikrates, still well preserved

today. Like the Xanthos and the Halikarnassos structures, this mini-monument stands on a proportionately very high podium; it is circular and has six Corinthian half-columns, the earliest structure to use Corinthian capitals on the outside. Devoid of sculpture, it is nonetheless crowned by oversized foliage, as a base in which to place the winning prize, the tripod.

Indicative of the shift away from the Doric and towards the Corinthian is the case of the Temple of Olympian Zeus in Athens, not far from the Ilissos River. Antiochos IV Epiphanes took the first steps necessary for a new building in 175 B.C.E. Construction began in 165 B.C.E. The building was completed in 124–125 B.C.E. It was continued until 131–132 C.E., during the reign of the Emperor Hadrian who opened the dedication ceremony for the largest temple ever built for Zeus.[158] It was a double peripteral marble structure of eight by twenty

Nereid Monument, Xanthos. c. 400.

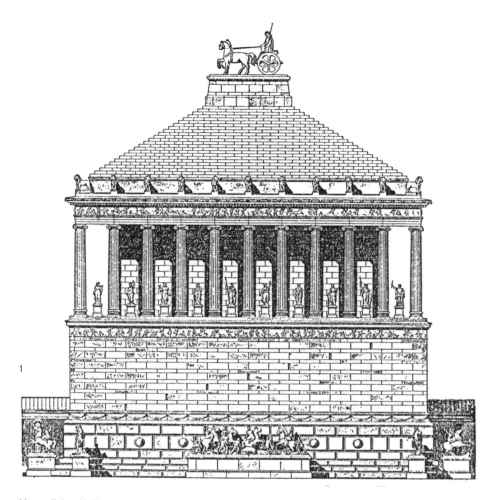

Maussolleion, Halikarnassos.
After Adler, Robertson, 1969.

2- Choragic Monument of Lysikrates, Athens.

double-row peripteral Corinthian colonnades with an extra third row across each end. It was designed by a Roman architect, Cossutius. However, rather than following contemporary Roman practice, it adhered to the design of the Heraion of Samos and Artemision of Ephesus, and in many respects the large Archaic temple it succeeded built by the younger Pisistratos, c. 515 B.C.E. On the other hand, when the question was raised as to the kind of colonnade and entablature to adopt for the temple, the Doric was dropped for the sake of the new kind, the Corinthian. The Corinthian required more labor to construct; however, it presented none of the Doric's inconsistencies.

In the Agora of Athens stands a curious octagonal structure, the so-called Tower of Aeolus, or "Tower of the Winds"—curious because of the rarity of its shape and use. At first glance, it appears to be simply

one more monument. In reality, this is the only surviving *horologion,* or water clock—a building-instrument whose design was attributed to Andronikos of Kyrrhus. Vitruvius refers to the construction of such *horologium rationes*—clocks, as well as other machines and instruments—for which he required the architect to know, among other things, "astronomy . . . and the order of the heavens."[159] However, the Tower of the Winds was more meteorological than astronomical or astrological. It mapped the movement of the sun and the winds, rather than that of the stars. Although constructed during Roman times, circa 37 B.C.E., its design characteristics resembled those of earlier Hellenistic rather than contemporary structures. Each side of the building had a sundial and, as in the case of the Choragic Monument of Lysikrates,[160] on the top of the roof rested a column. It had an octagonal shape

Tower of Aeolus, or Tower of the Winds, Athens.

The invention of the urban grid framework

As we have already mentioned, the architecture that emerged out of the Dark Ages in Greece was a new architecture, oblivious to previous Mycenaean or Cretan achievements in the region. As opposed to these previous palaces that involved large dense complexes—the building form being a fabric of open courts surrounded by rooms with hardly any freestanding structure—archaic architecture was one of freestanding edifices, mostly independent of each other. Gradually, as we have seen, since the time of the Propylaia of Athens and the stoae, buildings were to become space-containing, fabric-forming objects and structures that grew in relation to each other.

Since the fifth century B.C.E., with precedents that go back much before this time, another development has occurred that found its culmination in Hellenistic times: that of the orthogonal city grid plan inside which individual buildings were embedded. Hippodamos of Miletos is credited as the author of this system; not only did he design pioneering urban arrangements, he also—according to Aristotle[161]—wrote about them. His ideas were implemented in the city of Miletos—after the Persians had burned it—as well as at Piraeus commissioned by Themistocles, and at Thourioi.

At Miletos, during the first half of the fifth century B.C.E., Hippodamos planned a pattern of streets intersecting at right angles and more densely spaced in the northern part of the city. Though inserted in the northern part, the civic area of the city also touched the southern portion. All public and individual business was to be conducted in the civic area,

with a Corinthian capital, and supported a mobile bronze statue of the sea god Triton grasping a rod that functioned as a sail, indicating the direction of the wind as it turned. The building was entered through two prostyle porches, whose columns had capitals fusing the palm motive on their upper part with the Corinthian acanthus on their lower portion, and no base. The volume of the building was plain, but carried on each of its eight sides an oversized continuous frieze, bearing a relief that represented one of the eight winds. The building demonstrates the rich achievements of the Classical canon at that point in its ability to invent novel spatial arrangements to shelter and organize unprecedented complex functions, far removed from those of the early temples or stoae—the buildings from which it originated.

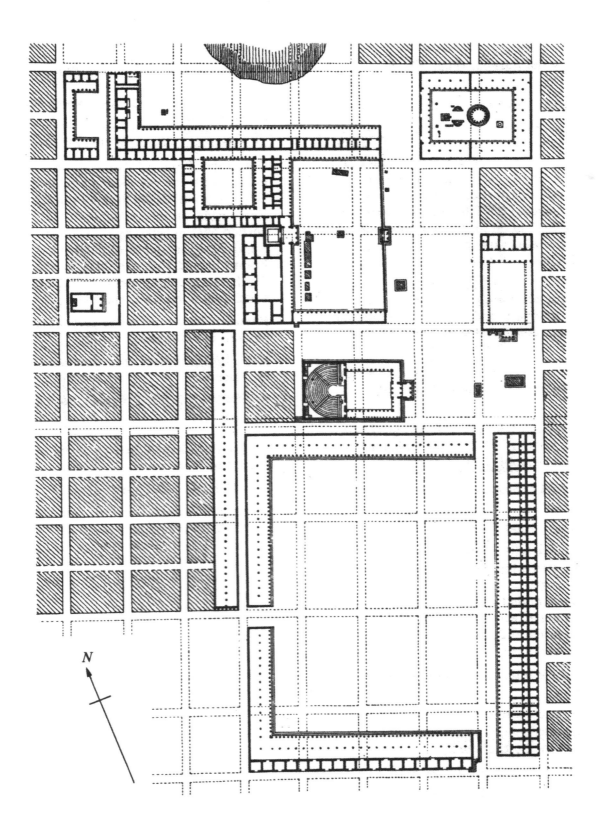

N

Agora area, Miletos.

0   50   100 m

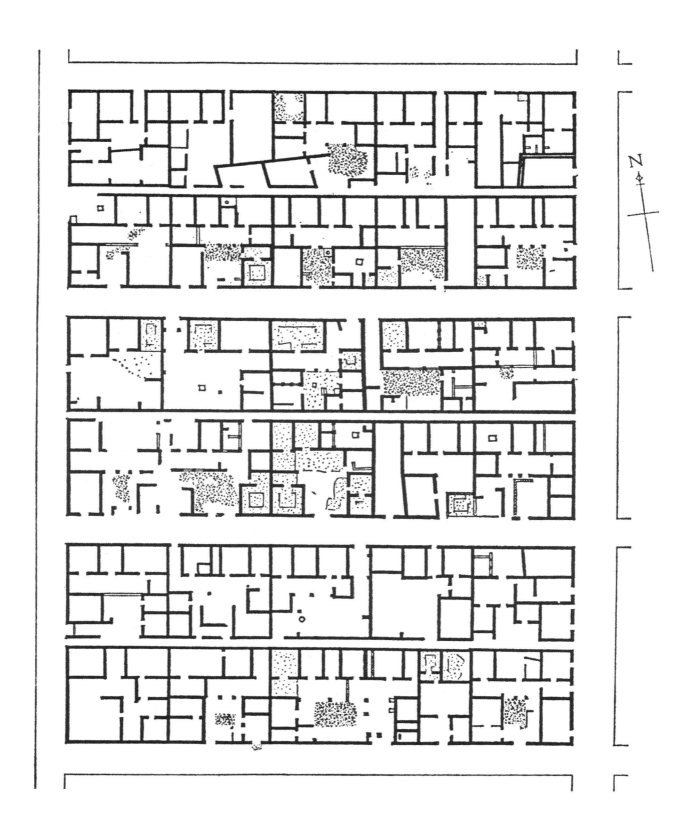

Olynthos, blocks of houses.
After Lawrence, 1983.

0   5 m

while the rest of the city became strictly residential. Thus the grid was a system applied not only to the blocks of the houses, but also to the design of public and open spaces. The agora became an integral part of the urban tissue with a fixed position and borders.

During the fourth century B.C.E., the system underwent further systemization. The cities created by Alexander the Great were similarly based on Hippodamean principles. Priene, for example, adopted the orthogonal plan on a sloping site with streets that included flights of steps. The agoras of the cities of the fourth and third centuries B.C.E. were to evolve into bigger and more elaborate complexes.[162] The stoa, as mentioned earlier, played a most important role and, in conjunction with new building types—*gymnasia* and *palaistrae*—formed building complexes. Stoae also begin to flank the main streets, thereby not only giving them a monumental appearance, but also enhancing environmental comfort and enabling social interaction.

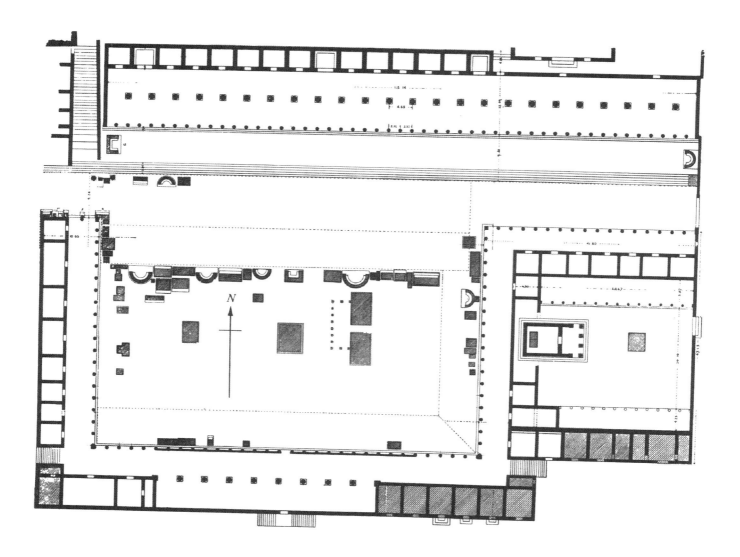

Priene, groundplan of center.

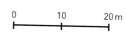

0   10   20 m

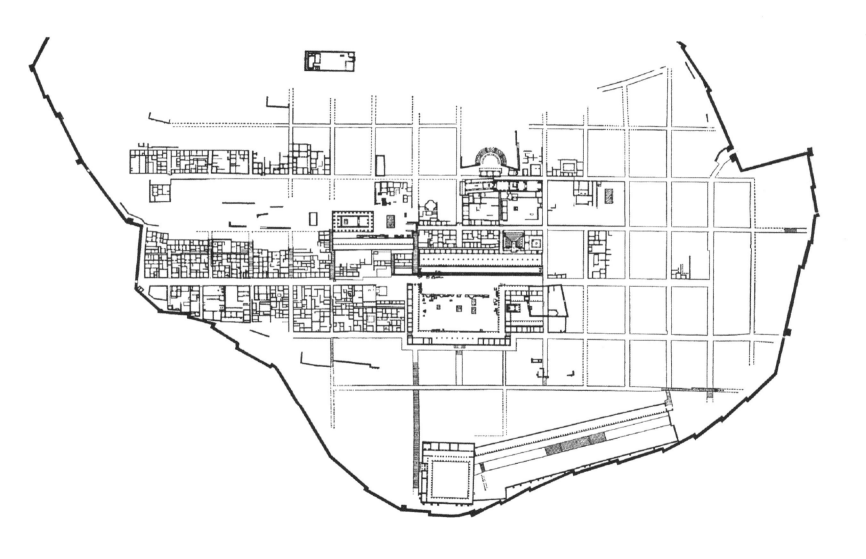

Priene, groundplan.
After Th. Wiegard and H. Schrader.

View of the Acropolis with Lycabettos Hill.
Photograph by Frédéric Boissonas.`

*"[Hephaestus] began by making a large and powerful shield... showing two
beautiful cities full of people. In one of them weddings and banquets were afoot...
the light of blazing torches. Youths accompanied by flute and lyre were whirling
in the dance, and the women had come to the doors of their houses to enjoy the show.
But the men had flocked to the meeting place, where a case had come up between
two litigants, about the payment of compensation for a man who had been killed.
... both were cheered by their supporters in the crowd... The other city
was beleaguered by two armies, which were shown in their glittering equipment.
... leaving the walls defended by their wives and little children,
together with the older men, they sallied forth."*

Homer *The Iliad*, Penguin, 1950. Trans. by E. V. Rieu, p. 349–350.

CHAPTER IV

HEARTH, *TEMENOS*, AND AGORA

Odysseus, the shipwrecked sailor, entering the palace of Alcinous as a suppliant, "sat down on the hearth by the fire ... as they all hushed in silence."[163] In his pioneering work,[164] Jean-Pierre Vernant has shown the connection between the hearth to which Odysseus attached himself as suppliant, and the virgin goddess, Hestia, who protects the *oikos*, the interior of the household and its contents. He has also shown that the significance of the goddess is strongly linked with Hermes, the god of the open and public spaces where men would meet, associated with commerce, theft, communication, and movement. Together, the two gods—essential elements of the *dodecatheon*, the system of deities of Greek polytheism—made up a framework through which the ancient Greeks conceived space, with each representing the extreme of a spectrum of private-public realms that encompassed the household, the sanctuary, the open place of the agora, and the paths crossing the countryside.

Throughout all levels of this hierarchy of realms lay the presence of a most significant element: fire. Fire was to be found in the Homeric palace of Alcinous. Fire embraced by the hearth occupied the heart of the *megaron*, of the Mycenaean acropolis. Starting from this hearth, a number of concentric rings grew outwards from the inside, finally arriving at the *propylon*—the gate that controlled the access to the whole complex. With the throne of the *wanax* on the side of the hearth, one can argue that there was "a centripetal organization located in the megaron of the palace and focused on the hearth where the ruler is responsible for the maintenance of the cult."[165]

Sacrifice and altar

Fire was present on the altar as an essential implement in sacrifice, the key ritual of archaic Greek religion. It occupied a central position not only in the sanctuary, but also in any other place where major political events of the

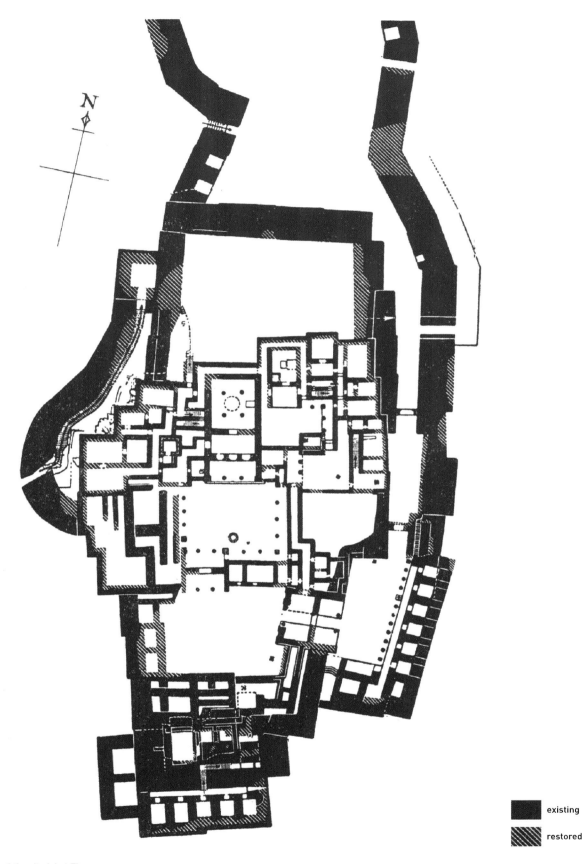

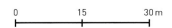

■ existing

▨ restored

Palace and south part of the citadel at Tiryns.
Late thirteenth century B.C.E.
After Müller, *Tyrins*, t. III, pl. 4, Lawrence, 1983.

0   15   30 m

community occurred, and were accompanied by sacrifice. During the sacrifice, in order to satisfy the gods, certain parts of the animal had to be completely burned upon the altar. The participants consumed the remaining parts—an act that was also part of the ritual and which took place next to the place of sacrifice. This collective meal that followed the sacrifice was fundamental in solidifying the community.[4] In contrast to Mycenaean society where this ritual was restricted to a certain group, in archaic Greece it was open, with equal rights being accorded to all members of the community. This accessibility represented the political constitution of the Greek *polis*—an institution based on the community of *homoioi*, the "similar" ones.

In the Homeric epic, sacrifice could be performed anywhere in the open air and often next to the sea. Sacrifices were also performed in a sanctuary. However, the question remains open of whether this sanctuary originated from the *megaron* of the Geometric period and of whether the Greek peripteral temple originated from it.[167] In the case of sacrifices that occurred in a sanctuary, a procession leading from the entrance of the sanctuary to the altar preceded the ritual.[168] During this procession, the animal and participants were adorned: the men being dressed in clean garments and the animal entwined with ribbons. The sacrificial basket was then carried on the head of a maiden, with the knife for sacrifice (*makhaira*) concealed beneath grains of barley, and water was brought in a vessel. When the procession arrived at the altar, the animal and the participants formed a circle around it. The ritual thus included a linear movement from the entrance to the sacred spot—the altar (*bomos*)—

where fire was present, as well as a movement encircling the spot of the sacrifice. The spatial arrangement during this last stage resembled that of an assembly where the audience encircled a speaker—the altar being the equivalent of the step (*bema*) occupied by the speaker.

The majority of early sanctuaries did not have a structure built especially for the altar. The original altar was made out of the ashes that were left from repeated sacrifices. Gradually, however, the altar became an architectural object—though in a few cases, as in the great ash altar of Zeus at Olympia, the original was never replaced.[169] The most ancient altars were at the Heraion on Samos (from the tenth century to 700 B.C.E.).[170] Their design was simple. By contrast, half a millennium later, the great altar of Zeus built by Eumenes II (197–159 B.C.E.) in Pergamon was set inside a colossal construction and had a complex organization within which the altar proper was only a small component. It included a massive sculptured frieze and was placed upon the plain base of a podium. A massive central flight led to the platform of the altar, which stood inside a court surrounded by a U-shaped Ionic colonnaded structure.

Common meals

Departing from the observation that the Temple of Apollo at Delphi contained within its interior space its own altar for sacrifices, a hypothesis was formed:[171] the original place where sacrifices occurred was the chieftain's dwelling.[172] The researcher in question, Mazarakis, sought to identify the spatial relation between the dwellings of rulers and communal religious rituals.[173] There was strong evidence that from c. 700 B.C.E. onwards, when temples became common within and outside settlements, and when the aristocracy came into power, these dwellings were transformed into temples. In some of them, sacred dining continued to take place: the temples providing hearths and benches, just as the chieftains' dwellings had done previously. At a later stage, the study suggests, these ritual functions were divided between separate specialized buildings: with the temple retaining the function of the house of the divinity and its cult image, the *hestiatoria* providing the meals, and the treasuries protecting the property of the sanctuary. However, it is still difficult to differentiate fully between cult buildings and rulers' dwellings. Furthermore, there is evidence that cult activity in the form of ritual communal meals, votive offerings, and altars preexisted in Greek sanctuaries (such as Olympia, or Samos), centuries before the building of the temples. The question of the evolution of religious sites thus remains unresolved.

The *temenos* and the open-air setting

Likewise unanswered is the question of how buildings inside a sanctuary related to each other. The ancient Greek word for sanctuary is *temenos*, from the verb *temnein*, "to cut." Indeed, sanctuaries in Ancient Greece were portions of land set apart from their surroundings by walls or boundary stones, the entrance being controlled by a gate (*propylon*). These markers indicated the portion of space within which special regulations of behavior had to be observed. At the Amphiaraeion of Oropos, a boundary stone reads: "*Horos*. It is forbidden to build inside these boundaries." Inside the *hieron* ("sacred")—as the sanctuary is also called—only a man in a state of purity, *hagnotes*, was allowed to enter. The opposite state, pollution, or *miasma*, include the violation of prohibitions related to sexual intercourse, birth, death, and murder.[174]

Close to the concept of *hieron* is that of *asylon*. This delineated the space that contained objects belonging to the gods, and that were neither to be destroyed nor taken away. From this derived the status of the *temenos* as a safe haven for people seeking protection—those who enter the *asylon* were considered the property of the god. The sanctuary of the classical period can therefore be seen as a spatial unit comprising elements related to ritual—which, in addition to temples, contained one or more altars, porticoes (*stoae*), dining places (*hestiatoria*), treasuries, and various votive offerings in the form of statues or buildings—and natural elements such as trees, shrubs, and flowers.

During the Archaic period, a gradual spatial reorganization took place, whereby the altar was moved from the center to east side of the periphery, the temple from the west side of the periphery to the center and the area for sacrifice from the west side of the periphery to the east. It has been argued further that this development implied a gradual shift from the invisible divinity in the sky, for which the sacrifice was intended, to the artifact or image of the divinity as a visibly manifest figure occupying a central position in its dwelling, generally eastward-facing. This change coincided with substitution of the internal axial single colonnade with the double one, and the gradual rise in importance of the function of the Greek temple as the dwelling place of the image of the god.

Temples, their contents, and divisions

In addition to its original, ancient cult image, referred to as *xoanon*—early *xoana* being believed to have fallen from heaven—the temple also housed other images that had been accumulated over time. These included votive offerings and valuable objects that were the property of the sanctuary, and were referred to as treasury, or thesaurus. Finally, it included relics of myths connected to the divinity, such as the olive tree kept in the Erechtheion. According to Herodotus, when the Persians destroyed the whole sanctuary by fire in 480 B.C.E., this tree also perished—only to grow thereafter "a new shoot eighteen inches long from the stump."[175] Cult images were anthropomorphic and precious. Due to its valuable materials, the statue of Zeus was fenced, as is indicated by the traces found in the paving and the walls. These images were the focal point for prayers, sacrifices and processions. Originally, they were simple pieces of carved wood, often believed to have fallen from heaven. They were easily transportable.[176] During the processions, following rituals that originated in the Near East, the cult image was temporarily removed, and treated as a human being. In Samos, the cult image of Hera was carried to the sea, purified, and given a meal of barley cakes. In Athens, the cult image was bathed. Also, in Athens the statue of Athena Polias was washed in the sea, near Phaleron, two months before the festival of Panathenaia. The origins of the ritual, called *Plynteria*, are Ionan. It was preceeded by the *Kyllanteria* during which the temple was cleaned.[177]

In temple inscriptions and literary texts are to be found two terms relating to the interior arrangement of the cella: *adyton* and *opisthodomos*. *Adyton* literally means, "not to be entered."[178] It restricts access and was applied to hero shrines, caves, subterranean structures, as well as to temples in whole or part and oracles. A well-known *adyton* was the hypaethral court of the oracular temple at the Temple of Apollo at Didyma that had to be consulted at night. Even more famous was the *adyton* of the seat of the oracle of Apollo at Delphi.[179] *Opisthodomos* means both the "back of a house" and the "back room of a temple." In some cases, the same term was also used in fourth-century B.C.E. inscriptions to denote the rear counterpart to the *pronaos* or front porch, before the *naos*. Herodotus is supposed to have read his *Histories* from the *opisthodomos* of the Temple of Zeus at Olympia,[180] and the Cynics are said to have filled an *opisthodomos* with noise.[181] An *opisthodomos* would also have housed valuable offerings.

Together with the cult image, the temple contained monumental votive offerings. This practice originated from the first offerings of the Geometric period that were deposited into tombs. In the eighth century B.C.E., this was replaced by the offering of objects to sanctuaries. It seems that

Sanctuary of Hera by Geneleos, Samos.
C. second half of sixth century B.C.E.
Photograph by Kienast.

offerings were considered a manifestation of power and prestige among the wealthy and aristocrats. The size of offering varied, occasionally being the building itself. Plato, with his aristocratic ideology and origin, was irritated by the display of wealth by those who "just won it," which served only to clutter open spaces.

Temenos, roads, and writing

Drawing on Egyptian and Mesopotamian precedents, lions and sphinxes had been used in votive offerings since the Archaic period. Human figures also appeared, such as those found on the sides of the Sacred Way leading from the *polis* of Samos to the extra-urban sanctuary of Hera. One example is the colossal male youth, or *kouros*, dated at 570 B.C.E.[182] Earlier *kouroi* have been found on the islands of Naxos and Delos. *Korai*, their female counterparts, were found in the Samian sanctuary. Around 560 B.C.E., the visitor to the sanctuary, moving from the gate towards the temple, would also have encountered another monument, unprecedented in ceremonial ways leading to Egyptian sanctuaries. Along the right-hand side of the path on a long base lay a recumbent figure, four standing female ones, and, at the end, a seated one with a dedication inscribed on the mattress beneath the recumbent figure, written boustrophedon and mentioning the names of the dedicators.

Since Phoenician writing was adopted and adapted by the Greeks, literacy spread fast and widely in a center from which diffusion was rapid and easy, such as the trading post of Al-Mina.[183]

The first written texts came from pottery and could be highly personal and lyrical, such as the one found on an eastern Greek cup in a child's grave on Ischia: "[I am] the famous drinking cup of Nestor. Whoever drinks from this cup, straightaway the desire of Aphrodite of the beautiful garland will seize him."[184] Within this context, inscriptions played a most important role in ancient Greek sites sanctuaries, agorae, and roads. They informed visitors as they moved around buildings and dedicated objects. They also provided company when read aloud, as the custom was for texts in ancient Greece at that time.[185] They commemorated the name of the dedicator and the god to whom it was offered, and acted as mechanisms for supplying publicity and fame—not only for a person, but also for whole communities and cities. Like contemporary forms of publicity, their spatial location was such that it would guarantee maximum visibility—on both sides of the streets, near the cult image of the god, and on the columns of the porticoes.

During the third century B.C.E., the authorities of sanctuaries were obliged to lay down decrees restricting the placement of such objects to protect the sanctuary buildings and ensure the smooth functioning of the place[186]—probably out of jealousy of the attention that visitors paid to them. Characteristically, in Euripides' *Ion,* the servant of Apollo asks Kreousa, who was visiting the sanctuary of the god at Delphi, if her husband had come accompanied her "for sightseeing or for consultation."

Sculptures drew equal attention. Visitors of temples were attracted by their appearance, but they were also aware of the names of the artists and sponsors. Here again inscriptions were part of the artifact proper. This is demonstrated in Herondas' *Mimiambus* in a dialogue between two women. One of the women exclaims of the statues they have encountered: "Oh, what a beautiful statues. ... Who was the craftsman that has carved this stone, and who is the dedicator?'" The other woman responds, "The sons of Praxiteles; don't you see these letters on the base? And the dedicator is Euthies son of Prexon."[187]

Identities, processions, and sanctuary locations

As we have already mentioned, the ancient Greeks thought of sanctuaries as parcels of land cut out from the rest of the surroundings. Sanctuaries, the roads that led to them and their relative position on a territory constituted a new cognitive spatial map. Together with a new legal framework of social behavior, *nomos*, this newly constructed map, *polis*, helped to bring together and anchor tribes whose previous organization had been more decentralized and of a mobile nature.[188] The Greek *polis*—often translated as "city"—actually signifies an institution; a specific way in which Greeks participated in a collective organization and their relation to a territory, rather than a dense urban settlement in the sense that "city" is used today. Its links with the older Mycenaean palaces appear, however, to be rather weak. Like the Greek alphabet, the *polis* emerged as a new invention. The basic components of this cognitive map were the sanctuary, or *temenos*; the *agora*, the residential areas; the *chora*, the land that fed the *polis,* and the roads that crossed through the territory interlinking sanctuaries.

In addition to structuring behavior within a group, the new cognitive map helped to organize intertribal relations. Working through common myths and communal rituals, it structured identity and territorial claims. Sanctuaries served as markers of the center and the boundaries of a *polis*. In particular, extra-urban sanctuaries were employed to mark off the limits of a territory, to affirm the control by the *polis* over the *chora,* or to point out new claims. The sanctuary of Hera at Perachora for instance, on the promontory facing Corinth, was located on an important road, reflecting the growth of Corinthian maritime power in the eighth century B.C.E., and served to demarcate the boundaries of the *polis* control.[189]

Processions were used to resolve problems of identity and territory between communities with pre-existing sanctuaries and centers, as in the case of the famous sanctuary dedicated to Demeter in Eleusis. This was linked to that in Athens in the vicinity of the Agora through the famous Sacred Way, and by the ritual of the Eleusinian procession.

There is strong evidence of the significance of the location of sanctuaries during the Archaic period in ancient Greece in establishing identities of communities and territorial claims over the land. Sites in which signs of previous civilization had been detected were reused by the Greeks of the Archaic period[190] as a means of constructing their identity and of answering questions of ethnicity. The choice of location of sanctuaries outside cities (extra-urban sanctuaries) was intended to circumscribe a territory.[191] They were, in a sense, establishing "liminal borders" or "ends," *eschatiai*—a term associated with the cult of Apollo, used for sending young conscripts doing their military service to the limits of a city's territory, before returning to take an oath as newly accepted citizens.[192]

The role of the sanctuary as spatial-political marker was enhanced by rituals—periodic festivals associated with the divinity of the sanctuary—that displayed territorial control and the legitimacy of this control. Other elements inserted in the landscape indicating the route of a procession, from a *polis* center to a periphery sanctuary (or in the reverse sense, a centripetal procession), called attention to the extent to which a *polis* claimed to control a territory. Periodic festivals within a sanctuary, or periodic rituals involving processions also manifested cooperation and conflict between a *polis* and its neighbors in relation to a territory. As de Polignac suggests,[193] initially such gatherings and sacrificial banqueting served to establish relations of "friendship"—*philia*—and instituted contacts between land neighbors, as in Olympia or Tegea, or between passing sailors, as in sanctuaries near the sea such as Heraion of Samos, Heraion of Perachora, and perhaps Brauron.

Processions linked the territory not only with the *polis* at large, but also with the constituent parts of the *polis*—the major streets, the agora, the acropolis, and the city sanctuaries—and as such were occasions to bring together the members of the community and to display publicly the membership, composition, and hierarchy of the groups that composed it.[194] Special rituals marked important points in the procession and their succession along the route created a sequence of landmarks—both religious and political—that were connected with special events.

In addition to the political or social reasons, the decision to locate a sanctuary was linked with beliefs about the relationship between the human world—mainly activities of production—and nature. There is no doubt that the sanctuaries of Artemis were intentionally founded on the edges of nature, inside the territory of hunting rather than building or agriculture. The presence of water, essential for Demeter, the divinity of female fertility, growth, and childbirth, was also a determinant in choosing a location for her sanctuary. In addition, as the ritual of this goddess required secrecy, her sanctuary was placed in a site that would provide physical isolation—even if it were to be found within the city.[195]

Zeus' sanctuaries were also often situated in remote rustic peak sites, associated with the god's role as mountain and weather god.[196] Poseidon's sanctuaries were often to be seen near the sea as at Isthmia and Sounion—here in the vicinity of the sanctuary of Athena, as the goddess of intelligence for the protection of navigators.[197] The location of these sanctuaries was also a landscape feature that could be seen from afar for orienting sailors, but also one which gave theme a sense of belonging, as attested by the following verses from Sophocles' *Ajax*: "I wish I were where the wooded cape, beaten by the surf, projects over the sea, beneath the high plateau of Sounion, so that I could salute sacred Athens!"[198]

Panhellenic sanctuaries: Olympia and Delphi

The foundation of extra-urban sanctuaries and their associated ritual activities not only reinforced the control of the *polis* over a territory, but also helped construct an ethnic identity for distributed

Temple of Hera, Olympia.
Photograph by Erich Lessing / AKG-images.

communities.[199] Such was the case of shrines at Pherai, that attracted the Thessalian *ethne*, or at Kalapodi, attracting the *ethne* from Phokis and Lokris, or in Arcadia, with its network of sanctuaries, such as the Temple of Athena at Tegea, due to Tegean synoecism. The case of southwest Arcadia and the sanctuary of Apollo at Bassai was similar.[200] This role becomes more obvious with the establishment of large Panhellenic sanctuaries (such as Olympia, Delphi, Nemea, or Isthmia) and the foundation of their games, periodically and gathering antagonistic communities and individuals from all over Greece and the colonies. The location of these Panhellenic sanctuaries was important for accessibility, but lay outside the orbit of territorial claims of individual *poleis*—serving all, but belonging to none.

Olympia's sanctuary is situated along the banks of the Alfeios River, that used to provide a passage in the northwest Peloponnesus, at its point of confluence with the River Cladeus, among a rich vegetation that included wild olives, which tradition said to have been brought from the land of the Hyperboreans and planted by Herakles.[201] Zeus was worshipped at Olympia, together with other gods including the goddess Hera—the earliest built temple of the site being hers. The more ancient altars inside the sanctuary included the ash altar of the Olympian Zeus, and altars to Earth (Gaia), Themis, and Hera. During the Early Iron Age, Olympia probably served as a meeting place for the mainly Peloponnesian chieftains of the west, to assert their status by making elaborate dedications, mainly in the form of metal objects with most characteristic being that of the *tripod*, a cauldron with three legs. The traditional date of the foundation of the quadrennial Panhellenic Olympic Games is 776 B.C.E. From c. 725 B.C.E., the games expanded, and the western regional event was replaced by a Panhellenic one.[202]

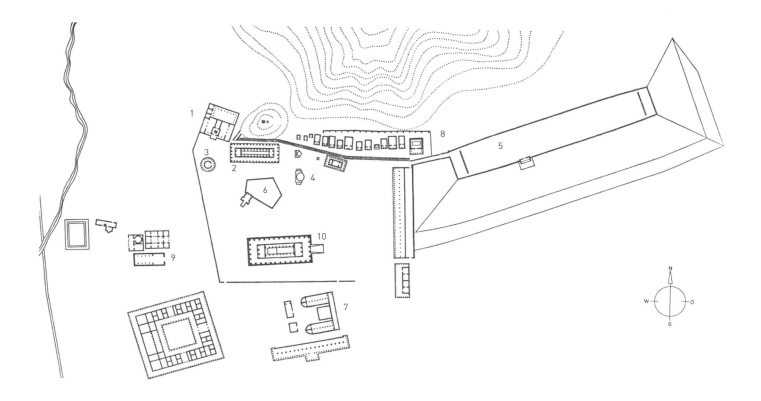

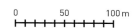

Olympia. General plan. Archaic period (sixth and early fifth centuries B.C.E.).
1. Prytaneion, 2. Temple of Hera, 3. Philippeion, 4. Altar of Zeus, 5. Stadium, 6. Pelopion,
7. Bouleuterion, 8. Row of treasuries, 9. Workshop of Phidias, 10. Temple of Zeus.
After Herrmann, 1972.

0   50   100 m

The Olympic festival, and the Pythian festival at Delphi, were held in August or early September, while the Nemean Games were held in late July, biennially between the Olympic and Pythian festivals. The Isthmian took place in April, perhaps because this was a brief sailing season in connection with the god Poseidon that was honored in the sanctuary.[203] The Olympic festival lasted for four or perhaps six days, and included a night of the full moon. The territory of Elis was regarded as inviolate, and at the site of Olympia, the gathering of competing Greeks was accompanied with the observance of a *sacred truce*. Hera's importance to the site is shown by the existence of a parallel festival to the main Olympics (*Heraia*) with its races of virgins.

The sanctuary included altars and the Pelopion, or tomb of Pelops, the temples of Hera and Zeus, a row of treasuries at the foot of the hill (built from the middle of the sixth century B.C.E.), and the *stadion*, initially extended inside the Altis, and later separated from it by the Stoa of Echo. Within the site of Altis were also found the shrine of Hestia; the Prytaneion of the Eleans (constructed in the fifth century B.C.E.), where victors were fed; the Metroon; the Philippeion (a building of the fourth century B.C.E., dedication of the Macedonian king, Philip); the workshop of Phidias[204] (where the sculptor worked on parts of the gold and ivory statue of Zeus); the Bouleuterion (council chamber, fifth century B.C.E.) where, at the beginning of the games, the athletes would take a sacred oath stating that they would not violate the rules, that they were free Greek citizens—not slaves—and that they had committed neither murder nor sacrilege. The same rules—not to be slaves, murderers or responsible for sacrileges—also applied to the spectators, with the exception that they could be barbarians (that is, not Greeks). Women were also apparently excluded.[205]

Likewise, Delphi was an extra-urban sanctuary whose ritual activities were associated with enhancing

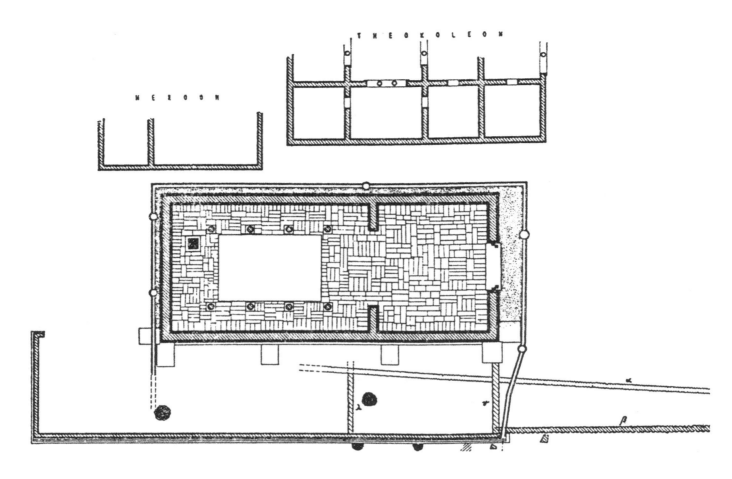

Phidias' studio at Olympia. 440–430 B.C.E.
After Herrmann, 1972.

the construction of a national, Panhellenic identity for distributed communities, as well as for helping the establishment of new colonies. The beginning of religious activity in Delphi is attested by the appearance of bronze votive objects c. 800 B.C.E., but was to intensify only during the last quarter of the eighth century—the period of formation and rise of the Greek *polis*—as is reflected in the increase in the number of dedications, and in the appearance of new categories of metalwork that coincided with the establishment of oracular divination. The Delphic festival, the Pythiad, was first established in 591 or 590 B.C.E. (or 586–585 or 582–581 B.C.E.). Modeled on the Olympic Games, it was initially an artistic competition, as a hymn to Apollo rather than an athletic contest, which was added afterwards.[206]

The emergence and rise of the activity of the Delphic oracle seem to have been related to the first wave of colonization of the eighth century B.C.E. Through Apollo's oracle, the sanctuary at Delphi was to influence the foundation of colonies and, especially, their location.[207] Pythia, the prophetess of the Apollonian sanctuary, delivered the oracles once a month, and this only during the summer— since from December until February, the god Apollo left Delphi for the land of the Hyperboreans. During this period, the honored god of the sanctuary was Dionysos. Pythias's answers were so confusing that they required the help of the "prophets" to be understood—and even then only partially.

The case of Athens: the Panathenaic processions

In order to understand in greater detail how some buildings of an ancient Greek *polis* were used, we

Temple of Apollo, Delphi.
Photograph by Waldemar Deonna.

Sanctuary of Athena Pronaia, Delphi.
Photographer unknown.

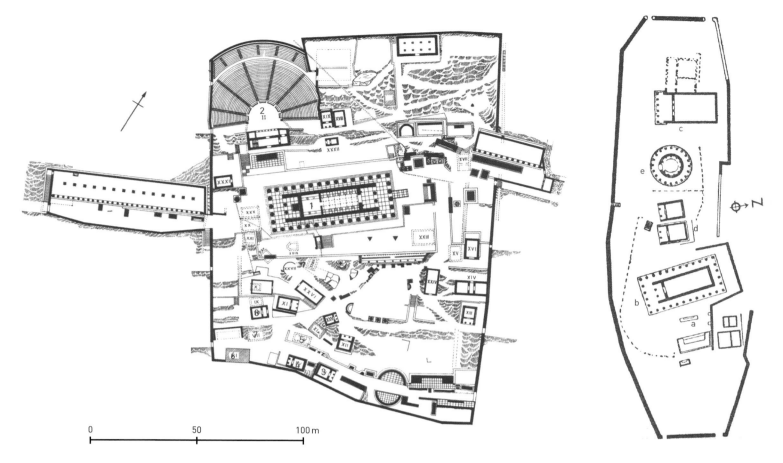

Plan of the sanctuary of Apollo, Delphi, seventh and sixth centuries B.C.E. 1. Temple of Apollo. 2. Altar. 3. Treasury of Siphnos. 4. Treasury of the Athenians. 5. Treasury of Cnidos. 6.Stoa of the Athenians. 7. Naxian Sphinx column. 8. Theater.
After Pouilloux and Roux, 1963.

Sanctuary of Athena Pronaia, Delphi. a. Altar of Athena. b. Temple of Athena II, 510 B.C.E. c. Temple of Athena III, fourth century B.C.E. d. Treasuries: on the left, the treasury of Massilia. e. Tholos,fourth century B.C.E.
After Gruben, 1978.

will focus on the case of Athens. The choice of such a large, complex, and rich—in terms of both money and structures—city, offers insights into meaning and function in ancient Greek architecture. Yet it also presents limitations: even with such an exceptional case, it is difficult to generalize about the rest of the Greek cities. Athens was the most characteristic and the same time least typical of the Greek *polis*—a case similar to that of New York and the rest of American cities today. We have therefore to proceed with caution, extrapolating conclusions about how other Greek cities functioned from the descriptions that follow.

We will take two approaches to Athens. The first will follow the Panathenaic procession, the most famous of all processions and the main festival of the city of Athens instituted to honor the goddess Athena, as reconstructed by archaeological and his-

torical research today. The second will take the route suggested by Pausanias in his *Guide to Greece*, that of an ancient "tourist," or *periegetes*.

The Panathenaic procession was probably founded in 566–565 B.C.E., coinciding with the establishment of the other great Greek festivals of Pythia (582 B.C.E.), Isthmia (581 B.C.E.), and Nemea (573 B.C.E.). The main festival—the Greater Panathenaia—was held every four years and was attributed to the tyrant Pisistratos, though many doubts subsist about this.[208] It was he who probably added to the event the athletic contest, as well as music contests and the recitation of the *Iliad* and the *Odyssey,* thereby attracting important artists from all over Greece. The main object of the festival was the procession of the *peplos*—bringing a specially woven robe for the wooden figure of the goddess Athena, housed in the Erechtheion—that was carried as a sail above a ship on wheels in Roman times. The procession was held the twenty-eighth of the month Hecatombaion[209] and set off at dawn. Starting at the Dipylon, the main gate of the city, and ending at the Acropolis, it followed the Panathenaic Way, crossed the Agora and the entire city via its principal thoroughfare. A special "Building for the Processions"—the Pompeion, dating from 400 B.C.E. and located between the Dipylon and the Sacred Gate—was used for the preparations. Himerius, an author of the Roman period, provided a vivid description of the route passing through the city in the fourth century C.E.: "The ship begins its voyage right from the gate, as from calm heaven. Moving from that point, as over a waveless sea, it is conveyed through the middle of the Dromos, which, descending from above, straight and smooth, divides the stoas extending along it on either side, where the Athenians buy or sell." The embroidered *peplos* represented the battle and victory of Athena over the giants. The ship carried priests and priestesses and, in size and appearance resembled a warship, thereby suggesting the naval strength of Athens. As with the sculpture of the Acropolis, victory was the unifying theme of the whole celebration.

The feast included cavalry and charioteer contests, with men in full armor jumping on and out of moving vehicles, or dancing.[210] Yet underlying this seemingly chaotic and variant composition, the Panathenaic procession enhanced Athenian unity and identity—political, social, and cultural. It affected the character of the landscape and the development of Athens. Its martial and mythological themes, employed in the iconography of artifacts that were positioned across the Panathenaic way, established a network of places that encompassed the whole city, creating a cognitive map of a unified spatial identity.[211] The whole event—including the sacrificial procession of the animals to be offered to the goddess Athena by the city of Athens, the Athenian colonies, and later all the members of the Athenian League—brought together the whole social spectrum and various age groups of Athenians, their colonists, and allies. The centripetal movement of the procession's route linked all the main areas of the city: the Dipylon gate, where the procession started; the neighborhoods of the craftsmen; the districts of the ceramists (Kerameikos); the area of the metalworkers (near the Hephaisteion); the civic center, the Agora; and the Acropolis, where a series of sacrifices were performed at the very end.

The order of the sacrifices on the Acropolis was determined by the topography of the sanctuary: the first being for Athena Nike, the second for Athena Hygieia on the altar just east of the southeast corner of the main block of the Propylaia, and the last on the great altar of Athena especially decorated for the occasion. Subsequently, the meat was divided and preparations began for its cooking. This final feast probably took place in Kerameikos, near the starting point of the procession.[212] The dining rooms of the Pompeion, which accommodated sixty-six dining couches, would have been used by the officials, the rest of eating taking place in the open air. The last part of the event was a fire ritual. The fire on the altar of Athena was lit with a torch that arrived at the Acropolis after a torch race that had started at the Eros altar in the Academy, outside Dipylon, passed the Agora and the building of the Prytaneion, where ambassadors and those rendering great state services dined at public expense. Aristophanes' remarks in the *Frogs* about the poor condition of the competitors due to overeating were well-known.

The case of Athens: Pausanias' tourist route

We return now to Athens to take a similar path following the itinerary of Pausanias from the outside to the center of the city. However, here we will be gazing at the buildings and artifacts that we meet on our way as detached ancient "tourists," rather than participating in a local ritual event.

The first landmark that captured Pausanias' gaze, "going up from Piraeus" and as he approached Athens—implicitly suggesting that the visitor to Athens should do the same—was "the ruins of the walls." Further on, as he came closer, he turned his eyes to observe "along the road very famous graves, that of Menander . . . and a cenotaph to Euripides."[213] Pieces of land the length of the way leading to the city were used as cemeteries, where tombs belonging to aristocratic families alternated with public ones. It was here that Perikles delivered his famous eulogy, the *Epitaph*, for the fallen of the first year of the Peloponnesian War, in 430 B.C.E., and rhapsodizing Athens, its citizens, and its democracy. The blending of religion and politics in the cemetery is further apparent in a stele dating from 336 B.C.E. that depicts Democracy crowning Demos, now in the Museum of the Attalus Stoa of the Agora in Athens.

Pausanias encountered the above-mentioned Pompeion—the special building between the Dipylon and the Sacred Gate, built in 400 B.C.E. with its rectangular peristyle and dining rooms on the north and west sides—that was used during the preparation of the Panathenaic processions. Next to "the gate to the Cerameicus there are porticoes, and in front of them" Pausanias stopped once more to look at the "brazen statues of famous men and women."[214] One of the porticoes contains shrines to gods. It is the house of Pulytion, at which it is said that a mystic rite was performed by the most notable Athenians."[215] The district of Kerameikos followed, "its name from the hero Ceramus."

Following Pausanias, one would then encounter the Basileios Stoa of 550 B.C.E. The building housed the office of the Royal Archon, one of the three magistrates of Athens with religious and legal responsibilities. On its walls and on upright stones, *stelae*, in front of them were inscribed the ancestral laws of Athens. It was here that Socrates had been required to appear when accused of impiety in 399 B.C.E. Entering the main space of the Agora, and continuing towards the west side, Pausanias indicated the buildings of political function. The Agora was a large, open square that tradition says was founded contemporary to Solon the Lawgiver's establishment of a legal framework for regulating life in Athens that was based, among other ideas, on a rudimentary type of distributive justice system. Before that time, during the Mycenaean period (1550–1100 B.C.E.) and Early Iron Age (1110–700 B.C.E.), the place seems to have been a burial area.

Following the constitutional reforms of Kleisthenes, considerable building activity took

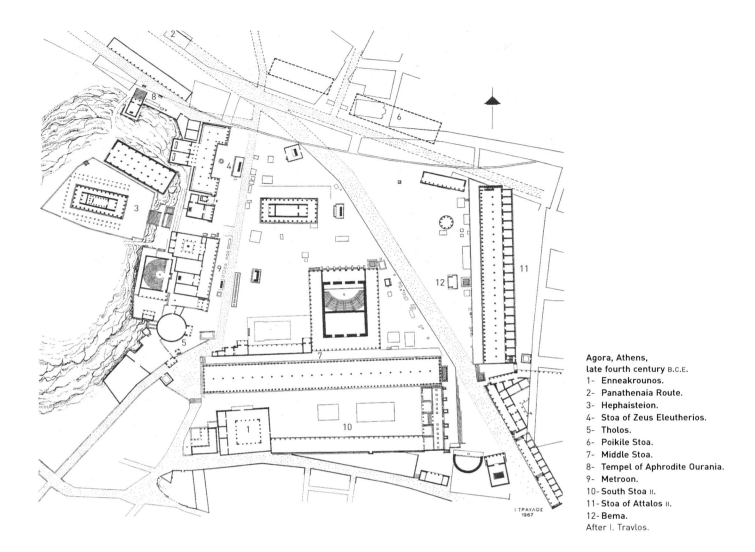

Agora, Athens,
late fourth century B.C.E.
1- Enneakrounos.
2- Panathenaia Route.
3- Hephaisteion.
4- Stoa of Zeus Eleutherios.
5- Tholos.
6- Poikile Stoa.
7- Middle Stoa.
8- Tempel of Aphrodite Ourania.
9- Metroon.
10- South Stoa II.
11- Stoa of Attalos II.
12- Bema.
After I. Travlos.

place at the site. From this period date the stones announcing to the visitor "I am the boundary of the Agora." This indicated the affinities between the Agora and the sanctuary as space-bound institutions that applied the norms of purity discussed above. Furthermore, near the boundary stones, as in sanctuaries, basins of holy water for purification rites were set up. Next to the Basileios Stoa, the grandson of the tyrant Pisistratos in 522 B.C.E. built the Altar of the Twelve Gods, from which all distances from Athens were measured.

In addition to the religious and technical-spatial significance of the place, Pausanias drew attention to its political importance, remarking that "a portico is built behind with pictures of the gods called the Twelve," and "on its wall opposite are painted Theseus, Democracy and Demos. The picture represents Theseus as the one who gave the Athenians

political equality."[216] Pausanias noted the strong link between religion and democratic politics, as demonstrated in the proximity between the "sanctuary of the Mother of the Gods" and "the council chamber of those called the Five Hundred, the Athenian councilors for a year. In it are a wooden figure of Zeus Councilor, Apollo . . . and (once more) Demos, together with paintings by Protogenes of the lawgivers, *thesmothetes*."[217]

Next to the early-fifth-century B.C.E. sanctuary of the Mother of the Gods was the Metroon—both sanctuary and house of the state archives—built in the second half of the second century B.C.E. Documents of public interest were also stored in the Bouleuterion, accommodating the meetings of the Council of Five Hundred. In its vicinity was the Tholos, the round building where "the Presidents (*Prytaneis*) sacrifice," which sheltered a

Demos, the people, crowned by Democracy.
Agora Museum, Athens.

"few small statues made of silver . . . [and] statues of [ancestral] heroes, from whom . . . the Athenian tribes received their names." In a spirit of servility and pragmatic accommodation, but also universality, and perhaps opportunism, Athenians were later to add Attalus the Mysian, Ptolemy the Egyptian, and the Emperor Hadrian to these ten original heroes.[218] However, one should also keep in mind that in the same spirit they also built in the Agora the altar to the "unknown god," thereby indicating the openness of their *polis* and to a great extent justify the freedom of speech. The building also served as the official notice board of the city. Drafts of proposed laws and lists of men called up for military service were posted here under the hero of the tribe concerned. One should not forget that reading was a permanent exercise inside the Agora and the public spaces of the city, and that literacy, together with publicity, was a presupposition of the political institution of democracy.

In the middle of the Agora was the Orchestra—a place with wooden grandstands for dramatic and musical contests. It was here that the statue of the tyrant slayers Harmodius and Aristogeiton, honored as the liberators of the city in 510 B.C.E. but by the time of Plutarch, however, referred to as victims of a love affair rather than heroes, was erected, suggesting the political use of the location and structure as an assembly place. Although the Agora's main use was civic as the buildings there indicated, it also accommodated informal gatherings and conversations.

The Agora of Athens to which Pausanias was now to take the visitor was also the market of the city. One could find everything there and in its vicinity. There were special quarters for fish and cloths; a stoa for flour may have been located on the Dromos; fish may have been sold near the Poikile Stoa, where bankers also worked; wine was traded in the Kerameikos near the gate; bronzes were made and sold near the Hephaisteion; books were to be found on the orchestra; slaves were sold at the Anakeion; there were sculptors near the law courts and a barbershop near the Herms. To quote Eubulus' *Olbia*, "you will find everything sold" here, from "figs and roses to waterclocks and indictments." In the second century c.e., Pollux was to add to this list cooks for hire.[219]

Towards the Hephaisteion and the Basileios Stoa, Pausanias would now turn to find statues, trophies, paintings, and dedicated brazen shields "smeared with pitch" to protect them from rusting. The Poikile Stoa followed, at the northern end of the

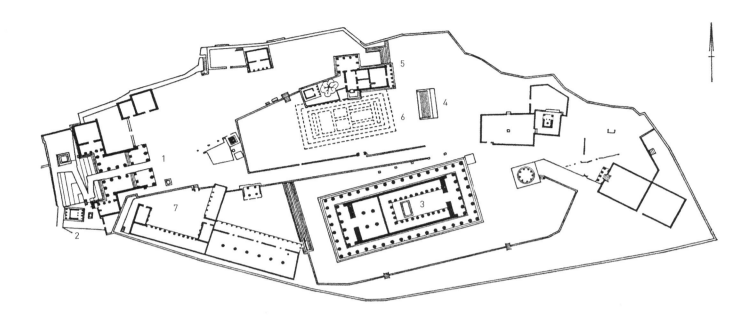

Acropolis of Athens, general Plan. After Stevens.
1. Propylaia, 2. Temple and Altar of Athena Nike, 3. Parthenon, 4. Altar
of Athena, 5. Erechtheion, 6. Old Athena Temple, 7. Buildings of
Artemis Brauronia. After Stevens, 1946.

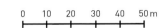

Agora, dated at 475–450 B.C.E. The building was south-oriented, and housed a series of large paintings by the famous painters Polygnotos, Mikon and Panainos. It had no specific destination and provided shelter for legal proceedings, summoning those who qualified to attend the Eleusian mysteries—sword-swallowers, jugglers, beggars, parasites, and philosophers. Zeno of Kition (c. 300 B.C.E.) used the stoa for his teaching—hence the name of his philosophical movement, Stoicism.

Before climbing to the Acropolis, Pausanias made a tour of the lower part of the hill, describing places where the memory of the war with Persia was still maintained. Indeed, before the Battle at Plataia, the Greeks swore an oath—the Oath of Plataia—that may be read in Book XI of Diodorus of Sicily's *Histories*. It begins with the declaration "I will not hold life dearer than liberty," and ends with the promise "I will not destroy any one of the

cities which have participated in the struggle [against the Persians] nor will I rebuild any one of the sanctuaries which have been burned or demolished [by the Persians], but I will let them be and leave them as a reminder to coming generations of the impiety of the barbarians."[220]

Pausanias then turned to the Street of the Tripods: "Leading from the Prytaneum," which "takes its name from the shrines, large enough to hold the tripods which stand upon them . . . very remarkable works of art."[221] From here, he moved to the shrine of Dionysos Lenaios, where the first dramatic contests were probably celebrated, and the shrine of Dionysos Eleuthereus.[222] The street was 2,400 feet (800 meters) long and it was here that the *choregoi*—rich sponsors of the choruses of the dramatic performances that were awarded a tripod as a prize—were obliged to set up this tripod. One such example was the Lysikrates Monument.

View of Temple of Athena Nike from the Propylaia.

After examining the "statues of poets, tragic and comic," Pausanias was to turn to the Theater of Dionysos, part of a cluster formed together with the shrine of Dionysos Eleuthereus and to examine the earlier constructions, the older Temple of Dionysos. It was here that the first drama was performed by Thespis in 534 B.C.E., followed by the dramas of Aeschylus, in one of which Agatharchus painted a scene introducing for the first time—according to Vitruvius'—a representation of space with tremendous repercussions for architecture. During the fourth century B.C.E., the orator Lykourgos undertook the construction of both the theater and the new shrine for Dionysos.

Pausanias' visit to the Acropolis included a rummaging through the major temples and their contents, observing that "in the temple of Athena Polias" was "a folding chair made by Daedalus, Persian spoils, namely the breastplate of Masistius,

who commanded the cavalry at Plataia, and a scimitar said to have belonged to Mardonius." He also strolled through the numerous votive offerings set up, cluttering the open space.

Before going back to the city, Pausanias turned to the bronze Athena, a "tithe from the Persians who landed at Marathon," the work by Phidias whose "point of the spear and the crest of her helmet are visible to those sailing at Athens as soon as Sounion is passed,"[223] expanding the imagined territory of Athens over the sea routes. The visit to the Acropolis ended by probing into its walls, an early part constructed by the Pelasgians, the original inhabitants of the Sacred Rock—at the time of Pausanias, the Arrhephoroi (young girls performing secret rites) being the only people living there.[62]

Following the tour of Pausanias on the Acropolis, it is clear that, as Eisenstein remarked, cited by Hurwit, "the Acropolis we traverse today is the

Theater of Dionysos, Athens.
Photograph by Frédéric Boissonas.

product of the nineteenth century" resembling very little what he called "the perfect example of one of the most ancient films"[224]—meaning the visual and thematic juxtapositions composing a real "montage." Even if this characterization is inaccurate and strongly anachronistic, it still captures the full wealth of contrasts, juxtapositions, and the character of the place. Nonetheless, even these dual descriptions of the role of the city offered above fail to grasp how buildings and space were interpreted and used at that time by the majority of the population. Both are in their own way exceptional. Yet neither deals with the way in which everyday chores were structured in the Athenian space, nor do they embrace the beliefs and desires through which the inhabitants of Athens—who were largely foreigners and slaves—perceived and exploited the constructed world that surrounded them, and one that is so alien to us today.

The question then remains: What is it about these structures that makes them so appealing and so significant to us today?

View of the Acropolis of Athens from the west.
Photograph by Frédéric Boissonas.

Hephaisteion, also known as the Theseion. South longitudinal section.
Photograph by Serge Moulinier.

"Leucippus and Democritus believe that the elements are the solid and the void . . . the material causes of existing things . . . the differences in atoms are the causes of other things . . . these differences are . . . shape, arrangement, position."

"Anaxagoras thinks that perception is by opposites, for like has no effect on like."
Theophrastus, *De sensu*, 27

"An unexpected harmony is better than an apparent one."
Heraclitus, fragment 54

CHAPTER V

THE POETICS
OF CLASSICAL ARCHITECTURE

In 399 B.C.E., in front of the Doric colonnade of the renowned Basileios Stoa, the most ancient stoa of Athens and seat of the Royal Archon, Socrates, the philosopher, met a young man, Euthyphro. Plato narrates the event in one of his earliest dialogues, the *Euthyphro*. Both Socrates and Euthyphro arrived at the Stoa on legal business: Socrates was prosecuted for being a "maker (*poietes*) of gods" and corrupting the youth—a charge that would lead to his death—and Euthyphro was to prosecute his father for murdering one of his servants. Apart from the reference to the Basileios Stoa, there is no other mention of architecture in the text. However, it does discuss issues that may inform us about how ancient Greeks viewed the world and architecture. As with most Platonic texts, *Euthyphro* has several levels of significance. It is a fascinating sociological and political document—though politically embarrassing for a contemporary reader, as we will discuss in the next chapter. At the same time, it is an important work in the history of the systematization of thinking dealing with the problem of definition of terms by referring a species to a genus: a problem we believe played an important role in the development of ancient Greek architectural thinking and spatial reasoning in general.

In the dialogue, Socrates claimed to be descended from Daedalus,[225] the celebrated mythical inventor, craftsman, sculptor, and designer of that formidable building—the labyrinth. However, he failed to mention the labyrinth in the text. Socrates discussed rather the archaic statues—the *xoana*—or one of the artifacts—the *daedaleia* or sort of "automata-toys"—that his ancestor Daedalus created, endowing them with the ability to "run away." Socrates asserted that he was like his ancestor in that he, too, made things that could move. His creations were "words that could run away and did not stay where one put them to stand." Furthermore, in contrast to his ancestor, Socrates boasted that he was a maker of "works that made *others* move." By this, he meant that he was not merely a craftsman of objects—despite his training as a sculptor—but a "craftsman" of *ways* of making objects. These

Temple known as the Basilica, Paestum.
Northwest corner column at sunrise.
Photograph by Serge Moulinier.

Parthenon, Athens. Southeast corner.
Photograph by Serge Moulinier.

ways he made available to be used by others. In other words, he was not simply a designer of products, but a designer of *methods*. To use John Pollock's metaphor, Socrates was involved in "cognitive carpentry."[226] Accordingly, the dialogue presents him as showing how one could reason correctly through the proper use of *species* and *genus*.

Socrates, who was a young man when the Parthenon was being built, was part of a major movement that contributed to what E. R. Dodds has referred to as "the transformation . . . [of] an untidy jumble . . . into a system of methodical disciplines."[227] Even if Dodds's assertion is too biased against archaic modes of thinking, refusing to concede that they were also organized around rules—albeit different from those characterizing contemporary disciplines—the fact remains that, between the end of the so-called "Archaic period" and the Classical times, Greece produced a new way of constructing and construing the world, which was unprecedented in its systematic rigor and embedded with new disciplinary institutions. There was no place for falsehood or accident in this system. The *Poetics* of Aristotle was one of the books that investigated this new way of doing things. Architecture was one of these disciplines.

When examining the evolution of Greek buildings, we see a step-by-step construction of this design method. This is accompanied by something broader—a system of spatial thinking for conceiving structures and places—or, more precisely, a *poetics* of architecture that would come to be known as the Classical canon. It is this design method and system enabling spatial intelligence that makes ancient Greek buildings so appealing. It remains implicit in their spatial structure, surviving the ravages of time—even if the actual fabric of the buildings is now in fragments and ruins.

The building as object

The process of this systematization of design—the making of what has been called the Classical canon—began slowly, following the emergence of the new type of spatial arrangement of buildings, consisting of detached, freestanding, and scattered Archaic volumes—the homes of chieftains or temples—that succeeded the vast, interconnected, and compact palatial or citadel complexes of the Mycenaean era. At the same time, the loosely structured nucleus of political organization, poor economy and meager technological knowledge characteristic of the Archaic communities that replaced the centralized, stratified, affluent, and literate Bronze Age regimes, began to expand and advance once more.[228] After a long period of stagnation, approximately as long as the Dark Ages, revolutionary changes—similar to those that would occur two thousand years later in Western Europe, leading to the Renaissance—probably initiated by advances in the technology of agriculture, led to a demographic explosion. According to Anthony Snodgrass,[229] by the end of the Bronze Age, where there had been three hundred twenty settlements, by the twelfth century B.C.E. there were only one hundred thirty, and in the eleventh century B.C.E., forty. Then, between 780 and 720 B.C.E., the population multiplied sevenfold. Similarly, community interaction declined and then grew back stronger during the same period.

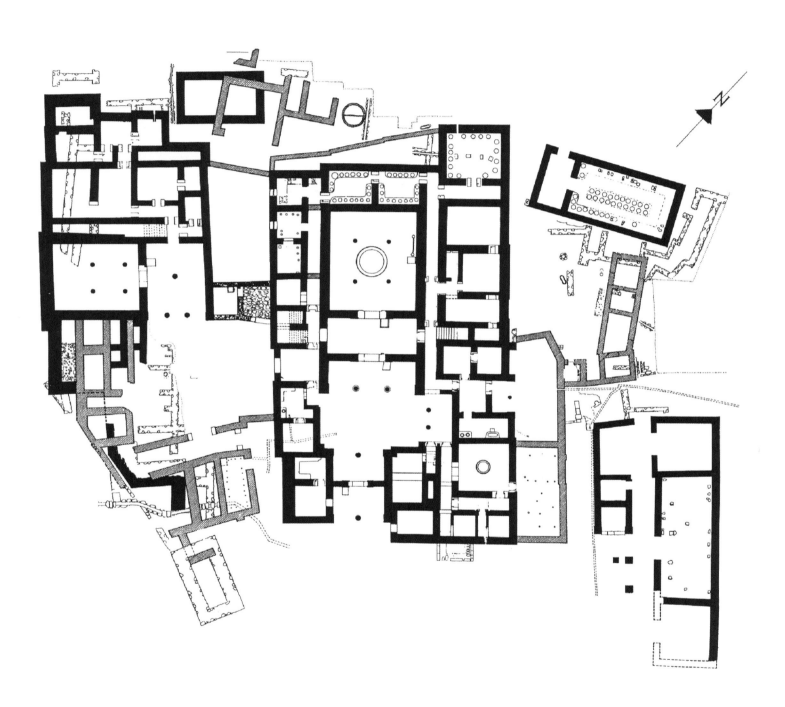

Palace of Nestor, Pylos.
General plan. C.1300.
After Travlos, 1966.

0   10   20   30 m

Hephaisteion, also known as the Theseion, Athens.
Soffits of the south peristyle.
Photograph by Serge Moulinier.

Temple of Hera, Paestum.
Photograph by Serge Moulinier.

Fundamental to this systematization was the discernment of entities out of endless sensory input, "individuate" recognizing them as "objects," developing categories to identify them, and referring to them as tokens, *kath' ekaston,* and as types, *kath' olou.* This is to a great extent what the dialogue of *Euthyphro* was about—although the beginnings of this way of thinking go back to the Ionians. Indeed, this was the challenge characterizing the initial struggles in the formation of the Classical canon in architecture.

In the absence of written texts, it is hard to demonstrate how this process took place in the very beginning. Were the rectilinear spaces of the supposed location of the king's throne next to the circular hearth in the midst of four columns that were contained within the compact Mycenaean palatial or citadel complexes, such as those of Tiryns or Pylos, seen by people at that time as "objects," entities belonging to known types of objects? Were

they construed as distinct spatial entities, in the way that eighth-century B.C.E. temples had probably been constructed? Perhaps Homer, a ninth-century B.C.E. poet, can help us in this. He had a name—*megaron*—for the main room of the palace used by the Mycenaean royalty. But what did Homer mean by this word? As is well known, Homer narrated events that occurred centuries before his time. His knowledge of theses events and their places was therefore blurred. Was he referring to the early thirteenth-century B.C.E. buildings or to the freestanding structures of his time in the manner of Herodotus in the fifth century B.C.E. when he referred to the Apollo Temple in Delphi as *megaron,*[230] or of Pindar's *Olympian Ode* of 472 B.C.E., when he wrote about the "golden pillars" of the porch of a "magnificent *megaron*"?

Things become more complex when one realizes that *megaron* is in fact of Hebrew etymology. Me'arah, a word in use even today, means "cave."

Temple known as the Basilica, Paestum.
The long north side.
Photograph by Serge Moulinier.

Leaving to one side the fascinating questions about origins and the possibility of information exchange—if not of workshops—within the Mediterranean world, the original meaning of the word indicates that the term referred to a kind of hollow space inside a compact mass, such as was the Mycenaean royal place, rather than the free-standing *megaron* of Homer's time. The fact that there was a name for this royal place suggests that people could point to *it* and consequently recognize it as an "object." Yet, did the term *megaron* have other implications beyond a reference to a specific token place? Could one talk about it as a type of space? Such questions that are very diffi-cult, if not impossible, to answer. One thing remains certain: by the end of the seventh century B.C.E., major changes occurred in architecture in Greece, giving rise to the emergence of free-standing temples substituting in importance the

"cave-like" central locations of the complexes of the Mycenaean era.

As we have already mentioned, a key design char-acteristic of this new type of building was the *pteron*, an external often irregularly shaped and spaced wooden colonnade. In all probability, it came about as a result of physical needs and pragmatic con-straints. It was used to protect from hostile weather both the walls of these special buildings—later called *naos*—made out of materials subject to easy decay, and the people gathering in their vicinity.

However, the colonnade continued to be used even when the walls of the *naos* were made out of hard durable stone. We also observe that by the end of the seventh century B.C.E., with few exceptions, the irregular colonnades surrounding the rectilin-ear and apsidal configured *naos* began to be replaced by regularly shaped and spaced columns forming a strict rectilinear configuration. In addition, during

Temple of Hera Argiva, Paestum.
The central nave from east to west.
Photograph by Serge Moulinier.

the same period, other components of the building appeared that were placed more consistently in
relation to each other. Characteristic is the case of
the triglyphs. Located initially along the horizontal frieze without any coordination with the supporting Doric columns—as for example in the Old
Tholos of Delphi or the Temple of Apollo in
Syracuse—by the end of the seventh century B.C.E.,
triglyphs were superposed on the axis of the
columns and in the middle of the intercolumnar
space. No socioeconomic, environmental, or technological reasons seem to have dictated this trend
towards spatial order.

Worldmaking, *kosmopoiia*

On the other hand, there is the possibility that it
was fear of *miasma*—pollution, and compulsion for

purity and purification, *katharsis* in its original
sense—that gave rise to the *temenos* as a precinct cut
off from the rest of the land.[231] Similar beliefs
and norms may also have led initially to the construction of these special buildings as cult structures—places distinct from their surroundings in
terms of their adherence to strict rules of spatial
layout. As a spatial entity within the territory of
the precinct, the *temenos* was a "*kosmos* within a
kosmos," or "a world within the world."[232] It was the
product of an act of purification, which in architectural terms was carried out by surrounding a
portion of space by an ordered colonnade and
arranging the components of the building within
this space in an orderly way. Ancient Greeks called
this "worldmaking," or *kosmeo*. Traces of this can
be found in ancient texts containing fragments of
Pythagorean theories. On the basis of these texts,
it appears that Pythagoras[233] was among the first

Temple known as the Concorde, Agrigentum.
The main access way and elevation to the temple's east side.
Photograph by Serge Moulinier.

ancient Greek philosophers to introduce *kosmos*, meaning the "world," as well as "order," and to link orderliness with *katharsis,* purification. However, already in Homer and Hesiod the word meant decoration of women. In addition, there is no evidence that concerns of ritualistic or divination purification guided the purgation of spatial anomalies in the design of buildings, the systematization of architectural thinking, and the formation of the Classical canon.

On the other hand, one can speculate that once the peripteral colonnade was introduced and given the cultural and intellectual development of the communities that initiated it, the colonnade began to be seen by these people in a different way. It started to have for them a visual, or to be more exact, a cognitive-spatial effect. In other words, the colonnade began to be perceived as defining the building as a distinct *object*. Like a wall, a colonnade delineates a parcel of space, providing a closure. In addition, the row of columns standing in front of the shaded surface of the wall of the *naos* produced a texture that contrasted more sharply with the background than the contrast produced by the texture of the mud-brick wall. The orderly arrangement—the spacing and shaping—of the columns reinforced the visual discontinuity, thereby generating a vibrant "illusory-contour"[234] that set the edifice, as an individual entity, apart from its surroundings. It created a *temenos*—no longer in a purificatory, but rather in a cognitive sense. It made a "*kosmos* within *kosmos*," or "world within the world,"[235] free of pollution and spatial anomalies. More significantly, by erecting a colonnade and arranging the interior components of the building in a coherent way, this was a major step in the pursuit towards the formation of a coherent system of architectural thinking and spatial reasoning.

Temple of Hera Argiva, Paestum.
The upper portions along the south side seen from the east at noon.
Photograph by Serge Moulinier.

Humans have become endowed through evolution with the ability to carve up the environment into objects. Objects are basic means without which the accumulation and organization of experiences into knowledge, reasoning, and communication—essential for survival—could not occur. In this sense, objects are not the "things" that constitute the world "out there," untouched by what humans have in their mind. They are instead things construed by the mind. They are "grasped,"[236] as one grasps physical things in the physical environment—except this "grasping" is done cognitively, within one's mind. On the other hand, although they are constructed "in the head," these mental objects are also constrained by the way things are "out there." Without this interaction between—metaphorically speaking—"hand and head," survival would have not been possible.

The process of construction of such mental objects—as one does by looking around, or walking down the street—can be passive, simple, and automatic. Yet, parallel to such effortless and automatic processes of recognition, identifying objects and reasoning about them is also an active, complex, and conscious process. It employs conceptual tools, systems of thinking, and methods that have been developed through history, and which are framed by each society's beliefs and desires. To quote Hilary Putnam, "there is no such totality as All The Objects There Are." It is individuals, institutions, and communities that "world make," deciding "what objects are in the world"—and these decisions have fundamental economic, social, and technological consequences. One can understand therefore the obsession of the Greek culture with identifying objects, *kosmoi* and *kosmemata*, in all areas of human activity and in architecture at this critical moment of their expansion. On the other

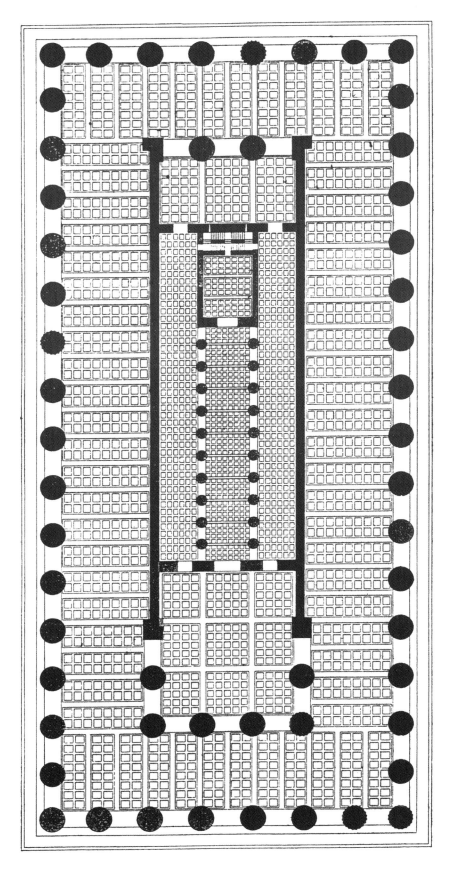

Temple G at Selinous.
Plan of the ceiling. 520–c. 475 B.C.E.
After Kohte, 1915.

hand, there is something unique about this period in ancient Greece that spans from the Archaic to the Classical period. To return to Socrates in *Euthyphro*, what occurred was not only the construction of one more set of objects, or one more possible world populated by a different set of objects, but the creation of a "work that gives to *others* the possibility" of "worldmaking": the making of a method of thinking.

Column and number

The making of systematic architectural thinking and what came to be known as the "Canon of Classical Architecture" owe much to the colonnade. The colonnade helped define the temple as object. Through the orderly shaped and spaced columns, it circumscribed an "illusory contour," producing a recognizable entity. At the same time, given the fact that it was itself an assemblage of physical, standardized entities—the columns, recognizable and countable themselves—it offered the opportunity not only of recognizing the temples as objects, but also of discerning similarities and differences between them, leading to a categorical system of buildings. It is clear therefore how standardizing the shape of columns and the space between columns was linked not only with a vague idea of "order," but also with a more tangible program of developing a taxonomy as part of constructing a system of design thinking. To put it, probably, more accurately from the historical point of view, the application of the peripheral colonnade made people aware of the possibility of developing a method of identifying and categorizing spatial objects, which in turn further reinforced the tendency towards standardization of columns and intervals.

This seems to be a very abstract and complex intellectual exercise; however, the process that occurred in architecture was not very different from those that took place in music, poetry, and certainly philosophy. The practical results of this development can be seen in the *Ten Books on Architecture* of the highly pragmatic Vitruvius. Compiling previous knowledge from previous writings, Vitruvius presented a classification of temples based on number—the number of columns of the front colonnade. The terms he used for this classification were Greek, thereby indicating that the Greeks had already developed the system. Thus a temple with a four-column front was called *tetrastylos;* with six, *hexastylos;* with eight, *octastylos;* and with ten, *decastylos.* In addition, he presented a second system of classification based on numerical relations: the ratio between the dimension of the diameter of the column of a colonnade and the distance between columns. Once more the terminology was Greek: *pycnostylos* with close columns, the intercolumnation being one-and-a-half diameters; *systylos,* "a little more open," with two diameters; *eustylos* with two and a half; diastylos with three, and *areaostylos* being even wider.

As we have seen, the standardization of the number of columns for the front colonnade and of the column and intercolumnation dimensions came into being gradually over the centuries. The systematization in question evolved in parallel with the development of the constructs of genus and

Temple of Demeter, Paestum.
Photograph by Serge Moulinier.

species—part of the overall systematization of spatial thinking and the formation of the Classical canon. Consequently, it is tempting to associate this development in Greek architecture towards what we might call "elementarism" and orderliness—that is, seeing buildings as units made out of other units and number—with the search by Greek thinkers[237] to invent an elementarist and number-based system of representation of the world. Pythagoras' representation of *kosmos* used elementary units and numbers, and his notion of orderliness was the arrangement of spatial entities expressed in numbers.[238] In the domain of music and "auditory thinking," Pythagoras achieved a major breakthrough. He connected sound with number—the length of the monochord strings.

However, other attempts by his followers were not as convincing—such as the demonstration by Eurytus as reported by Alexander of Aphrodisias in *Met,*[239] defining man as the number two hundred fifty and then taking an equal number of colored pebbles and filling with them a rough sketch of a man he had done before. Moreover, influenced by Pythagoras, Plato in his writings particularly his famous passage of *Timaeus,* represents the world through "divisible bodies," *ta somata meristou,*[240] and number. However, with the exception of Vitruvius' Book V on theaters, there is no strong evidence that Pythagorean ideas guided decisions about the number of columns of the *pteron* and their distances. The fact is that temples differed from each other in terms of the number of columns of their front and side. As we have seen, for the Temple of Apollo in Bassai and for the earlier Temple of Apollo in Corinth the arrangement

was 6×15—but for other temples it was 6×12, 6×13, 6×14, or 6×17 for some unknown numerological or cosmological reason. If one looks over the long list of ancient Greek temples and examines the number of their columns, no ordering system can be found and no general rule suggests that the selection of these numbers had to do with Pythagorean or Platonist models of the world. Nevertheless, late Medieval and Renaissance architects reading *Timaeus* in conjunction with Vitruvius and the Bible developed a syncretist system, within which Pythagorean and Platonist ideas were to play a most important role. Yet while this system claimed universality and adherence to the rules of antiquity, it had very little to do with Greek architecture as it was produced in its time.[241]

Taxis and *merologia*

The classification of temples by Vitruvius based on number as discussed above may appear weak from the point of view of systematization. It was strictly a descriptive tool, limited in its potential to help design buildings and organize space. In spite of this, the introduction of the *pteron* in ancient Greek architecture was very significant. Its role was once again related to the categorization of buildings, though in this case the system used instead of number was topology: relations of adjacency of parts, *meroi*, irrespective of their shape and size. With the development of a system for dividing the space of a building into parts and identifying their relations—a *merologia*—the first step towards a systematic method of design was taken.

Temple of Hera, Paestum.
Photograph by Serge Moulinier.

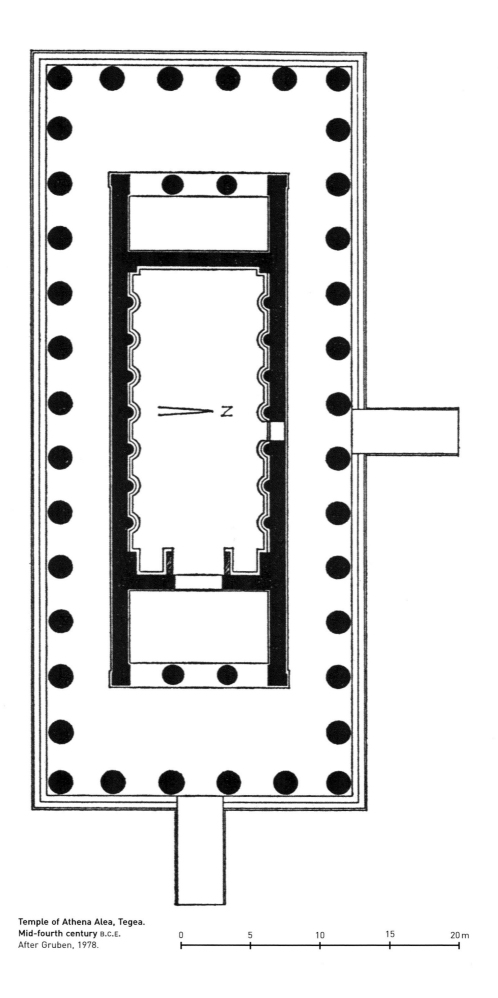

Temple of Athena Alea, Tegea.
Mid-fourth century B.C.E.
After Gruben, 1978.

0   5   10   15   20 m

Vitruvius at the very beginning of his *Books* discusses the division of the space of a building in an ordered manner. He uses the Greek word *taxis*, and translates it into Latin as *ordinatione*, stating that it is one of the "constitutes" of architecture. Yet, as he proceeds further, trying to distinguish it from what he calls in Greek *diathesis*, and in Latin *dispositione*, the discussion becomes unclear—especially when the concept of *ideae* is introduced. This he considers as being related to *ichnographia, orthographia*, and *scaenographia*, while in fact they are ways of representing plan, elevation, and perspective of buildings respectively. A clearer discussion about ordered division of space into parts and taxis, as sequential ordering of objects is found in Aristotle's *Metaphysics*.[242] *Taxis* and beauty, *to kalon*, are juxtaposed with disorder, *ataxia* and *aischron*. He refers to this ordering, together with shape and position, as basic constituents of Democritus' system of nature. However, *taxis* is simply Aristotle's interpretation of *diathige*—the term used by Democritus—which corresponds to Aristotle's beliefs and preoccupation with static spatial organization as found in another of his texts, the *Poetics*. The book provides a "method"[243] for the "making" of tragedy. There is no direct reference in the text to architecture. However, it does turn several times to the making—the *poetics*—of other artifact objects, as well as to how animals or any "object," *apan pragma*, are made and under what conditions they are "well-made," *kalos*.

According to the *Poetics*, such an object has to be made out of "sweet" stuff, or "pleasant speech." Furthermore, most importantly it has to be "complete" and "whole" (*teleon* and *holon*) and to be comprehended as a whole. Thus, in order to be "easily taken in by the mind" and to be "easily taken in by the memory" it must be of a certain size: neither too large, nor too small. In addition it has to be made out of parts, *moria*, and these parts are to be arranged in an "orderly way," *tetagmena*.

Tripartite schema

Vitruvius provides a way of looking at temples according to how a colonnade relates to the body of the *naos*. In *Ten Books on Architecture*, he lists temples according to the position of the colonnade in relation to the *naos* and again uses Greek terms, suggesting that the Greeks had already developed this system. According to this, a temple can be: *prostylos*, having columns in front; *amphiprostylos*, with columns on both front and back; *peripteral*, with a colonnade all round; and *naos en parastasin* or *in antis*, with no colonnade and with pilasters terminating the walls of the *naos*.

The taxonomy is obviously descriptive. However, by examining more closely the categories proposed, one finds—as the prefixes *pro-*, *amphi-*, and *peri-*, indicate—an underlying conceptual spatial structure, "an articulated structure that encodes the decomposition of objects into parts."[244] In addition, it relates these parts spatially to each other. In other words, a peripteral temple was seen to be made out of a *naos*-part with a *pteron*-part in front, a *pteron* behind, and one *pteron* on each of its two sides. What emerges schematically is a tripartite frame[245]—or diagrammatically a three by three, nine-square matrix-array whose central part is

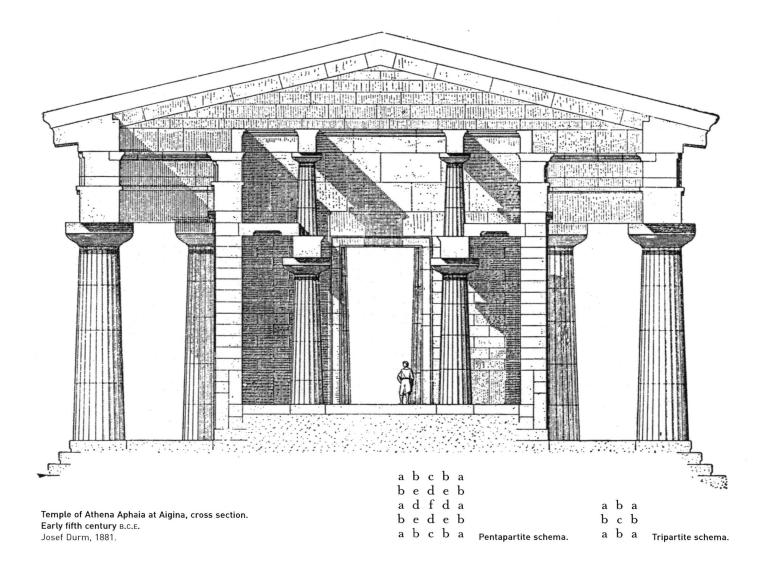

Temple of Athena Aphaia at Aigina, cross section.
Early fifth century B.C.E.
Josef Durm, 1881.

```
a b c b a
b e d e b
a d f d a          a b a
b e d e b          b c b
a b c b a  Pentapartite schema.   a b a  Tripartite schema.
```

occupied by the *naos* and the peripheral parts by the pteron. Oriented in the landscape, these *pteron*-parts may be called the east, south, west, and north, and from the point of view of one approaching the temple, they may be called front, back, left, and right.

The framework could be extended in all three dimensions by introducing the categories of middle, up, and down. Its rather straightforward, simple structure is easy to grasp, and once adopted, it became a standard tool for spatial composition. During the Renaissance, it was schematized by Cesariano, who assigned letters to each of the parts of the array.[246] By the end of the eighteenth century, it was further schematized and made easier to operate by J. N. L. Durand, who represented the tripartite framework through axes instead of squares.[247] Durand's system of representation

made it easier to comprehend the hierarchical recursive structure of nested tripartite frameworks. The method was initially aimed at the students of the École Polytechnique, but by the second part of the nineteenth century, it was adopted by a very large number of architects. It helped categorize buildings in general and keep track of alternative possibilities of composition of space at a preliminary "pre-parametric" level. However, in his effort to be efficient and effective Durand suggested a linear process of composition from the coarsest array to the most detailed, thereby reducing the complexity of partitioning whether one composes an artifact or scans it to understand how it is composed. Nothing of the kind was suggested by any of the ancient Greek authors—nor even by Vitruvius—who wrote about *taxis* in relation to poetry or rhetoric.

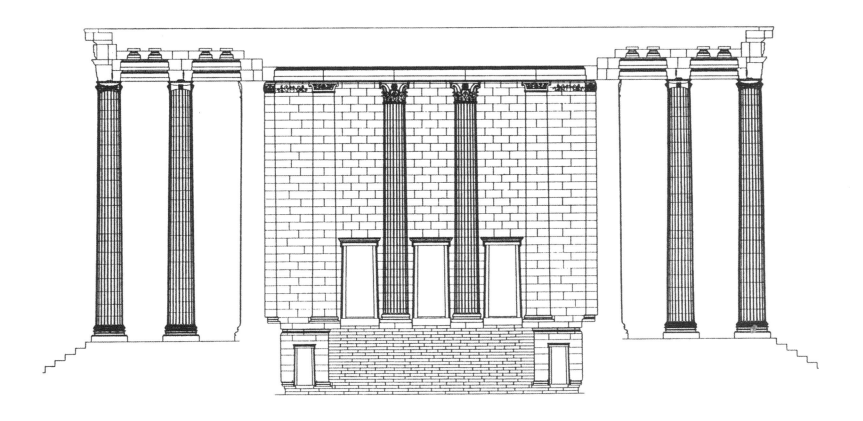

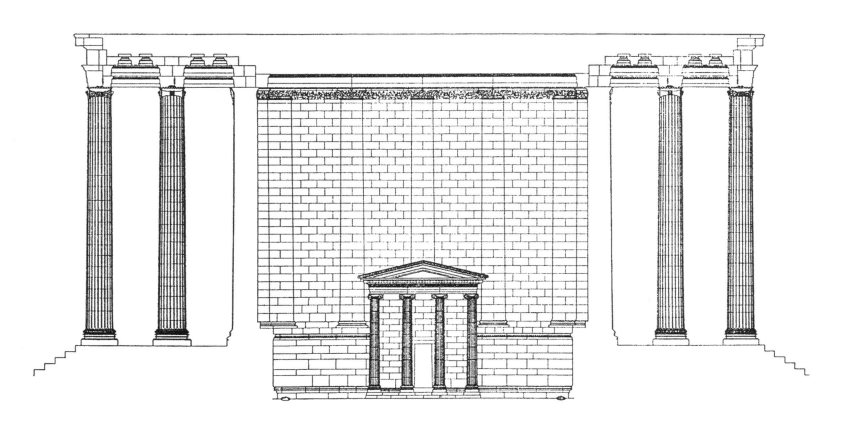

Temple of Apollo, Didyma, Miletos.
Cross section.
After H. Knackfuss. H. Berve and G. Gruben, 1978.

As mentioned above, according to the *Poetics,* a "complete" and "whole" has to be *tetagmenon,* divided and arranged orderly in parts. As opposed to Vitruvius, Aristotle states explicitly the tripartite, normative organization of an orderly arranged work. A whole is defined as having a "beginning, middle, and end." The issue here is not the number three of the parts—they can more divisions in a work as we will see later—but rather the requirement of closure, implied in the notions of beginning, *arche,* and end, *eschaton,* sandwiching a core part, the middle, or *meson. Taxis* and tripartition—as a rule for arranging, *tattein,* a discourse to make it "easily graspable," *eusynoptos*—was recommended once more by Aristotle in his book on *Rhetoric,* which was written after the *Poetics.* Here Aristotle splits the middle part of the discourse into two in order to express the duality between the statement of a legal case and the proof—an essential articulation in a speech intended to persuade.

Tripartition for Aristotle was both a descriptive and explanatory framework to represent, scan, and analyze existing works. But it was also a normative schema prescribing how to make new works and arrange their parts. Aristotle did not invent it. It had an earlier and wide-ranging history in other cultural modes that run parallel with the emergence of the *peristylion* and the disappearance of the single central colonnade in temples. Corax from Syracuse had already recommended this in the first book on rhetoric (second part of the fifth century B.C.E.); he also discussed the possibility of inserting two intermediary parts to arrive at a five-part organization of a speech. Soon after, following the early tripartite plan of the old temple in the Argive

Heraion, Alcman was to compose three part poems. Tripartition is canonized as a formula known as "the three of Stesichorus"—*strophe, antistrophe,* and *epodos*—referring to the name of Stesichorus of Himera (632–556 B.C.E.),[248] who invented it at about the time of the tripartite plan of the temple C at Selinous. Drawing on the seventh-century B.C.E. schema of Terpander,[249] a poet-musician from Lesbos who developed a closed seven-part schema in sharp contrast to the open arrangement of Homer's epics, Pindar elaborated in his *Odes* the triad schema inserting between them transitional parts. The result was a five-part schema. This schema recalled the five-part division that was already present in the Temple of Artemis in Kerkyra (Corfu) and which evolved at the time of Pindar in the Temple of Aphaia at Aigina, and Zeus in Olympia. Occasionally Pindar articulated even further the *pentapartite* schema by inserting into it two more divisions to arrive at a seven-part schema, following Terpander's older version. As the middle part of a *naos* was occupied by the most important cult object of the temple—namely, the sculpture of the resident god—so the middle of the Pindaric ode, called characteristically the navel, *omphalos*—associating the center of the body of the poem with the center of the human body—was occupied by the presentation of a key myth.

The above analysis referred mainly to partitioning in relation to the short axis of the building. The same breakdown of the plan of the building applied in reference to the long axis, and the same division of the space in three parts was found persistently: from the archaic temple of Artemis in Kerkyra, with a *pronaos, naos,* and closed *adyton,* to the classical Temple of Apollo Epikourios at Bassai, and the late fourth-century B.C.E. temple by Pythius with a very shallow *opisthodomos* as a third part. The most canonical case is the temple of Artemis Leucophrene that Vitruvius admired, as well as the writing of its architect, Hermogenes. As we saw before, the temple is peripteral and the *naos* is divided into the *pronaos, naos* proper, and *opisthodomos*. However, despite the fact that the proportions of the three parts of the building are 2:2:1, Vitruvius in his book suggests 2:3:2. This brings back not only the problem of the reliability of the theoretical text of Vitruvius as reflecting both the practice and theory of ancient Greek architects, but also the question of what makes a building canonical, and more importantly, what exactly defines the canon. This problem will be discussed later.

Before that, we should return to one aspect of the canon—once more to tripartition and to its wider significance. In his book on *Rhetoric*, Aristotle talks about the *prooimion*, the beginning of a speech as being analogous to the *prologos* in poetry, and to the *proaulion*, the prelude in flute playing.[250] They are all "beginnings"—*odopoiesis*—preparing the way for what is to come. Pindar makes equally explicit the analogy between space and discourse organization in his Fourth Olympian Ode by using the analogy between *prologos* and the frontage of a project: the beginning of a work, *ergou prosopon*, shines far away like "the golden pillars of the front of a porch," *prothyro*, announcing the building, *megaron*. This parallel, as well as the other homologies in partitioning systems from different modes of expression, was not brought here with the intention

to suggest any general "world view" of the time. It was rather to suggest that for communities so curious, open, and competitive as the Greek at that time, it was rather normal to exchange information, question, criticize and learn "across disciplines," to use a contemporary expression. This is in shown in texts such as the Socratic dialogues, but also in the places such as the agorae with their stoae and public places for eating. In addition, the preoccupation of the Greeks with these homologies of orderly arrangement, *taxis* and *kosmos* in poetry, drama, speech, music, and architecture, indicate their commitment to discovering the common intelligence that generated them. And some—like Anaxagoras, friend of Perikles—believed that "order was made," *kosmopoiia,* and that the "mind" was the "machinery," or *mechane,* that made it.[251]

Earlier in this book, we saw how the development of a design method, an architectural *poetics* in ancient Greece, was manifested by efforts to define the building as a "whole object"—a fundamental prerequisite towards constructing a system of spatial thinking for a design method, that was to become the architectural Classical canon. We have also seen how these efforts were facilitated by the creation of the *peristylion*—that is, by surrounding the *naos* with a row of columns. The columns formed an illusory contour circumscribing a bounded area, thus defining it as a thing, *to on,* that one could point and refer to. A more regular shaping and spacing of the columns of the *peristylion* significantly enhanced the creation of this entity. Later, we proceeded to examine how the colonnades and walls of temples enabled the perception of the internal space of the temple as being segmented, discerning spatial discontinuities, and parsed into constituent parts: those of the *naos* and the *pteron*. The emergent tripartite *taxis* was a schema of interconnected parts—an array that worked as a system of representation, a spatial frame registering *where* lower-level objects, like the columns and the other components of a temple are located. It is a "cognitive map," or "plan of places," all of which are spatially related to each other topologically, relative to which one can describe where: for example, a column appears in relation to another column or to a door, and indeed in relation to the whole building. The spatial plan is equivalent to Aristotle's plan of the tragedy in *Poetics* within which one can specify where an action is to occur and where an actor will enter and engage in an action with another actor.

It is important to note that this array map informs where objects are independently from the viewer. This is what has been called an "absolute" or "allocentric" arrangement. That is, one can *think* about the arrangement of columns, doors, and statues and their position in relation to each other without *looking* at them from a personal point of view.[252]

The kinds of architecture

Having discussed the level of the design system of Classical architecture that refers to *where* objects are within the building, *taxis*, we will now move on to the next level that refers to *what* kind of objects are placed within it.[253] Rather than taking the temple as a single object, we will first focus on the column. We will segregate this from the rest of the *pteron* and

identify it as an "object" nested within the building-object. The choice of the column is based on the historical fact that the column was the object through which the concept of *kind* within the Classical canon of architecture was developed, both logically and morphologically.

In other words, having examined how a building is partitioned we will now investigate how columns, are "individuated": what are the spatial means through which they are recognized, identified and—in the spirit of challenge of the dialogue *Euthyphro*—how they relate to genus and species. Finally we will generalize this discussion by showing that the observations about columns can be attributed to any other "object" that enters into a building and populates its parts—pilasters, walls, banisters, doors, windows, ceilings, door panels, pedestals, and even movable furniture, such as tables, chairs, and lamp stands.

A final word about the use of the term "kinds" versus "orders" before we proceed with the analysis proper: throughout this text, we have used the concept of "kind" rather than "order." There is no reference to "orders" of architecture in ancient Greek texts. When authors such as Pausanias wanted to identify a building they would simply call it Doric, Ionic, or Corinthian. In his endeavor to systematize architectural thinking, Vitruvius used the term *genera*—that is, "kinds." The term "orders" came into play gradually after the Renaissance[254] by extension of the concept of "order" as a translation of the Greek *taxis*. With few exceptions, Serlio used the term *genera,* as did most of the Italian and French theoreticians of architecture in the seventeenth century.

Parthenon, capital detail.

Doric, Ionic, and Corinthian kinds of columns may be categorized as follows: 1) their subdivisions into constituent parts and the number of the imbedded subdivisions in these parts; 2) the relative size of these subdivisions, their proportions— the primary concern of Vitruvius and post-Renaissance Classical architecture;[255] 3) the configuration of their profile.

We will start by examining the parts into which a column is segmented. We will look into the vertical subdivisions rather than the whole array as we did above, segmenting the plan of the building. In other words, we will apply once more the framework of *taxis* decomposing the column in order to see how it is divided into parts and, as with the overall plan of the temple, we will apply it recursively.

Looking at the buildings and the ancient Greek (and Roman) texts that refer to the buildings, we find that all ancient Greek columns—whether Doric, Ionic, or Corinthian—divide into a capital and a shaft. Doric shafts reach the ground directly, but Ionic and Corinthian shafts have a base. The Classical canon, as adopted by the Romans and as developed during the Renaissance, could not tolerate the Doric exception and frequently added a base to the column (see the canonical table of the kinds of architecture by Serlio at the beginning of this book). However, a more archaeologically correct Perrault, in his translation of Vitruvius, drew the Doric column without a base. Yet, so strong became the tendency to universalize the rules governing the kinds of architecture that when European travelers came in contact with the baseless Greek Doric, they were very often initially shocked.

Broadening now our view, away from the column and expanding our selective attention to encompass the whole building from the skyline to its foundation, we recognize the column as a part inserted between two parts—the entablature (for which no Greek term exists) above, and the stylobate (*crepidoma*) beneath. Subsequently, scanning the stylobate we find that frequently (but not always) it is made up of three parts, as a three-stepped supporting platform. The entablature is also composed of three parts. In Doric buildings, these are the *epistylion* (architrave), the triglyph-metope, and the *geison* (cornice). In Ionic buildings, they are the *tainiai* (fasciae)—the *zoophoros* (frieze), and the cornice architrave. In conclusion, we observe that tripartition is present here, too. Moreover, tripartition is also to be found applied to some of the nested parts. The Ionic cornice divides into the *sima*, *geison* proper, modillion dentils, and the fasciae that are usually made up of three bands. Tripartite is also the organization of the Doric triglyph-metope composed of a middle part between two *taeniae*. The middle part is tripartite in the vertical sense: the metope being flanked by the two triglyphs, which in turn, as the name indicates, are also composed of three vertical bands.

If we now narrow our attention to each of the three parts of the column—capital, shaft, and base—we recognize that they also are partitioned into three subordinate components. The Doric capital is segmented into abacus, echinus, and necking: the Ionic into abacus, volutes, and echinus. Despite its apparent complexity, the Corinthian capital is tripartite too. It is divided into abacus, volutes, and acanthus entities. Sixteenth-century theoreticians, such as Serlio and Philibert de l'Orme, tried

Temple of Hephaistos.

to make the tripartition of the Corinthian capital explicit by overlaying its form with analytical diagrams.[256]

We will now proceed to scan the shaft. The Doric shaft has a higher part, the necking; a middle part, consisting of twenty flutes meeting in sharp ridges or arrises; and no closure, or lower part, ending abruptly. The Ionic and Corinthian shafts are tripartite. Their middle part is always fluted. The flutes are more numerous—twenty-four—than in the Doric, and, in contrast to the Doric, they meet in narrow flat strips. The Ionic shaft is inserted between a lower short part—composed usually of three, minimal parts: an *astragal,* a convex roundel; a *taenia,* flat fillet; and the *apophyge,* a concave sweep—and a top part made out of an astragal band or an elaborate lotus and palmette border (framed further by astragal bands), as in the unique fifth-century

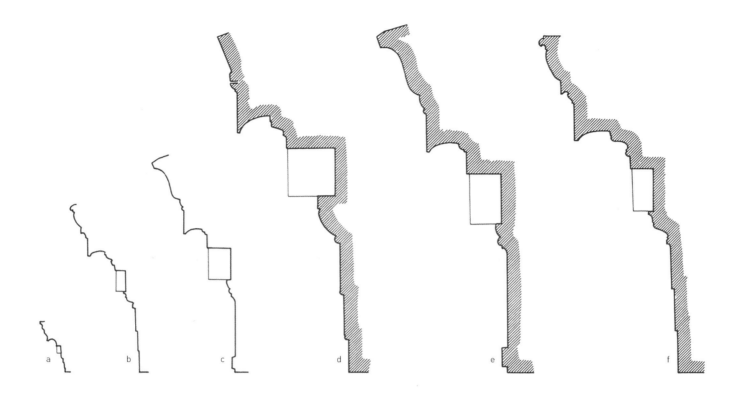

Entablatures, fifth and fourth centuries B.C.E.
From left to right:
a. Sarcophagus from Sidon.
b. Erechtheion at Athens, Caryatid Porch, 421–405 B.C.E.

c. Monument of the Nereids at Xanthos, 400 B.C.E.
d. Ionic Temple at Messa, Lesbos.
e. Monument of the Nereids at Xanthos, c. 400 B.C.E.
f. Erechtheion at Athens, Caryatid Porch, 421–405 B.C.E.

B.C.E. Ionic temple at Locri Epizephyrii in southern Italy or in the Erechtheion.

As mentioned earlier, the Greek Doric column has no base. The canonical base of the Ionic and Corinthian columns is again broken down into three parts. Scanning the base of the Erechtheion, we easily recognize its tripartite profile consisting of: 1) an upper *speira* or torus, a convex molding; 2) a middle part, the *trochilus* or scotia or cavetto, a deep concave molding; and 3) a lower part, once more a *speira*. The Ionic base of the Erechtheion was widely imitated. It is clearly tripartite. Its profile, as shaped by a succession of cymatia in contrast to each other, helps the observer perceive it as being articulated into constituent parts. The straight is followed by the curved, the concave by the convex, the protruding by the indented, and the flat by the inclined. The juxtaposition of these coupled shape properties is reminiscent of Roman Jakobson's "binary oppositions" in linguistics.[257] The effect was that the profile offered maximum discontinuities of contour that permitted better segmentation into parts and accurate identification of the column. Light falling on these folds made the profile more forthcoming.

The same procedures were applied to the columnar elements in the horizontal sense. Just as the Attic-Ionic base presented the most characteristic "vertical" profile case, using minimal configuration means by applying the organization of "binary oppositions" to maximize contour discontinuity, the "horizontal" profile of the Doric shaft did so with equal effect. The soft waves of the concave flutes meet in razor-sharp edges and follow each other forming the convex circular outline of the column shaft.

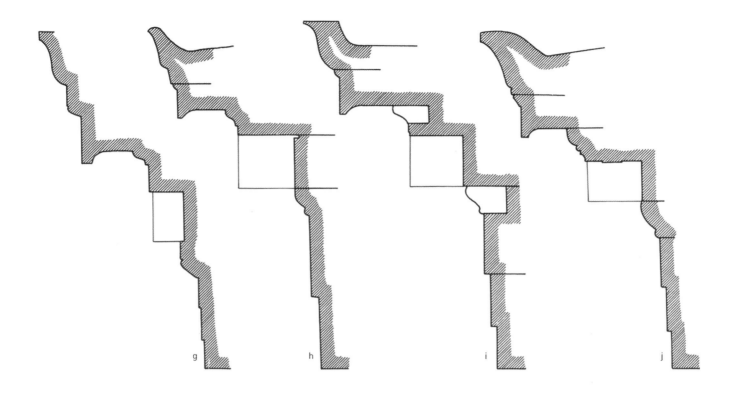

g. Sarcophagus from Sidon.
h. Zeus Temple at Labranda, mid-fourth century B.C.E.

i. Mausoleion at Halicarnassos, c. 353 B.C.E.
j. Temple of Athena at Priene, 334 B.C.E.
Schwandner, 1996.

Similar devices for contour shaping, and the same use of "binary oppositions" between three-dimensional configurations were employed with equal intelligence and thoroughness in sculpture—both in the modeling of the body and the modulations of the pleats of the fabric, as in the Erechtheion caryatids, as well as in the bas-reliefs of the Parthenon. Interestingly, when referring to the profile of contours, Aristotle used the concept of *rysmos*,[258] a form of the word *rythmos* implying flow and movement in the succession of these shapes in space.

The process of recursively partitioning columnar components, sectioning and imbedding parts within parts, is not an infinite regression. One finally arrives at a limit, components that cannot be divided further—the elements, *stoichea,* of architecture, beyond which no more spatial divisions are possible. This limit appears as a result of practical and cognitive constraints. One could not carve a piece of stone beyond a certain dimension without breaking it. But there are also shapes that cannot be geometrically decomposed further into even simpler shapes—the so-called "primitive shapes."[259] Greek architecture had a name for this "element" that was "formally indivisible into another form," as Aristotle defined it in his *Metaphysics*.[260] It was called the *kymation,* meaning "little wave"—although as a molding, its simple geometric shape also included *taeniae,* or long rectangular prisms. The Canonical cymatia were the Doric or hawksbeak, the Lesbian or cyma reversa, the Ionic ovolo or cyma, and the Egyptian or cavetto. However, although the forms discussed above, comprising the Ionic base, *speira* and *trochilus,* also fall under the definition of the indivisible *stoiea,* they were not called cymatia.

Temple of Hera, Paestum.
Photograph by Serge Moulinier.

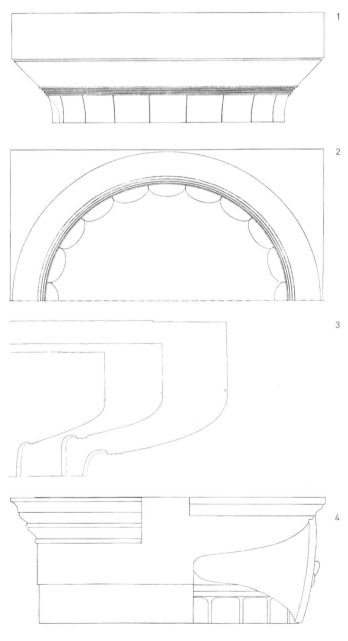

1, 2 - **Temple of Artemis Epidauros. Doric capitals.**
3 - **Temple of Artemis Epidauros. Doric capitals, side view.**
4 - **Temple of Athena Pronaia, Delphi. Ionic capital. Fourth century** B.C.E.
After Roux, 1961.

Temple of Hephaistos, Athens.

Temple of Hephaistos, Athens.

Like the elementary forms that constituted the Ionic base, cymatia were small in size, but extremely important in their role of making up the profile of the various components of the building, and thereby serving to distinguish and identify the kinds of architecture. In other words, they specified the *what* of the objects that occupied the parts of the world of the building. Biederman, a contemporary cognitive scientist and visionary expert called such simple primitive recognition components *geons*[261] (for geometrical *ions*), the idea in this case being the minimum number of elementary elements to classify any concrete object. Biederman concluded that three would suffice. The normative cymatia of the Classical canon came very close to the Biederman *geons*, which, together with the application of the tripartite

schema, might suggest why the Classical canon has been so engaging.

Like almost every aspect of Greek architecture, the form of the cymatia originated outside Greece. However the way in which they were combined, and modified in the process of combination appears to be very much a Greek product. The number of types of cymatia in Classical architecture was very small. The complexity and variety of the profiles used by the genera was generated through the combination of these simple ingredients. Seen from the perspective of the canon, the cymatia appear to have undergone modifications in interaction with each other. There is a much discussed, cryptic short fragment attributed to the *Canon*, the book written by Polyclitus on sculpture: "goodness arises through *to para micron*."[262] Perhaps *to para micron*

Erechtheion. Detail of Ionic base.

Erechtheion. Detail of Ionic base.

meant many numbers. However, there is also the possibility that it meant that the success of design depends on "the smallest detail"—the elementary *stoicheia*, or cymatia.

As stated above, the analysis of the "kinds of columns" was generalized for all other "objects" that enter a building and populate its parts. For a contemporary reader, this might sound arcane—but for someone who knew about "styles" just before World War II, the idea was obvious: columns, pilasters, walls, banisters, doors, windows, ceilings, door panels, pedestals, and even movable furniture, such as tables, chairs, and lamp stands that were placed together in a space have to be congruent, unless clashes between kinds were a deliberate part of the design. The great invention of the Classical canon was to put together the system of *taxis*, or partitioning

of space, with the system of *genera,* or the kinds located within it. What this schema supplied was, on the one hand, a device for identifying an object by parsing it into constituent parts—while, locating these parts in reference to each other. This was a contribution to the systematization of spatial thinking as a whole because it demonstrated within a particular domain of application, the building, what contemporary cognitive science calls the subsystems of "what" and "where" in spatial thinking, and the intelligent interaction between the two.[263]

Metric structure

The analysis of the parts that composed the vertical organization of a Classical Greek building may

Erechtheion. Detail of Ionic base.

Erechtheion. Detail of Ionic base.

appear to a contemporary reader detailed, complicated, and tedious. Certainly, they do not differ in this respect from the analysis of ancient Greek poetry. On the other hand, just as in the case of reading Homer, Sappho, and Pindar, while they can be enjoyed read as ordinary phrases, without the level of scansion they cannot be enjoyed as poetry.

We have seen how ancient Greek buildings—not only temples but also thesauri, stoae, and propylaia—can be understood as objects construed and constructed recursively through a hierarchy of nested parts-objects. The levels of the hierarchy were not uniform. The first level divided the building into parcels of space. The second level identified and articulated objects into kinds to populate these parcels. The third level, as we will

now see, places elements within the parts and relates them to one another. Vitruvius describes such a system, which he calls *symmetria*, as an interpretation of the Greek word for proportion. *Symmetria* is based on a common unit of measurement—the *embatis,* or modulus in Latin. According to Vitruvius, this can be achieved by choosing as a base the thickness of the column and deriving from it by multiplication or division all dimensions of the elements of the building. Number therefore is a key device. This is convenient for the whole of Vitruvius' approach to architecture, which departs from the doctrine of *mimesis.* Vitruvius does not mention the term and does not develop any general theory. Here the idea of imitation implied "extracting from the human body" proportions and transposing them to buildings,

Erechtheion, Caryatid detail.

Propylaia.

on the basis of the belief that number underlies the articulation of the body and that the human body is "constructed by Nature in a way that its members correspond to the configuration of the whole." Part of Vitruvius' argument is that the ancient Greeks had already applied this method because their units of measurement measures were "collected from the human body"—the finger, the palm, and the cubit. In addition, the body contains what the Greeks call "*teleon*," or "perfect numbers."[264] As examples, Vitruvius refers to the numbers six and ten, and repeats Plato's claim that things and numbers correspond. Vitruvius' ideas were to have an enormous impact on European architectural theory since the Renaissance. But they were also strongly opposed. On the other hand, they do not seem to be applicable in most cases to

ancient Greek buildings and to lead to any general conclusion about how ancient Greeks conceived their buildings. As the name suggests, *symmetria* identifies a condition of concordance between the all components of an object, whether natural or artificial. However, the system of proportions, as interpreted by Vitruvius reduced this concordance to numerical relations only. Not only this fail to cover other, perhaps even more fundamental, aspects of agreement between elements, the elements themselves and elements and the building as a whole, but also it set up numerical rules that were empirically inapplicable to Greek buildings, as Antoine Desgodets and Claude Perrault had already discovered about Roman architecture in the seventeenth century.[265] Furthermore, it is neither rigorous enough in terms of how exactly

Parthenon East frieze, slab VII, detail (Louvre).

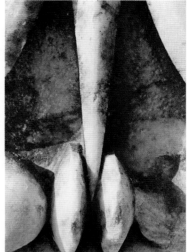

Dart and astragal, detail, Priene.

numbers relate to an architectural element, nor abstract enough to generalize about all the components of a building.

Thus there is a need to select features—distinctive features—that are both sufficiently abstract and specific for representing significant relations between the elements of a building, and between the elements and the building as a whole. Once more the columnar element and the colonnade are generic. As stated before, a series of columns form "subjective contours" and consequently object boundaries. Yet, on the basis of relations between each other they also form a "group" or a "spatial architectural pattern." Once more we are faced with an "object," a "pattern"—one of an intermediate scale, larger than the column itself, but smaller than the whole building or its

partitions. In other words, columnar patterns are contained inside the divisions of *taxis*. Sometimes the concept of "rhythm" is applied in the sense of what makes a number of columns distinguishable as a group. Vitruvius referred to rhythm, but indirectly via the concept of "*eurythmia*," which for him was proportion, blurring this with *symmetria,* which, of course, is not bilateral symmetry although it has been translated as such.

Forming larger patterns through grouping architectural components, such as columns, is a cognitive operation very similar to that of assembling a stream of cymatia and other elementary contours into larger entities as we have seen above. Interestingly, Aristotle applied the term *rysmos*[266] (a form of the word *rythmos*) to the profile of an object. This term applied in his age mainly to the

Temple of Hera Argiva, Paestum. South fluting of the south column *in antis* from the *opisthodomos*.
Photograph by Serge Moulinier.

metric and time patterns of dancing. To avoid confusion, it is perhaps better[267] to adopt a more abstract term such as "stressed" or "accentuated," and "non-stressed" or "non-accentuated,"[268] in relation to spatial elements. Within the framework of this categorization of architectural components, the column is a stressed component, the void between columns a non-stressed one; similarly, pilaster is juxtaposed with wall components, or wall component with an opening, a window or a door.

Metric patterns are objects made out of object-components. As such they should follow the norm of termination we discussed above. The convention of the Classical canon has been that the termination ought to be on a stressed component, as in an anapest or an iambic metric unit offering a sense of closure. In addition, in architecture there has been a tendency to amplify stress by either increasing the size of the stressed component, or in a complementary way, by decreasing the non-stressed intercolumnar distance—or both, as in the termination of Doric temple colonnades.

Metric patterns are seen as objects themselves, made out of object-components. As objects, they relate to each other as objects do. They form themselves into patterns, or are patterns of patterns. They stand behind, over, next to, or are embedded within other patterns. The rule applied when metric patterns relate to other metric patterns is to align stressed components with those stressed vertically and horizontally. This can be seen clearly in the organization of the building aligning columns with superposed triglyphs, columns, consoles, ornamental gutters, sculptures, and antefixes. This created a major and intractable problem and one that we will come across later—the scandal of the Doric termination.

Parthenon capital fragment.
Photograph by Goette.

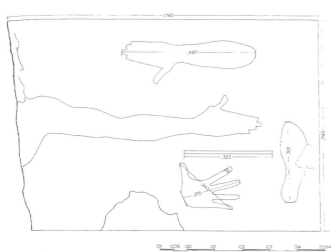

Metrological relief, Salamis.
Drawing by Ifigenia Dekoulakou-Sideris (1990).

Figures

Figures in Classical architecture are relations that are unique and that cannot be parsed, being too complex to be reducible to elements or simpler patterns, and fitted into a system. Some figures are like templates, and they can usually be approached through lists and definitions: some simple "if-then" rules. Figures have been identified and applied in poetry, rhetoric, and music. Their application in ancient Greek architecture is rather modest in comparison to that of Roman times. Vitruvius remained silent about their use in architecture. However, another Roman author, Cicero,[269] may help us categorize them in a very general way, borrowing from his discussion on figures in rhetoric. He divided figures into two

Roman and Greek base profiles.
1. Paestum.
2. Saturnia.
3. Cosa, Basilica.
4. Tivoli, rectangular temple.
5. Rome, Temple of Veiovis.
6. Rome, Forum Boarium, round temple.
7. Rome, Palatine, fragment.
8. Rome, Forum Boarium, rectangular temple.
9. Rome, Argentina, temple.

10. Rome, Forum Holitorium, temple.
11. Rome, temple in Via delle Botteghe Oscure.
12. Delos.
13. Athens, Older Parthenon.
14. Athens, Temple of Athena Nike.

15. Agora A 2891 and 2892.
16. Propylaia.
17. Erechtheion, north porch.
After Shoe, 1969.

Ionic capital, detail Attalos Stoa.

kinds—the overt and the subtle. Overt figures are *parallelism, alignment,* and *contrast.* As we have already seen, Hermogenes was particularly successful in the application of alignments. From the Archaic period, alignment was a basic device to bring about spatial coherence. The use of a drawn grid has been suggested,[270] and this is very probable since such a device was used from earlier times in Egypt. Many efforts to identify such patterns in ancient Greek buildings have been made, one of the best known being A. Thiersch's analysis[271] of the ground plan of the Erechtheion, applying both parallelism and contrast. There is little evidence, however, that such an application was related to how ancient Greeks looked at buildings.

Some subtle figures are: 1) *aposiopesis*[272] or ellipsis, which means silencing or leaving out a part, a component, element, or pattern; 2) *abruption,* interrupting a part, a component, element, or pattern; 3) *epistrophy,* returning to a part that appeared previously. Even the most canonical building, the Parthenon, contained such exceptions and they overpopulated the Erechtheion. As opposed to the overt figures that operated by agreement with the overall system of the canon, subtle figures appear to work against it. Yet, they have the opposite effect. By seemingly contradicting the order of the canon through a local anomaly, they reinforce it by demonstrating its global application. Some of these silences, interruptions, and returns were motivated by the imperative of experimentation and finding something new. Many were the result of conflicting constraints, as in the case of the Propylaia. The effect, at least for us today, is one of liveliness— the sparkle of the complex activities, beliefs, and desires by a complex society such as that of Athens.

Temple of Aphaia, Aigina. Fragments from Terracotta Acroteria
from the west elevation and from the east pediment.
After Furtwängler, 1906.

One must confess that the Propylaia form not only a more pragmatic, but also a more exciting building than the restoration proposed by Dinsmoor.[273]

Subtle figures became increasingly applied in Classical architecture during the late Renaissance Mannerist period and played a key role in the work of Palladio.[274] Their use increasingly signaled the rise of a counter movement in architecture—an anti-Classical approach that we will discuss in the next section.

Synthesis, a new system

As we have already seen, the systematization of ancient Greek architecture—the canon and its tripartition rule—was not enforced from the top down. The adventures of the Ionic base, documented superbly in the work of L. T. Shoe,[275] encapsulate the explorations and experiments that almost all components of ancient Greek buildings went through before arriving at a canonical—one should say "institutionalized"—form. Indicative of this is the fact that one of the basic canonical components—the "entablature" discussed above—had no Greek name although, as the buildings suggest, it was clearly treated as an "object." It is far removed from the facts, therefore, to talk about the intention behind each decision of architects in ancient Greece to put together a canon. It is equally inappropriate to judge their works as conforming or not to such a canon, which was only formed retrospectively.

For this reason, if one tries to apply the canon type of the columnar bases analyzed above over the tokens of whole production of bases in Greek antiquity, one will be disappointed. Most ancient

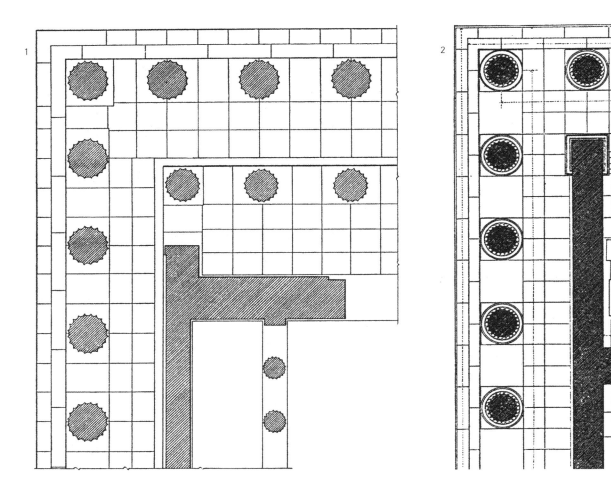

1

2

The evolution toward a greater coordination of elements. Parthenon, Acropolis, Athens. Plan of paving on front and side.
After Lawrence, 1983.

Temple of Athena Polias, Priene.
After T. Wiegand and H. Schrader, 1904.

Greek Ionic bases, especially in Asia Minor, were neither tripartite nor as elementary as the Attic variety. The scotia element ranged from the elaborate arrangement of the sixth-century B.C.E. Temple of Hera in Samos to the relatively simple base of the Temple of Athena Polias in Priene, with two scotiae inserted between three layers of double astragals. The Erechtheion Attic-Ionic base was canonized after a long series of a very elaborate explorations borrowing Oriental Levantine elements, combining them, and modifying them by changing dimensions, adding, and subtracting torie, scotiae, and plinths, and elaborating them further by introducing horizontal flutings. Such was the interchangeability of the components that in their restoration efforts major archaeologists confused capital and base elements, as in the case of Koldewey's restoration of the Neandria capital.[276]

Architects explored design possibilities during the Archaic period, and even later during Classical times, without maps and without a preconceived target. The experiments took place at regional centers distributed around the Mediterranean. We can see them in Aeolia, Ionia, Sparta, and especially in southern Italy where there was a constant interchangeability of Doric and Ionic spatial arrangements, cymatia, and cymatia combinations, without any clear idea that they were developing a "pure style." But the search was not random. There was a tendency to move by fission and fusion of forms—a sense of ascending and recognition of arriving at a peak, such as the Attic-Ionic base.

The process resembled evolution, as explained in François Jacob's classic paper *Evolution and Tinkering.*[277] Ancient Greek architects looked for

Library of Ephesus.
Photograph: AKG-images.

immediately open paths in a space of conflicting constraints and provisional possibilities within a rugged and multi-peaked landscape.[278] The process was not linear but parallel. Many trials occurred in different regions leading to various local outcomes. Some of these products disappeared without being influential—including the more provincial experiment to fuse the Doric with the Ionic capital at Amyclai; the attempt at the Propylon of Samothrace (285–246 B.C.E.) to bring together eastern Ionic and western Corinthian kinds by introducing two porches at both ends of the building with different kinds of columns for each; and, finally, the prestigious experiment of combining buildings and columnar elements in the Erechtheion in the Acropolis that was finally to inspire new architecture only in the twentieth century. Others were influential but

in a subtle way, leaving behind no overt traces—the Aeolic column is a case in point, to be rediscovered only centuries later by archaeologists.

The architectural system and the associated design method emerged gradually and selectively from the bottom up. However, there were also conceptual breakthroughs punctuated by top down interventions: the writing, for example, of an influential book, Polyclitus' *Canon,* or the invention of a new kind of column, in the Apollo temple of Bassai, and a few years before the inclusion of the Doric and Ionic in the Parthenon and in the most experimental and innovative secular work, the Propylaia. Moreover, at about the same time another equivalent breakthrough occurred in Aeschylus' introduction of the second actor and in Sophocles' third advancing the conceptual "dialectic" power of the tragedy.

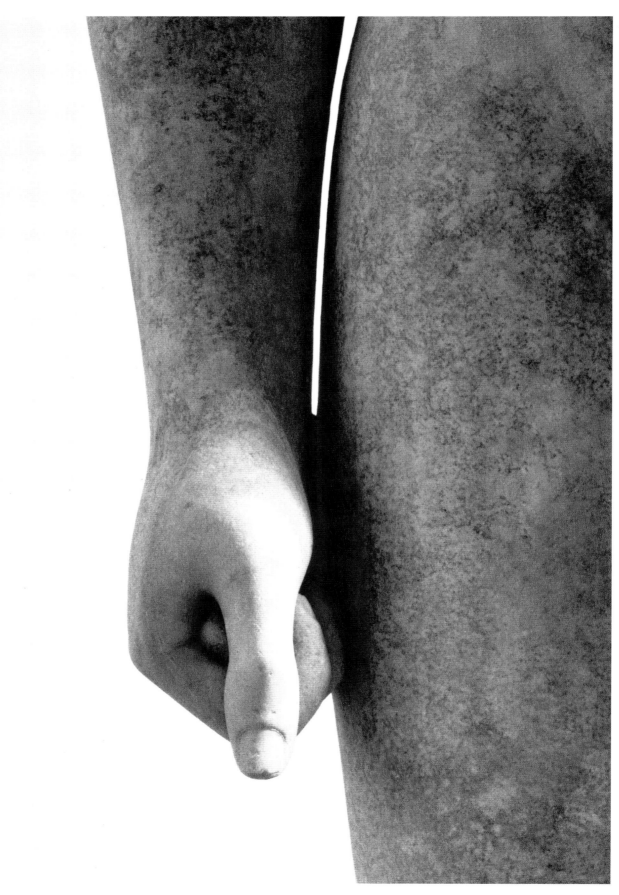

Kouros, Vathy.
Photograph by Gehnen.

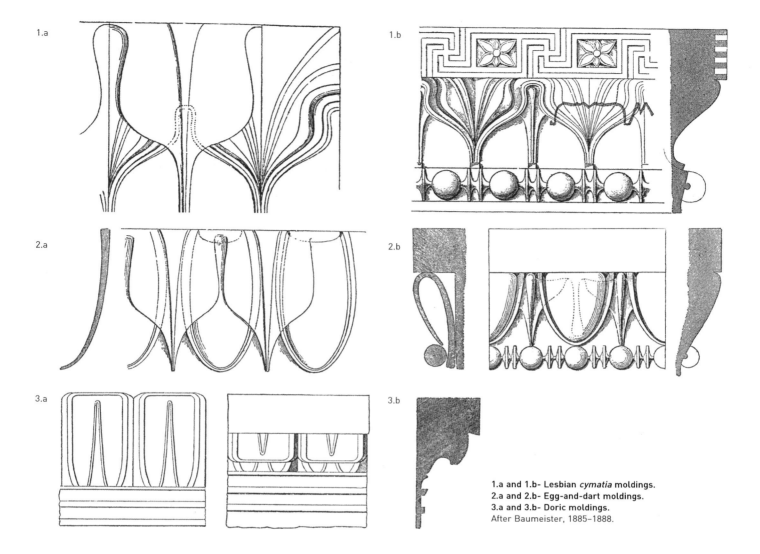

1.a and 1.b- Lesbian *cymatia* moldings.
2.a and 2.b- Egg-and-dart moldings.
3.a and 3.b- Doric moldings.
After Baumeister, 1885–1888.

The significance of bringing together the Doric, Ionic, and Corinthian kinds under the same roof was not just "syncretist." It was the invention of a new conceptual framework of architecture. Within this new framework, the initial idea of *taxis* and its specific tripartite schema was developed further into a spatial system within which each part was associated with a specific architectural kind: the outside and the lower with the Doric, and the inside and higher with the Ionic, Corinthian being the last in this ranking of penetrating and rising in space. The schema was used in several buildings and most explicitly in the Stoa of Attalos in Athens: as we have seen, the more "Egyptian-Orientalist" palm capital was the resurrected ancestor that replaced the Corinthian column here. Yet it was the Romans who made extensive use of the system,

exploiting its potential—the most striking example being the amphitheater of the Colosseum. Here we see the results of this potential having achieved a structure within which one can easily identify specific places, despite its large scale and repetitive fabric. The European Renaissance further developed the system by elaborating on both the idea of *taxis*-zone and kind in large building complexes, as well as in the smallest and most intimate space of a room.

Thus, one can argue that it was not only the existence of the different kinds of architectural components—the Doric, Ionic, and Corinthian—and the need to reconcile them into a syncretist home, (perhaps for political reasons forging local regional idioms into an "international Panhellenic" cosmic cosmopolitan Universalism?) that advanced the

Doric *cymatia.*
After Shoe, 1952.

creation of this synthesis. It was also, and perhaps more significantly, the need for developing a more specialized and differentiated conceptual spatial framework for functional, institutional, social, political, and cultural requirements, that led architects to *recruit* existing kinds of architecture and reinterpret them into a new hierarchical topological system. Classical architecture achieved a method of bringing together the "*what* and *where*" of the world of the building with the potential of extending it to conceive other possible worlds.

Optical corrections

One of the enigmas of the evolution of ancient Greek architecture is why there should have been a strange turn towards irregularity, at the very moment we see the systematization of architectural thinking coming to a peak and the convergence of regional experiments forming a universal canon of Classical architecture with the projects that followed the end of the Persian invasion. Was it a reaction against the dangers of standardization and mechanization of architectural production at the time of invention of so many rules, or was it a development of a countermovement?

Neither *taxis* nor the taxonomy of the *genera* or the metric relations can explain this phenomenon. These irregularities were manifested in Poseidonia or Paestum, and first noticed by Claude-Mathieu Delagardette. But it was Joseph Hoffer who first described them as results of a conscious effort to "avoid the rectilinear," "infuse the lifeless forms of art with a breath of living Nature," and fill us "with

wonder and astonishment at the *refinement* of feeling they express." Furthermore, in the epigrammatic words of Adolf Michaelis, a Strasbourg professor of classical archaeology and author of a basic work on the Parthenon, they "produce an effect of life" (*Lebendigkeit*).[279]

Another view presented these irregularities not as "refinements," but as anomalies caused by carelessness in the execution, or by the structure sagging over time due to sinking foundations and settling ground. There has been also a claim that the upward curvature of the stylobate was intended merely to ease the flow of the water away from the floor of the building. However, this reason fails to account for the presence of the bending, even if the soil was composed of rock, as Dinsmoor[280] remarks, referring to the Parthenon; nor does it explain the rest of the deviations, such as the tilting of the columns or, as we have seen in several cases, the irregularity of their inter-columnar space. In addition, as discussed above, recent discoveries by archaeologists have shown that the entasis of the columns in the Temple of Apollo at Didyma was constructed geometrically, and thus intentionally.[281] Yet there is no corresponding ancient Greek document explaining what the intention was.

There is also Vitruvius. He did discuss such departures from regularity as being due to optical reasons, to correct visual phenomena known today as visual illusions. Here, his notion of *logos opticos* is clear. There is a reason and reasoning involved for these incongruities to occur. Buildings are made to be seen—at least if the spectator focuses on *Venustatis* aspects in a project. However, seeing

Stoa, Priene. Corner column.

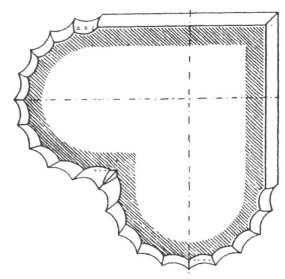

South stoa of the north market at Miletos,
section of heart-shaped corner columnar element. 150 B.C.E.
After Gerkan, 1922.

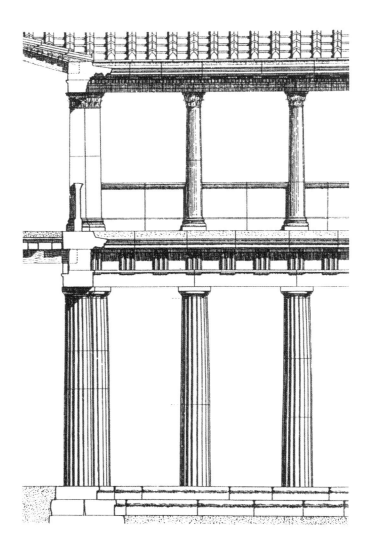

Stoa, north market at Miletos, section. 150 B.C.E.
After Gerkan.

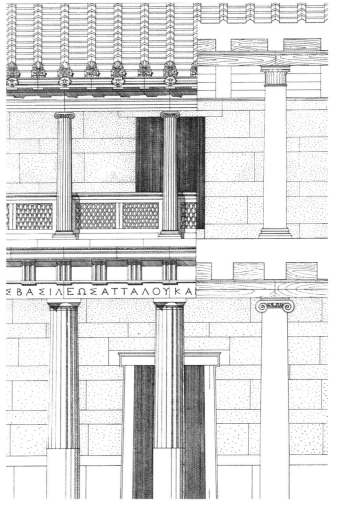

ΣΒΑΣΙΛΕΩΣΑΤΤΑΛΟΥΚΑ

Stoa of Attalos, Athens, elevation. 159–138 B.C.E.
Front view.
After Travlos, 1980.

happens through the eyes and the eyes cheat, *occulus fallit,* and this we have to compensate by calculation, *ratiocinatione.* Vitruvius[282] explained many of these intended falsities to overcome and restore true regularity and harmony. Thus he recommended for the *araeostyle* temples an increased diameter to overcome the effect of the air passing through the enlarged interval between columns because the "air consumes and diminishes the perceived diameter." He also asked for a swelling in the middle of the columns, which he referred to by the Greek word *entasis.* Furthermore, he cited a drawing at the end of his book, which unfortunately did not survive. Other suggested compensatory measures include the inclinations of cornices to adjust the "length of the line of vision," *longior visus linea,* between designed detail and observer. Interestingly, Vitruvius failed to mention that in Ionic temples such corrections were less prominent than in their Doric counterparts. Moreover, when recommending correction rules for Doric temples, he asked the designer to consider and apply by analogy what he had already said about Ionic ones.

Vitruvius derived his ideas mainly from Lucretius, who was writing half a century earlier, and whose *De Rerum Naturae* presented a theory of vision and perception, arguing that "the nature of the phenomena cannot be comprehended by the eyes," which are passive receptors and subject to deception. For understanding, one needs the power of reasoning. And reasoning according to Vitruvius meant optical corrections.

How much of Vitruvius' theory of optical corrections was known to the Greeks or accepted by Greek architects in their work? There is a fragment attached to the so-called "Damianus" manuscript, occasionally attributed to the Hellenistic mathematician, engineer, *mechanikos,* and inventor of machines and specialists on the art of making automata, *automata-poetikis,* Philon of Byzantion, and a very similar passage by a contemporary and of the same background, Heron of Alexandria[283]— both of the late second century B.C.E. Both recommended to designers "compensations" to overcome optical deceptions. The Damianus passage argues that "since things do not appear as they are in reality," designers should try to discover means to provide the correct size and shape in appearance. Philon, also a mathematician and engineer and probably older than Heron,[284] made a fascinating historical claim that architecture evolved through a long series of "trial and error" of designing "adding and subtracting" to make buildings appear regular by compensating for optical errors. This might be taken as implying an intuitive process of artistic improvisation. However, considering the complexity of the structure of the temples and coordination of the construction work, as well as the context of the writings of Heron and Philon, who were mathematicians-engineers, it is clear that this process was rigorous. It required the mathematics of three-dimensional geometry, together with some scientific assumptions about nature and vision. Indeed, Euclid's *Optics* dealt with very similar points. In this sense, the problem of errors and corrections appears simply technical.

Democritus,[285] whose ideas we have already discussed above, and who asserted "we know nothing

Temple of Hera Argiva, Paestum.
Photograph by Serge Moulinier.

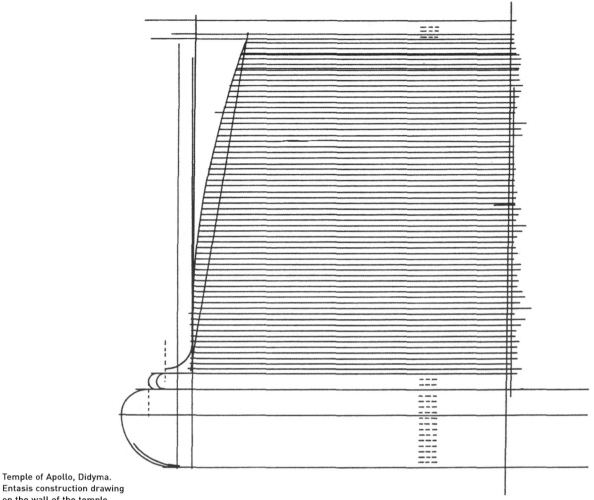

**Temple of Apollo, Didyma.
Entasis construction drawing
on the wall of the temple.
After Haselberger, 1985.**

accurately in reality," had already prepared the philosophical underpinnings. Our visual knowledge, the image, *emphasis*, depends on "the condition of our body," as well as "emanation," *aporroai*, of "those things that flow upon the body and invade it." This implied not so much the impossibility of knowledge as the importance to know the exact limitations of the instruments through which we acquire knowledge. Also implicit is the notion that the "absolute"[286] representation of the world, or "allocentric" map, had to be complemented by a representation that was explicitly dependent on the viewer's position. This suggested that a canon should be supplemented by an "egocentric" map representing the arrangement of columns, doors, and statues and deciding their place and configuration by framing them in reference to a viewer-centered frame.

Unfinished and *assyndeton*

Close to the problem of exceptions to the norm of *teliotes*, as universal regularity and order in a work, to the idea of "refinements" and optical corrections, is the problem of the unfinished in ancient Greek buildings. The *hemiteles*,[287] as the Greeks referred to it, was not a major concern. However, the *non-finito*, as Vasari called it, discussing the work of Michelangelo, became increasingly a major point of dispute in aesthetics and retrospectively a subject of discussion in relation to ancient Greek architecture. As we mentioned above, the norm of perfection, *teleon*, dominated Greek thinking—whether it was aimed at the constitution of the world, *kosmos*, or the composition of the work, *ergon. Apergasia Telea,* perfection in a work was a merit and received praise. Vitruvius was after perfection in

Parthenon, Athens. Stylobate along north side.
Photograph by Serge Moulinier.

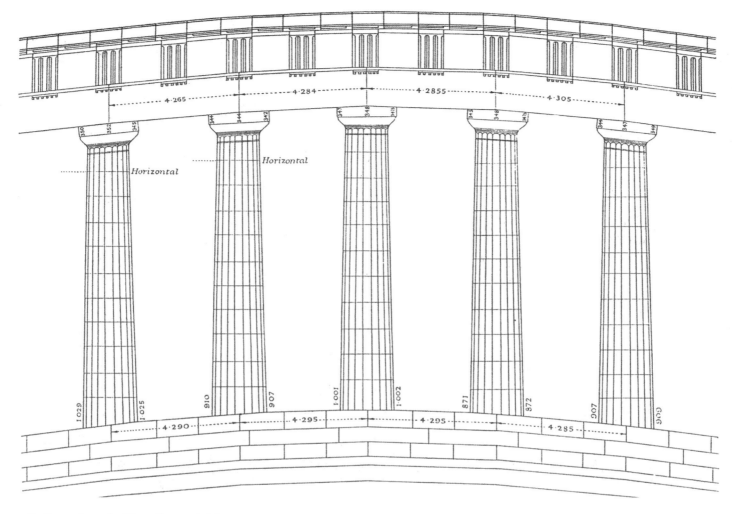

Parthenon, Acropolis, Athens. Exaggerated diagram
of distortions of north colonnade.
After Lawrence, 1957.

his search for certain proportions. *Telea* should be
the action-plot contained in a tragedy according to
Aristotle's *Poetics,*[288] and by implication the tragedy
itself should have this quality of *teleon.* Perfection in
this sense was something very pragmatic and tangible: the presence of a closure, *peras,* in the work
and the application of a device, such as the con-
cluding part, *epilogos,* to achieve this. From the perspective of production of a work, the work was
perfect when there was nothing more to add. The
concept of *hemiteles*[289] as applied by Vasari, by
Roman writers about painting, and by recent writers on ancient Greek architecture referred to an
unfinished act of design—thus something unfinished physically in the work that can be identified
by roughness of texture and missing parts. The
Heraion of Olympia, the Selinunt Temples G and
F, the Naxos [door] temple of Apollo, and perhaps

the best-known example, the Athens Propylaia
contain physically unfinished details needed for
erecting and placing the various pieces of stone
such as the *ancone,* handling bosses. The reasons for
their incompletion are in most cases known.
Circumstances, such as war, interrupted construction and subsequent conditions did not permit the
completion of the project. However, one may speculate that they were left as they were—unfinished—
because they were meaningful or pleasant to look
at. There are Pliny's[290] passages praising unfinished paintings by a list of ancient Greek painters,
including the "famous Apellis," remaining in a
sketch form, *lineamenta,*[291] "for in these the sketch-
lines remain visible the original thoughts of the
artists." Furthermore, in an unprecedented way
reminiscent of Ruskin's beliefs about touch, truth,
and authenticity, he asserts that in these rough

Parthenon, west pediment. Back view of figures.
Photograph by Hellner.

lines one finds the "artist's hand." To what degree such concerns with memory and authenticity played a role in leaving a building in a state of *ateles* in ancient Greece is hard to say. As contemporary viewers of these unresolved pieces in works of antiquity, we are moved by coming into contact with the human act of making of a work, sharing a sense of community. Yet, in addition, we have a deeper pleasure: from being passive spectators, we are given the active task of completing the unfinished process and in doing so become participants in the effort to grasp the system of spatial intelligence, construe and construct it in the poetics of the Classical canon. Thus, as emphasized before, the application of the canon was never seen as a pedantic or mechanical exercise.

This may be supported by the suggestion made by Aristotle in his *Rhetoric* that an epilogue in a speech should be made to lack consistency—not in the sense of being incoherent, but in being "disconnected," *assyndetos*,[292] lacking explicit links or with connections not yet placed, thus "unfinished." After going to great pains to analyze a complete and coherent system, this is not the only moment that Aristotle turns around to demonstrate the existence of aspects of the world that could not fit into it, and to use the system proposed to suggest the necessity for a complementary one for thinking beyond the system's confines. Thus, next to his *Topics*, he produced his *Rhetoric* and *Poetics,* to his *apodeixis*, his *enthymeme*.[293] To this belongs his concept of "strange," *xenikon*,[294] in the *Poetics* that he even extends to the level of *barbarismos*, which—within the framework of the rigorous system of the *Poetics*—provides a mechanism for avoiding being "commonplace," *tapeinon*, which he considers highly undesirable.

In addition, in keeping with the theory of poetics, ancient Greek tragedy is a source of pleasure—"tragic pleasure," *tragodias edone*—not in static *taxis*, but in the construction, *systasis,* of the work. This offers not only a smooth succession of ordered objects, but also a problem and a solution, *ploke* and *lysis*: the higher the complexity, *peplegmenos,* of the process, the greater the "attraction and leading of the soul," the *psychagogeia*.[295] Thus *taxis* is interrelated to the "reversal of expectations," *peripetia,* and "recognition," *anagnorisis*,[296] as equally important dynamic ordering devices.

It is in this context that one should look at the subtle figures referred to previously—such as *aposiopesis, abruption,* and *epistrophy*—as indispensable ingredients of the Classical canon, together with *taxis*, kinds, and metric patterns. And it is probably for this reason that ancient Greek architects decided to incorporate into the Classical canon the scandal of the Doric. Rigorous, but reductionist and intolerant, and with his typical urge to solve at all costs the problems of ambiguity and inconsistency that would confuse those more pragmatic contractors and clients, Vitruvius did not hesitate to recommend the suppression of the Doric. Joining the opinion of other Greek architects, who might have been motivated not only by theoretical concerns, but also by "regionalist" interests and personal motivations,[297] he called it "confused and inconvenient," in order to avoid the continuation of the anomaly.

On the other hand it can be argued that by developing this system ancient Greek architecture, like Euclidean geometry, so obsessed with closure and perfection, embodied at the same time *ploke* and *lysis*[298]—a never ending chain of questions and answers, a meta-system sowing the seeds and showing the way, for developing alternative "anti-Classical" anti-systems. This however intensified the presence of the riddle that haunted Socrates: How one can lead a "good life."

Temple of Artemis, Segesta. Unfinished *krepidoma.*
Photograph by Serge Moulinier.

Propylaia, Acropolis.
Photograph by Walter Hege.

View of Parthenon from the Theater of Herodes Atticus, Athens.
Photograph by Frédéric Boissonas.

CATHARSIS, CRITIQUE, CREATION

"Men fail to notice what they do after they wake up, just as they are not aware what they do when asleep."
Heraclitus of Ephesus

"And the creation of... the worlds... is that into which destruction, too happens... for they pay penalty and retribution [diken]... for their injustice according to the assessment of time [chronou taxin]."
Simplicius, *Physics* 24, 17

"Mind is infinite and self ruled."
Anaxagoras, fragment 12

Was the development of Classical Greek architecture related to the evolution of a way of life and, more specifically, to a particular social and political framework? The answer obviously has an effect on the question put forth at the beginning of this book: Why Classical Greek architecture today?

Today, after years of accumulating evidence supporting each side, the right response to the first question is that ancient Greek buildings worked on two distinct levels—just as in reading Plato's dialogue *Euthyphro* involving Socrates referred to above, there are two distinct lines of argumentation happily cohabiting in the text. The first, involving values and action, demonstrates Socrates' brutal disregard for human rights, and is embarrassing for a contemporary reader, while the second concerning Socrates' brilliant methodology of thinking is both fascinating and admirable for the same reader. As distinct from *Euthyphro,* however, there is a point where the two lines intersect: the social, political, and spatial design thinking not only coex-

isting in the same structure, but also collaborating.

Clearly, the emergence and development of Classical architecture coincided with that of the institutions of *polis* and democracy. Yet, there is no correlation between architectural spatial organization and the political regimes that commissioned or used these buildings. There is neither overt nor buried symbolism of *polis* or democracy in the plans or details of ancient Greek temples or stoae that have to do with political or social structure or values. Conceivably, there are such connections with the sculpture embedded in these buildings—but this is altogether a different story.

Polis and democratic values were expressed, without doubt, in the geometrical layout of new colonial Greek towns by the end of the sixth century B.C.E., where the regularity of the rectangular grid facilitated the equal distribution of lots to the citizens reflecting universal, distributed, and approximately equal political rights. The political concept of equality under the law, *isonomia,* as expressed in the writings of Hippodamos of Miletos, had its equivalent in the *isomoiria* of the allocation of landshares and *isodomia*—applied here to the sameness of buildings, rather than to the individual stonepieces. However, one has to keep in mind that the grid-based spatial arrangement was originally conceived and applied practically by 2000 B.C.E. in Mesopotamia and Egypt—the grid being the Egyptian hieroglyph to represent "district" (*hesp*)[299]—where it had very little to do with the institutions of the Greek *polis* or democracy. To a modest degree, ancient Greek sanctuaries used some kind of grid coordination system for building complexes,[300] which was probably derived by projecting the lines of the exterior walls of one building to another.[301] To some degree, this urban grid reflected the grid applied in the spatial arrangement of temples[302] and other important public buildings that was relatively elastic during the Archaic and early Classical periods and increasingly consistent since the fourth century B.C.E. when the irregular column spacing disappeared.

The emergence and growing dominance of the square grid in these buildings chronologically correlated with the foundation of the city-state. Yet its use as an ordering device for spatial divisions and dimensioning of building elements was not related to *isonomia*, or to any similar concepts expressing the values of equity or equality, *isotis,* linked with the institutions of the *polis* or democracy.

From another point of view, however, but still in the urban scale, the absence of a "royal," absolutist power in the institution of the Greek *polis*— aristocratic, tyrannical, or democratic—was reflected in the absence of a central, unique place, a "carved in" *megaron,* in the Oriental or Mycenaean sense. From the eighth century B.C.E. onwards, ancient Greek settlements were characteristically spatially "anarchic" with the occasional freestanding *megara* distributed strategically but not centrally. This absence of organization of space between buildings was presented in the past as proof of the ancient Greek "mentality," according to which the concept of "void" was another name for "nothing," but lacking a concept that represented space between objects. This of course is very wrong because pre-Socratic philosophers, as well as Aristotle, had developed concepts to represent relations between and within object entities. As we discussed in the previous chapter, it appears that artifacts, sculpture or buildings, were designed with an "object-centered" frame of reference in mind, rather than a "visual egocentric" one—at least up to the fourth century B.C.E. In this case, it may be claimed that the reason for giving priority to this frame was "social" or "political" in the sense of lack of interest to develop any centrally coordinated system given the absence of central power. By the third century B.C.E., an "allocentric" coordinating framework—the rectangular grid—appeared to play an increasingly dominant spatial organizational role, and this correlates with the ascendancy of the importance of the activities of the agora. But this does not relate to any particular political system.

The development of Classical architecture and the drive to create a unique, coherent system of forms—a canon—has to do with the construction of a Hellenic identity and the process of what Gregory Nagy called Panhellenism.[303] As with other cultural expressions, architecture was part of a movement that aimed to reinforce claims of ethnic purity and superiority intended to advance Athenian and subsequently Greek hegemony and expansion. The founding of a new Greek settlement was accompanied by the foundation of a temple building associated with foundation cult and foundation myth-and-hero-making poetry. Typical claims of ethnic purity and superiority are to be found in the strange Platonic dialogue *Menexenus*. Here Socrates, taking a feminist position alleging that Aspasia was the real author of Perikles' renowned oration in Thucydides, narrates from memory another of her funeral speeches in which she refers to Athens as a laudable "woman mother . . . helping Greeks against Greeks in the cause of freedom." According to Aspasia, who interestingly came to Athens from Miletos and was not Athenian, the Athenians were superior because they were pure-blooded, *amigeis,* "unadulterated by barbarian stock," like "Pelops, or Cadmus, or Aegyptus or Danaus," who were only by "name Greek."

Perikles depicted the political system of Athens as being equally free of outside influences, not owing to "laws of neighbors," ignoring the Mesopotamian and Egyptian borrowings in the long-term drawing up of the Athenian constitution. In a similar manner, the Athenians saw the Classical architecture of Athens as unique, its characteristic quality of simplicity being intentional. In the Platonic dialogue *Critias,* the Temple of Poseidon was referred to as belonging to the "barbaric kind" because of the extensive use of gold, silver, and ivory in the interior, echoing Perikles' declaration in the same oration that Athenians "cultivate refinement without excess."

These efforts to forge a national identity, however, were carried out within a characteristically open framework of exchange of goods, reciprocal flow of information, and a remarkably unrestrained circulation of people. Once more, Perikles stressed in his oration the operation of this dynamic openness, set up through institutional structures, supported by the explosion of media encoding and processing information, and sustained by advancements in the technology of transportation, as it was applied in Athens. On the other hand, Athens was not unique in this. As we have already seen, both Asian and Italian settlements, as well as many mainland Greek cities, openly imported and assimilated outside forms—as attested by the distribution of plan arrangements, details, and technology of the buildings. Without this openness to knowledge, to cosmopolitan technicians—who provided not only "impulses" and "inspiration," but also the very "building blocks" for design innovation—and without a network infrastructure serving their circulation, it would not have been possible to create the new poetics of ancient Greek architecture and the Classical canon.

The "agonistic" framework that dominated Greek culture further assisted the objectives of forming distinct identity and maintaining creativity. It covered a large range of performances—athletic and military, as well as artistic. The very concept of the canon was derived from the institution of contest. Etymologically "canon" (or *kanon)* was an imported concept derived from the Akkadian or Hebrew and meant "rod" or "stick" and by extension "measuring rod."[304] Canon in Greek appears in reference to a tool, the ruler, used in building construction to keep forms straight and to measure distances. In Polyclitus' book of the same name, referred to previously, it probably meant measuring unit, thus rod, and was used to generate a modular system to coordinate the dimensions of the human body in a sculpture. Vitruvius described a similar system for specifying the sizes of all elements of temples. However, "canon" was also used during the Hellenistic period in the sense of "canonical," meaning a standard of the highest quality, a first class group of objects thus "classical"—to be used as a model to derive rules for further practice. This norm of excellence was derived after a contest, deliberation, and finally judgment, *crisis [krisis]*. It was carried out by a group of judges, *kritai*, belonging to the Museum of Alexandria. On the other hand, as Nagy suggests,[305] the institution of "*agon* and *crisis*" that followed from collective judgment was not originally Alexandrian. Its roots go back as far as the pre-Classical period, involving contests of poetry and music, *rhapsodoi*. As such, the beginnings of the idea of the canon as a set of rules to organize practice derived from a chosen prototype by a group who argue and vote is not despotic but democratic.

The link of Classical architecture to the rule of law is even deeper. We have already discussed the concepts of *taxis* and *kosmesis* as rule-constrained, *nomimon*, disposition, applied to the domain, *kosmos*, of space referring to a rule-constrained arrangement of parts of space. We have also mentioned the application of the same concepts to time, referring to the rule-constrained arrangement of segments of time, a concept applied in ancient Greek poetry, music, and rhetoric. As space units are occupied according to some rule, *kosmounde*, by nested physical objects characterized by size—for example in the "good arrangement of a building"—so segments of time are occupied according to some rule by actions and events having duration as in the "good arrangement of a song." What is common to both domains is that a "good world," *eukosmos*, results from the presence of *nomos*. *Nomos* has been linked with *taxis* and *kosmesis* from the Archaic period onwards. In addition to time and space, it was applied to several more concrete and complex domains including the human body, as well as society itself in the "constitution of a *polis*."

Since archaic times, *taxis*, *kosmesis*, and *nomos* have thus been linked with the domains of the body, the soul, and society. Whatever the content of the argument, this is clearly demonstrated in the analogical relations underlying Plato's dialogue *Gorgias*,[306] where "*taxeos kai tou kosmou*" is explicitly linked to the house, *oikia*, to the temperance of the soul, *sofrosyne*, and to justice, *dikeosine*.

Despite such speculative parallels between psychological and social organizational norms and spatial order, it is improbable that ancient Classical buildings, with their intricate spatial divisions, articulations, and arrangements, were used as a kind of "paradigm" to produce moral and political ideas through the mechanism of spatial inferences. However, the *eunomon kekosmemenon* building could be seen—to cite a phrase of Aristotle when talking about a musical instrument—"for purification, *katharsis*, rather than instruction, *mathesin*." The mental "therapy" achieved through purification of thinking is not carried out by adding new knowledge, but by creating a new consciousness of what we already know.

To explain this claim by Aristotle, we have to go back to Heraclitus' complaint that, despite lessons, "men fail to notice what they do after they wake up, just as they are not aware what they do when asleep." Indeed, one can reread Heraclitus and Aristotle, taking into account some results of current research in cognitive science on the problem of "bias"—as present today as it was during antiquity. As a result of bias, people fail to arrive at the correct judgment about most important issues: not so much because they lack information, but because of what has been called "reasoning illusions." As if they are "still asleep," people's thinking is circumscribed by and anchored in received opinions, which they refuse to challenge. As Heraclitus suggested, they fail to interact with the reality that surrounds them, to reflect on their beliefs and to scrutinize their presuppositions. As a result, their lives are uncreative, but also amoral—if not immoral.

Furthermore, as contemporary studies have demonstrated, the fact of supplying more information does not help to free people from bias. Different means are required for "de-biasing." According to the *Poetics,* ancient Greek tragedy— through *logou katharsis*—played such a role. By adopting, as the *Poetics* suggest, the double strategy of *hedismeno logo,* "sweet discourse," the disturbance of an *ainigma,* "riddle," and the shock of *xenicon,* "estrangement," tragedy enhanced a new view of the world—what Aristotle called *anagnorisis,* "discovery."[307] This recasts the world, exposing those inconsistencies in its assumptions, and confronting the *ploke* or denouement of conflicts between its accepted dogmas. Ultimately, it censures the lack of *nomos*—not only in the mind and its interpretation of nature, but also in the world of human relations and the organization of society.

Perhaps the spatial logos of the Classical canon, *taxis* and *kosmesis,* together with the Doric and Ionic kinds, the metric patterns, and the overt and subtle figures, did play a similar role through comparable devices of riddle, estrangement, and *anagnorisis.* Like tragedy, it provided a tool for creating new worlds and responded to the question of "how to live." Its buildings—to cite once more from Heraclitus a celebrated reference to the Delphic oracle—"neither speak out nor conceal, but give a sign." They bring about an awareness of the possibility of *eunomia*—a very free translation of which may be "the creation of good rules to live by."

NOTES

Prologue

1   O. Spengler (1926).
2   M. Heidegger (1989).
3   T. Hamlin (1940).
4   R.K. Logan (1986).
5   W. Burkert (1992).
6   I. Malkin (1987).
7   C. Morgan (1990).
8   J.M. Edmonds (1940).
9   W. Burkert (1992).
10   Ibid.
11   J. J. Coulton (1977).
12   W.S. Heckscher (1937-38), pp. 204–220;
     R. Weiss (1973), p.10.
13   G. Vasari (1550, 1568).
14   H. Pirenne (1939)
15   D.C. Dennett Jr. (1948).
16   R. Klibansky (1939).
17   C.H. Krinsky (1967).
18   Current research has stressed the distributed
     regional origins of the kinds of architecture of
     Classical Greece. See B.A. Barletta (2001), and
     P.P. Betancourt (1977).
19   Vitruvius, *De Architectura.*
20   Aristotle *Historia Animalium* I, pp.15–20.
21   L. Lefaivre and A. Tzonis.
22   R. Krautheimer (1942-43), pp. 1–34.
23   L. Lefaivre and A. Tzonis.
24   Vitruvius, *De Architectura.*
25   R. Wittkower (1962).
26   Serlio's was the first original architectural
     treatise written in a modern language to be
     published.
27   A. Palladio (1570).
28   L. Lefaivre and A. Tzonis.
29   C. Perrault (1683).
30   J.D. Le Roy (1758, revised 1770).
31   J. Stuart & N. Revett (1762–1830);
     See Wiebenson, (1969).
32   1770 edition, p. 3.
33   Theologian and bishop of Cambrai.
34   A. Pope (1731); A.A. Cooper Shaftesbury, Earl
     of (1711), a stalwart Whig and reformist who
     believed in parliamentary authority.
35   G. Highet (1985). See Rousseau's collaboration
     with C. W. Gluck to reform music through a
     revival of Greek tragedy.
36   M.A. Laugier (1753)
37   L. Lefaivre and A. Tzonis (2004)
38   J.J. Winckelmann (1762).
39   J.F. Blondel (1675-1683).
40   *Literary Correspondence* (May 1, 1763).
41   G.B. Piranesi (1769).
42   M.A. Laugier (1753). See also M. Ribart
     de Chamoust (1783).
43   Goethe (1772).
44   E.M. Butler (1935).
45   E.M. Butler (1935), p.27.
46   B. Snell (1953).

Chapter I

This chapter owes much to F. A. Cooper and N.
J. Kelly's research on the temple of Apollo, Bassai.
47   R. Martin (1976).
48   Pausanias, *Guide to Greece*, VIII.
49   F.A. Cooper (1978).
50   F.A. Cooper (1978)
51   F.A. Cooper (1978)
52   After the Greek Revolution, Gropius came to
     Athens as a consul and became one of the
     charter members of the Archaeological
     Society of Greece, founded in 1837, with the
     immediate task of excavating the Acropolis of
     Athens.
53   F.A. Cooper (1978)
54   G. Roux (1976).
55   *The Morning Chronicle*, January 27, 1816.
56   The *Expedition Scientifique de Morée* executed
     further measured drawings of the temple in
     1833 and at 1853 by Denis Lebouteux. From
     1902 to 1907, the Archaeological Society of
     Athens undertook a program of restoration of
     the temple. The temple suffered in the
     earthquake of 1956 and a thunderstorm of
     1966. Today, the temple's foundations, laid out
     on soft subsoil, have distorted the horizontality
     of the stylobate, and several parts of the
     building have crumbled due to the changes of
     temperature to which limestone—the main
     building material—is sensitive. Since 1983, the
     building has been systematically restored and
     remains covered with a protective tent.
57   F.A. Cooper and N. J. Kelly (1996)
58   W.B. Dinsmoor (1950).
59   F.A. Cooper and N. J. Kelly (1996)
60   Ibid.
61   Ibid.
62   For a comparison between narrative
     organization in Herodotus and figures see
     J.L. Myres (1973), pp. 62–63.
63   F.A. Cooper and B.C. Madigan (1992),
     pp. 27–31.
64   C. Vatin (2001), pp. 381–387.
65   F.A. Cooper and N.J. Kelly (1996),
     pp. 367–68.
66   R. Osborne (1987), pp. 12–16.
67   N. Yalouris (1979), pp. 89–104.
68   Clement of Alexandria, "Stromateis,"
     Miscellanies.

Chapter II

69   Darwin's definition of evolution.
70   O. Murray (1993), p.12. See also R. Osborne
     (1996); A. Schnapp-Gourbeillon (2002);
     A. M. Snodgrass (1971)
71   J.J. Coulton (1993).
72   J.J. Coulton (1993).
73   J.J. Coulton (1993).
74   J.Camp and E. Fisher (2002)
75   K. Kilian (1980)
76   A. Mallwitz (1981). I. A. Papanikolaou (1990)
     rejects the hypothesis of a lineage from
     the *megara* and *oikoi* of several shapes
     of the Geometric period to the Greek
     peripteral temple of the seventh century
     B.C.E., since Hekatompedon I of Samos,
     Apollo of Eretria.
77   M. Petropoulos (1996-97).
78   A. Bammer (1990); (1991).
79   A. Mazarakis-Ainian (1997).
80   Pindar, *Olympian Odes*, 13, *Isthmian Odes*, 13.
81   E.L. Schwandner (1990); C. Wikander (1983).
82   H. Robinson (1976), p. 205.
83   R.F. Rhodes (1984); N.L. Klein (1991);
     E.R. Gebhard (2001).
84   E.R. Gebhard (2001).
85   O. Broneer (1971); E.R. Gebhard and
     F.P. Hemans (1992).
86   Egypt, Megiddo, Ramat Rahel and Samaria:
     Y. Shiloh and A. Horowitz (1975).

87 Tel Dan, Hazor, Megiddo, Taanach, Beth-Shean, Samaria, Ramat Rahel, Jerusalem, and Gezer: E.R. Gebhard (2001)

88 T.C. Mitchell (1982). "Israel and Judah until the revolt of Jehu (931–841 BC)," *The Cambridge Ancient History vol. 3, part 1: The Prehistory of the Balkans, the Middle East and the Aegean World, Tenth to Eighth Centuries BC*, under the direction of J. Boardman, I.E.S. Edwards, N.G.L. Hammond and E. Sollberger, Cambridge, P.P. Betancourt (1977).

89 A. Mallwitz (1981).

90 J.J. Coulton (1976); C.A. Pfaff (1990).

91 E. Akurgal (1983).

92 P.P. Betancourt (1977).

93 P.P. Betancourt (1977), p.123; R. Martin (1955–56), pp.119–32.

94 P.P. Betancourt (1977) lists these scholars: 'Proto-Ionic' is used by W. B. Dinsmoor; 'Aeolic' by K. Schefold (1938), D. S. Robertson, and Akurgal; 'Eolo-Ionic' by R. Vallois, etc. See also J. Boardman (1959), and Y. Shiloh (1979), Wesenberg (1971) calls these capitals 'Volutenkapitelle'

95 J. Boardman (1959); B. Wesenberg (1971)

96 Pausanias. *Guide to Greece* V, 16, 1.

97 Herodotus, *Histories*, II, 97, II, 178–180.

98 G. Rodenwaldt (1939).

99 B.A. Barletta (2001).

100 J.J. Coulton (1979).

101 G. Gruben (1993); (1997).

102 L.S. Meritt (1969).

103 J.J. Coulton (1976); P. Bruneau and J. Ducat (1983).

104 Vitruvius, *De Architectura*, VII, 12, 16.

105 Pliny, *Historia naturalis*, XXXIV, 83.

106 G. Gruben (1960).

107 A.W. Lawrence (1983); U. Muss (1994); C.A. Picón (1988).

108 G.E. Mylonas (1957); I.M. Shear (1999).

109 D.S. Robertson (1943).

110 A.W. Lawrence (1983).

111 G.E. Mylonas (1957); I.M. Shear (1999).

112 Herodotus, *Histories*, III, 57–58; Pausanias, *Guide to Greece* X, 11, 2.

113 G.E. Mylonas (1957); I.M. Shear (1999).

114 P. Amandry (1953) identifies it with the victories of Mycale and Sestos of Cimon over the Persians in 479–478 B.C.E. See also J.F. Bommelaer and D. Laroche (1991)

115 J.F. Bommelaer and D. Laroche (1991); P. Amandry (1953).

116 B.A. Barletta (2001), pp. 99–100.

117 S.P. Morris (1992).

118 P. Friedländer (1949), n. 139A.

119 J.A. Bundgaard (1957).

Chapter III

120 Herodotus *Histories* VIII, 55.

121 K. Jeppesen (1958).

122 J.J. Coulton (1977).

123 A.W. Lawrence (1983), beginning of chapter 15.

124 F.C. Penrose (1888).

125 W.B. Dinsmoor (1950), p.161.

126 M. Korres, G.A. Panetsos, T. Seki (1996), p.12.

127 J.M. Hurwit (1999), pp. 310–11 on Plutarch and funding.

128 I. Travlos (1980).

129 J. A. De Waele (1990).

130 P. Hellström (1988), pp. 107–121; Strabo *Geography* XIV1, 14.

131 J.M. Hurwit (1999).

132 J.A. Bundgaard (1957).

133 J.M. Hurwit (1999).

134 J.A. Bundgaard (1976); T. Tanoulas (1996), pp. 114–123, 129.

135 De J. A. Waele (1990), p.64.

136 I. Travlos (1980), pp. 213–227.

137 W.B. Dinsmoor (1950).

138 A comparable movement from regional design conventions to a *koine* has been observed in the design of artifacts of a different scale: pottery. However, buildings were not an economic product subject to sale and exportation. Their fabrication was much slower and, as we have seen, involved the collaboration of a large number of specialized craftsmen whose activities had to be coordinated and planned far in advance. The centripetal-centrifugal development of rules of design, as a canon or *koine*, involved a more distributed network of regional centers and a more complex cluster of techniques and methods. Yet this did happen.

139 R.A. Tomlinson (1963) Vitruvius, *De Architectura*, IV. 3.

140 W. Konigs (1983), pp. 134–176.

141 Vitruvius, *De Architectura*, III. 6.

142 Vitruvius, *De Architectura*, III. 2 & III.3.

143 R.A. Tomlinson (1963).

144 R.A. Tomlinson (1963); K. Jeppesen (1958).

145 F. Seiler (1986).

146 A.W. Lawrence (1983); R.A. Tomlinson (1963).

147 K. Jeppesen (1958).

148 R. Osborne (1987), pp. 12–16.

149 K. Jeppesen (1958).

150 K. Jeppesen (1958), p.70.

151 L. Haselberger (1980), pp. 191–215; L. Haselberger (1985), pp. 114–122; L. Haselberger (1983a), pp. 90–123; L. Haselberger (1983b), pp. 111–119.

152 Vitruvius, *De Architectura*, VII. 11.

153 Pausanias, DollG., II. 27. 5.

154 P. Coupel and P Demargne (1969).

155 P. Pedersen (2001/2002), pp. 97–130.

156 Pliny, *Naturalis Historia* 36, pp. 30–31.

157 K. Jeppesen (2002a), pp. 207–218.

158 J. Travlos (1988), pp. 402–411.

159 Vitruvius, *De Architectura*, I c. ix.

160 A.W. Lawrence (1983).

161 Aristotle, *Politics* IV, 1,2, 16; W. Setuller et al. (1989).

162 R.E. Martin (1951); R. Martin (1956).

Chapter IV

This chapter draws on the research carried out by Thoebe Giannisi, *Chant et Cheminement*, doctoral thesis.

163 Homer, *Odyssey*.

164 J.-P. Vernant (1965).

165 J.C. Wright (1994).

166 J.-P. Vernant (1979), pp. 37–132.

167 W. Martini (1986), pp. 23–36; E. Drerup (1969); B. Bergquist (1967).

168 W. Burkert (1985), pp. 55–64.

169 D. Rupp (1983), p.102; H. Schleif (1934), pp. 139, 156.

170 D. Rupp (1983), p.103.

171 A. Mazarakis-Ainian (1988), pp. 105–119.

172 A. Mazarakis-Ainian (1997), p.286.

173 W. Burkert (1985).

174 B. Bergquist (1967).

175 Herodotus, *Histories,* VIII, 50.

176 For the Taurian Artemis, see Euripides, *Iphigeneia,* 977; for the Palladion Athena, see Apollodorus, *The Library* 3.143; W. Burkert (1985) n.84 II 5 3; I.B. Romano (1988) p.129.

177 I.B. Romano (1988); E. Simon (1983).

178 M.B. Hollinshead (1999), pp. 189–218.

179 Archaeological research has been unable to identify the exact location within the temple of the *adyton,* or to determine its architectural nature. For Herodotus, the *adyton* was located within a *megaron* and had a seating capacity for visitors. In Euripides' *Ion,* the *adyton* was the place of consultation of the oracle. Ancient descriptions of the temple also included an iron throne at the entrance of the cella from which Pindar had intonated hymns to Apollo. In the front lay the hearth of the goddess Hestia, and an *adyton* on two levels: the ground floor housing the gold statue of Apollo and a lower ground floor divided perhaps into two parts, the *oikos,* where those in quest of the oracle would have sat, and the *antron* where the Pythia was seated near the *omphalos,* or "navel-stone," regarded as the tomb of Python or Dionysos by the Greeks. It is not possible, however, to identify those parts of the Delphic temple as presented in ancient sources, with the parts that archaeological research has discovered. The paving stones in the interior of the cella have not been found, and research gives only the following information: the cella was divided into three parts, possibly four. The east part, close to the entrance, after the *pronaos* porch, was paved, and was accessed via two lateral doors. This part of the cella— the first to be entered—was separated by a stone wall between the two first interior columns from the following central part of the cella. As regards the central part of the cella, we have no information. Its west part—the deepest area of its interior—was not paved, but no element has been found to support the hypothesis that it was on a different level to the rest. Finally, at this west part, there was an interruption of the south colonnade.

P. Amandry (2000), pp. 9–21, esp. pp.20–21.

180 Lucian, *Herodotus,* 62.1.

181 Lucian, *Fugitivi,* 7.

182 H. Kyrieleis (1996).

183 O. Murray (1993).

184 *Greek Historical Inscriptions,* no.1.

185 J. Svenbro (1993).

186 F. Sokolowski (1962), no.107; F. Van Straten (1992), pp. 270–271.

187 M.B. Hollinshead (1999).

188 A.M. Snodgrass (1977).

189 F. De Polignac (1995), p. 15.

190 C.M. Antonaccio (1994), pp. 79–104.

191 F. De Polignac (1995); (1994), pp. 3–18.

192 P. Vidal-Naquet (1981), pp. 151–75.

193 F. De Polignac (1995); Strabo, *Geography.*

194 F. De Polignac (1995); F. Graf (1996); S. Georgoudi (2001), pp. 153–71.

195 S.G. Cole (1994), pp. 199–216.

196 C. Morgan (1990) pp. 26–28.

197 M. Detienne and J.P. Vernant, (1974).

198 Sophocles, *Ajax,* 1216–22.

199 C. Morgan (1997).

200 Ibid.

201 Pausanias, *Guide to Greece,* V, 7, 7.

202 C. Morgan (1997).

203 Ibid.

204 Pausanias *Guide to Greece,* V, 15,1.

205 Pausanias *Guide to Greece,* V, 13, 10.

206 Pausanias *Guide to Greece,* X, 7, 2.

207 C. Morgan (1997).

208 J.L. Shear (2002).

209 E. Simon (1983).

210 I. Travlos (1980); E. Simon (1983).

211 J. Travlos (1988).

212 E. Simon (1983).

213 Pausanias, *Guide to Greece,* I, 2, 2.

214 Pausanias, *Guide to Greece,* I, 2, 4.

215 Pausanias, *Guide to Greece,* I, 2, 5.

216 Pausanias, *Guide to Greece,* I, 3, 3.

217 Pausanias, *Guide to Greece,* I, 3, 5.

218 Pausanias, *Guide to Greece,* I, 8, 5.

219 Pollux; Eubulus.

220 Diodorus of Sicily, *Historical Library,* XI, 29, 3–4.

221 Pausanias, *Guide to Greece,* I, 20, I.

222 Pausanias, *Guide to Greece,* I, 20, 2.

223 Pausanias, *Guide to Greece,* I, 28, 2.

224 J.M. Hurwit (1999).

Chapter V

225 S.P. Morris (1992); F. Frontisi-Ducroux (1975).

226 J.L. Pollack (1995).

227 E.R. Dodds (1951), p.236.

228 A.M. Snodgrass (1980).

229 A.M. Snodgrass (1980).

230 Homer, *The Iliad,* I. 396; *The Odyssey,* XVII. 604, XVIII, 198.

231 M.N. Nilsson (1952) ch. III.

232 N. Goodman (1981).

233 G.S. Kirk and J.E. Raven (1963).

234 R. Jackendoff (1992), p. 22.

235 N. Goodman (1981).

236 H. Putnam (1992), pp. 109–33.

237 G.S.Kirk and J.E. Raven (1963).

238 G.S. Kirk and J.E. Raven (1963), p.314; Aristotle, *Metaphysics,* 127.9, 1092b8.

239 Alexander of Aphrodisias, *Metaphysics,* 827, 9, commentary on Aristotle's *Metaphysics,* N5. 1092b8.

240 Plato, *Timaeus,* 35–36.

241 L. Lefaivre and A. Tzonis (2004).

242 Aristotle, *Metaphysics,* 985b10-20. It was contained in Democritus, *Megas Diakosmos* and *Micros Diakosmos* (Little World System) probably written around 440 B.C.E. However, as A.P.D. Mourelatos (2003) has argued "*taxis*" was one of Aristotle's terms, misinterpreting the more dynamic concept of Democritus.

243 Aristotle explicitly refers to *methodou* in the opening paragraph of his book.

244 An expression used by Jackendoff (1992, p. 44) in reference to Marr's model for representing geometrical and topological properties of physical objects.

245 A. Tzonis and L. Lefaivre (1986).

246 C. Cesariano (1521); A. Tzonis and L. Lefaivre (1986).

247 A. Tzonis and L. Lefaivre (1986).

248 J. Sandys (1968).

249 *Onomasticon,* Pollux.

250 Aristotle, *Rhetoric,* III, xiv, 14.

251 Aristotle, *Metaphysics,* I. iv, 15.

252 P. Bloom, M.A. Peterson, L. Nadel, and M.F. Garret (1999).

253 On the "*what* and *where*" cognitive system, see P. Bloom, M.A. Peterson, L. Nadel, and

M.F. Garret (1999), and R. Jackendoff (1989).

254 L. Lefaivre and A. Tzonis (2004).

255 Ibid.

256 A. Tzonis and L. Lefaivre (1986).

257 R. Jakobson, C.G.M. Fant, and M. Halle (1952).

258 A.P.D. Mourelatos (2003).

259 S. Ullman (1996).

260 Aristotle, *Metaphysics*, V, III.

261 I. Biederman (1995).

262 J.J. Pollitt (1974).

263 P. Bloom, M.A. Peterson, L. Madel, and M.F. Carrel (1999).

264 Plato, *Republic*, V, 4, 6. Euclid, *The Elements*, 7.

265 L. Lefaivre and A. Tzonis, eds. (2004), Introduction by A. Tzonis.

266 Aristotle, *Metaphysics*, I, iv.

267 R. Jakobson, C.G.M. Fant, and M. Halle (1952).

268 G. Nagy (1994), p. 18. This is the path taken by W.S. Allen, who avoided in literature the term rhythm, opting for "a system that operates in terms of stress." See G. Nagy (1994), p. 27.

269 Cicero, *Ad Herennium*, I, iv, and *De Inventione*, I, xvii.

270 J.J. Coulton (1977).

271 A. Thiersch (1889).

272 Hermogenes, *L'art Rhetorique*, 361.12 and 419.16.

273 W.B. Dinsmoor (1950), pp. 200–202.

274 A. Tzonis and L. Lefaivre (1986).

275 L. Shoe Meritt (1969).

276 P.P. Betancourt (1977), pp. 66–67.

277 F. Jacob (1977).

278 S.A. Kauffman (1993), p. 33.

279 Quoted in W.H. Goodyear (1912).

280 W.B. Dinsmoor (1950).

281 L. Haselberger (1983b) and (1985).

282 Vitruvius, *De Architectura* III., c. iii. 10–13.

283 Damianus, *Optica*. ; Heron, *Definitiones*, 135.13.

284 T. Heath, (1981).

285 G.S. Kirk and J. E. Raven (1963), p. 423.

286 P. Bloom , M.A. Peterson, L. Madel, and M.F. Garret (1999).

287 A. Kalpaxis (1986) and J.A. Schmoll (1959).

288 Aristotle, *Poetics*, XXII. 23.

289 J.A. Schmoll (1959).

290 Pliny, *Naturalis Historia*, 35.145.

291 J.J. Pollitt (1977).

292 Aristotle, *Rhetoric*, III. 19. 6.

293 Aristotle, *Rhetoric*, I.

294 Aristotle, *Poetics*, XXI. 22; Aristotle, *Rhetoric*, III. 11.

295 Aristotle, *Poetics*, VI. 27.

296 Aristotle, *Poetics*, XV. 16 ; Aristotle, *Poetics*, X. 4.

297 R.A. Tomlinson (1963).

298 Aristotle, *Poetics*, XVIII. 4.

Epilogue

299 Aristotle, *Politics*, II, viii.

300 M. Jammer 1970.

301 Juko Ito, (1988); (2002). The first example the Poseidon sanctuary at Sounion.

302 There is an exception here of the tholos, which is based on a translation of the square grid coordinates to polar ones.

303 G. Nagy (1990).

304 W. Burkert (1992).

305 G. Nagy (1990).

306 Plato Gorgias, 504 d–e.

307 Aristotle, *Politics*, VIII, vi, 4–6.

TERMINOLOGY

DORIC ORDER

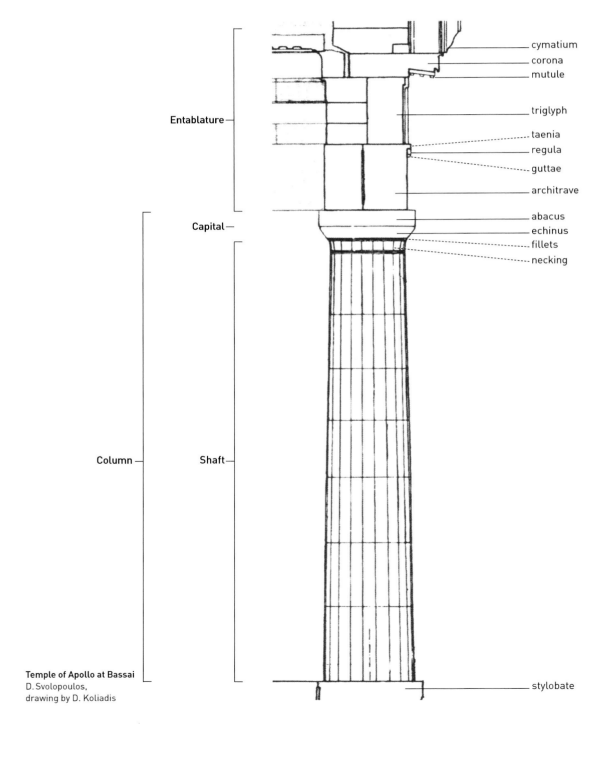

Entablature

Capital

Column — Shaft

cymatium
corona
mutule
triglyph
taenia
regula
guttae
architrave
abacus
echinus
fillets
necking

stylobate

Temple of Apollo at Bassai
D. Svolopoulos,
drawing by D. Koliadis

IONIC ORDER

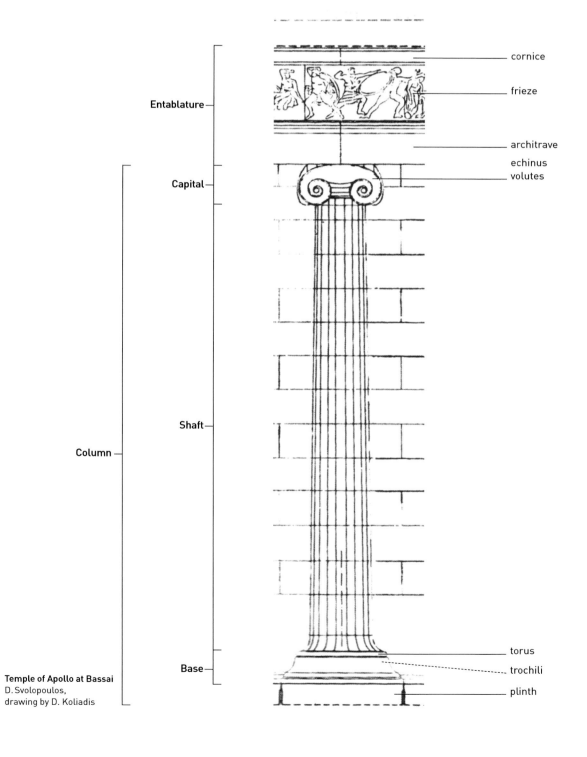

Entablature
- cornice
- frieze
- architrave

Capital
- echinus
- volutes

Column

Shaft

Base
- torus
- trochili
- plinth

Temple of Apollo at Bassai
D. Svolopoulos,
drawing by D. Koliadis

CORINTHIAN ORDER

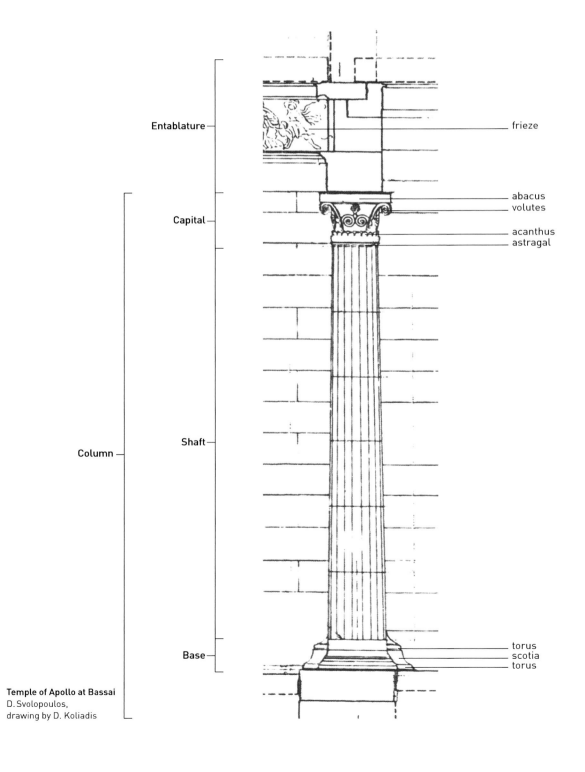

Entablature

frieze

Capital

abacus
volutes
acanthus
astragal

Column

Shaft

Base

torus
scotia
torus

Temple of Apollo at Bassai
D. Svolopoulos,
drawing by D. Koliadis

LAYOUT OF A GREEK TEMPLE

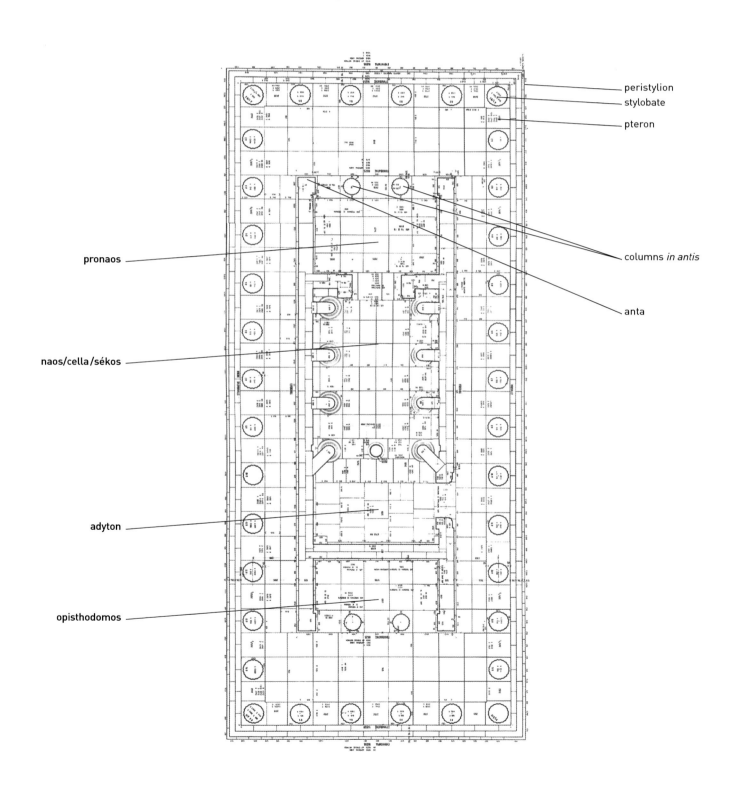

peristylion

stylobate

pteron

columns *in antis*

pronaos

anta

naos/cella/sékos

adyton

opisthodomos

MAPS

THE ANCIENT GREEK WORLD

Paestum

Metaponto • • Taranto

Sybaris •

Locri •

Messine •

IONIAN SEA

• Segesta

Selinous •

• Morgantina

• Akragas

Megara Hyblaia •
• Gela
Syracuse •

Sicily

Thrace

Macedonia

• Pella

Vergina •

Olynthus •

Thasos

Samothrace

Mt. Olympus ▲

Lemnos

Troy •

Neandria •

Dodona •

Thessaly

Iolkos •
Dimini • •

Klopedi •

Thermi •
Mytilene •

Phrygia

Pergamon •

Lesbos

Euboea

Chios

Larisa •

Lydia

Phocaea •

Sardis •

Thermon •

Mt. Parnassus ▲

Delphi •

Lefkandi •

Orchomenos •
Lebadea •

Oropos •

AEGEAN SEA

Smyrna •
Clazomenae •

Ithaca

Thebes •

Rhamnos •

Belevi •

Perachora •

Eleusis •
Athens •

Ephesus •

Corinth •

Aigina •

Pirseus •

Samos

Magnesia •

Elis •

Sikyon •

Aphaia •

Thorikos •

Andros

Priène •

Nemea •

Mycenea • •

Tyrns

Sunium •

Miletus •

Lycia

Olympia •

Hermione •

Syros

Delos

Didyma •

Caria

Bassai •

Tegea •

Cyclades

Megalopolis •

Peloponnese

Messene •

Paros

Naxos

Halicarnassos •

Sparta •

Siphnos

Cos

Pylos •

Melos

Phylakopi •

Thera

Akrotiri •

Rhodes

Cnidos •

Lindos •

Kythera

Vroulia •

Kydonia •

Knossos •

Arkhanes •

Prinias •

Gournia •

Gortyn •

Crete

TRADE NETWORKS IN ANCIENT GREECE

Marseille

Emporium

Paestum

Carthage

Malta

CYPRUS

Enkomi

Vouni

Pyla

Kition

Paphos

Tamassos

Scythia

Olbia

Pontus

Sinope

Trapezus

Heraclea Pontica

Tarento

Aphrodisias

Al Mina

Telmessos
Xanthos

Babylone

Cyprus

Knossos

Crete
Phaistos   Gournia

Byblos
Sidon

Meggido
Judaea
Ashdod   Jerusalem
Askalon

Apollonia
Cyrene
Euesperides

Alexandria

Naucratis

Hermopolis

CHRONOLOGY

All dates here are B.C.E.

PERIOD	POLITICS AND CULTURE	CONSTRUCTION OF BUILDINGS
3000	Beginnings of Minoan Culture in Crete	
c. 3000–2000	Development of Mediterranean "polyculture"	
	Old Kingdom in Egypt	
	Sumerian period in Mesopotamia	
c. 2200	Earliest Cretan palaces	
	Middle Kingdom in Egypt	
2100	Arrival of Mycenaean Greeks	
c. 2000	Destruction of many European sites	
	Old Babylonian period in Mesopotamia	
c. 1700	Earthquakes destroy Cretan palaces	
	New Kingdom in Egypt	
c. 1500–1450	Earliest Mycenaean tholos tombs	
	Hittite Empire dominates	
1450	Mycenaeans take over the Cretan Palace	
1400	Beginning of Assyrian domination of central Mesopotamia	
c. 1400	Earliest Mycenaean palaces	
c. 1370	Palace of Knossos destroyed	
c. 1300		Palace of Nestor at Pylos
1230	First settlements of the Israelites in Canaan	
1220	Destruction of Troy VIIa	
1200	Destruction of Mycenaean sites in Greece	
1200	Hittite Empire destroyed. "Peoples of the sea" repulsed from Egypt	
Late thirteenth century		Palace and citadel at Tiryns
1150	Destruction of the citadel of Mycenae	
1100–1000	Invasion of the Dorian Greeks	
1050	Use of iron in Greece; renewal of contacts with Cyprus	
1050–950	Migration of Ionian and other Greeks to the Aegean and the coast of Asian Minor	
c. 1000	Complete destruction of Mycenaean palace culture	
1000–960	David king of Israel	
1000–750	Age of Phoenician	
975	Hero's tomb at Lefkandi	
960–931	Solomon king of Israel	
c. 900–800	Early revival of population and agriculture. Iron for tools and weapons	
800	Euboeans and Cypriots establish a trading post at Al Mina	

PERIOD	POLITICS AND CULTURE	CONSTRUCTION OF BUILDINGS
776	First Olympic Games	
775	Euboeans establish trading post in the Bay of Naples (Ischia)	
753	Foundation of Rome	
c. 750	Spatial and social organization of Greek city-states	
c. 750–700	Greek alphabet created on Phoenician models. "Hoplite" in the Greek world. Oracle of Apollo at Delphi already famous	
750–700	Homer and Hesiod	
c. 750–550	Greek colonies throughout Mediterranean	
690–650		Temple of Poseidon at Isthmia
675	Lycurgan reforms at Sparta	
c. 657	Cypselus tyrant at Corinth	
650–625		Old Temple at the Argive Heraion
c. 630	Sappho of Lesbos born	
625–585	Periander tyrant of Corinth	
c. 625–545	Lifetime of Thales of Miletos	
621	Draco's code of law	
c. 610–540	Lifetime of Anaximander of Miletos	
c. 610–600		Temple of Athena at Ancient Smyrna
600	Foundation of Massilia	
c. 600–	Chattel slavery	
Sixth century	Temple of Artemis at Ephesus	
594	Solon, archon at Athens	
580–570		Temple of Artemis at Kerkyra
570 or 550		Temple C at Selinous, Sicily
560–556	First tyranny of Pisistratus at Athens	
560–546	Croesus king of Lydia	
Mid sixth century		Temple A at Neandria
545	Conquest of Ionian Greeks by the Persians	
545	Persian capture of Sardis. End of Lydian Empire	
c. 540	Tyranny on Samos	
539	Persian capture of Babylon. Return of the Jews from exile	
534	First tragedy performed at City Dionysia in Athens	
c. 530	Pythagoras emigrates to southern Italy	
528	Death of Pisistratus. Athens ruled by Hippias	
525		Temple of Hera IV (of Polycrates) at Samos

PERIOD	POLITICS AND CULTURE	CONSTRUCTION OF BUILDINGS
510	Athens free from tyranny	
508	Reforms of Cleisthenes at Athens	
499	Ionian Revolt	
494	Sack of Miletos and end of Ionian Revolt	
490	Battle of Marathon	
482	Discovery of silver at Laurium in Attica	
480	Battles of Thermopylae and Salamis. Athens and Acropolis sacked by the Persians	
479	Battles of Plataea and Mycale	
477	Delian League	
476	Pindar's First *Olympian Ode*	
475	Bones of the hero Theseus to Athens	
472	*Persae* of Aeschylus	
465	Helot revolt	
c. 460		Temple of Zeus at Olympia
458	Building of Long Walls from Athens to Piraeus	
458	*Oresteia* of Aeschylus	
454	Treasury of the Delian League moved to Athens	
451	Perikles' law on citizenship	
449–444		Temple of Hephaistos at Athens
447	Athenian building program	
447–438		Parthenon at Athens
447–432		Parthenon at Athens Acropolis
445–426	Herodotus of Halicarnassos active	
437–431		Propylaia at Athens Acropolis
431	Thucydides begins his history *Medea* of Euripides	
431	Peloponnesian War	
431	First Spartan invasion of Attica	
430	Plague at Athens	
430	Democritus of Abdera, Hippocrates of Cos, Socrates, and Protagoras of Abdera active	
430	Funeral oration Perikles	
c. 430		Olynthos, blocks of houses
429	Death of Perikles	
429	Sophocles Oedipus Tyrannus	
429		Temple of Athena Nike at Athens Acropolis

PERIOD	POLITICS AND CULTURE	CONSTRUCTION OF BUILDINGS
Probably 429–c. 400		Temple of Apollo at Phigalia-Bassai
423	*Clouds* of Aristophanes	
421	*Peace* of Aristophanes	
421–405		Erechtheion at Athens Acropolis
415	*Trojan Women* of Euripides	
414	*Birds* of Aristophanes	
411	Athenian democracy temporarily abolished.	
	Lysistrata of Aristophanes	
404	Capitulation of Athens. Installation of regime of the Thirty	
403	Fall of the Thirty. Restoration of democracy at Athens	
399	Trial and execution of Socrates	
396–347	Plato active	
395	Thucydides' *History* published	
384	Aristotle and Demosthenes born	
After 370		Tholos at Epidauros
359	Philip II becomes king of Macedonia	
c. 353		Mausoleion at Halicarnassos
Mid fourth century		Tholos of Epidauros
Second half of fourth century		Theater of Epidauros
348	Death of Plato	
347/6–329		Arsenal of Philo at Piraeus
340		Temple of Athena at Priene
338	Philip defeats Athens and Thebes at Chaeronea	
336	Philip murdered. Accession of Alexander	
335	Aristotle begins teaching at Athens and founds the Lyceum	
	(Peripatetic school)	
334	Alexander crosses into Asia. Battle of Granicus	
Dedicated in 334		Temple of Athena Polias at Priene
333	Victory at Issus	
331	Foundation of Alexandria. Victory of Gaugamela	
330	Burning of Palace of Persepolis	
327	Marriage of Alexander and Roxane	
326	Alexander crosses the Indus.	
	Army's mutinies at Hyphasis River	
323	Death of Alexander in Babylon	
322	Deaths of Aristotle and Demosthenes	

PERIOD	POLITICS AND CULTURE	CONSTRUCTION OF BUILDINGS
c. 320–301	Macedonian general Antigonus and son Demetrius try to establish a large kingdom in Greece, Macedonia and the Near East	
310	Zeno of Citium establishes the Stoic school in *Soa Poikile* at Athens	
307	Epicurus establishes philosophical school at Athens	
306–304	"Successors" of Alexander declare themselves kings	
301	Battle of Ipsus	
300	Ptolemy I founds Museum of Alexandria. Euclid active	
300		Temple of Artemis Cybele at Sardeis
c. 300		Temple of Artemis at Epidauros
Third century		Priene, Agora
Third century and later		Temple of Apollo at Didyma
279	Gauls invade Macedonia and Greece Archimedes active	
Mid third century		Temple of Apollo at Didyma
239–130	Greek kingdom in Bactria	
238–227	Attalus of Pergamum against Galatians. Becomes master of Asia Minor and takes royal title	
174		Temple of Zeus Olympios at Athens Hellenistic
167	Desecration of Temple at Jerusalem, Antiochus IV and statue of Syrian god Baal. Macabean Revolt	
c. 165		Pergamon, Altar of Zeus
159–138		Stoa of Attalos at Athens
150		Temple of Apollo Smintheus in the Troad
148	Fourth Macedonian War. Corinth sacked, Macedonia becomes Roman province	
c. 130		Temple of Artemis Leukophryne at Magnesia
30	Death of Cleopatra VII, queen of Egypt	

BIBLIOGRAPHY

ABBREVIATIONS

AA	Archäologischer Anzeiger
ABSA	The Annual of the British School at Athens
AEph	Αρχαιολογική Εφημερίς
ActaAArtHist	Acta ad archaeologiam et artium historiam pertinentia
AJA	American Journal of Archeology
AM	Mitteilungen des Deutschen Archäologischen Instituts, Athenische Abteilung
AntCl	L'antiquité classique
AntJ	Antiquaries Journal
ASAtene	Annuario della Scuola archeologica di Atene e delle Missioni italiane in Oriente
BABesch	Bulletin antieke beschaving, Annual Papers on Classical Archaeology
BASOR	Bulletin of the American Schools of Oriental Research
BCH	Bulletin de correspondance hellénique
BEFAR	Bibliothèque des Écoles françaises d'Athènes et de Rome
CRAI	Comptes rendus des séances de l'Académie des inscriptions et belles-lettres
EpigrAnat	Epigraphica Anatolica. Zeitschrift für Epigraphik und historische Geographie Anatoliens
Fondation Hardt	Fondation Hardt pour l'Étude de l'Antiquité Classique
Gnomon	Gnomon. Kritische Zeitschrift für die gesamte klassische Altertumswissenschaft
Hephaistos	Hephaistos. Kritische Zeitschrift zur Theorie und Praxis der Archäologie und angrenzender Wissenschaften
Hesperia	Hesperia. Journal of the American School of Classical Studies at Athens
IstForsch	Istanbuler Forschungen
IstMitt	Istanbuler Mitteilungen
JbZMusMainz	Jahrbuch des Römisch-Germanischen Zentralmuseums
JdI	Jahrbuch des Deutschen archäologischen Instituts
JHS	Journal of Hellenic Studies
JWCI	Journal of the Warburg and Courtauld Institutes
ÖJh	Jahreshefte des Österreichischen archäologischen Instituts in Wien
OpAth	Opuscula Atheniensia, Stockholm
OpRom	Opuscula Romana, Stockholm
Peloponnesiaka	Πελοποννησιακά. Περιοδικόν της Εταιρείας Πελοποννησιακών Σπουδών
RA	Revue archéologique
RdA	Rivista di archeologia
RM	Mitteilungen des Deutschen Archäologischen Instituts, Römische Abteilung
SIMA	Studies in Mediterranean Archaeology
Qedem	Qedem. Monographs of the Institute of Archaeology, Hebrew University in Jerusalem
QS	Quaderni di storia

ANCIENT AUTHORS

Apollodorus	*The Library*	Lysias	*For the Cripple*
Aristides	*Panathenaicus*	Pausanias	*Guide to Greece*
Aristophanes	*Frogs*	Pindar	*The Odes of Pindar*. Edited and translated by
	Clouds		Sir. J. Sandys. London and Cambridge, Ma., 1968.
Aristotle	*Categories*	Plato	*Cratylus*
	Generation of Animals		*Critias*
	Historia Animalium		*Euthyphro*
	Metaphysics		*Laws*
	Nicomachean Ethics		*The Republic*
	On Interpretation		*Theaetetus*
	Poetics		*Timaeus*
	Politics		
	Rhetorica ad Alexandrum	Pliny	*Historia naturalis*
	Rhetoric		
		Plutarch	*On Music*
Athenaeus	*Deipnosophistai*		*On the Malice of Herodotus*
			Parallel Lives
Cicero	*Ad Herennium*		*Pericles*
	De inventione		*Quaestiones Romanai*
			Solon
Diodorus of Sicily	*Historical Library*		*Spartan Institutions*
			Theseus
Euclid	*The Elements*, edited and translated		
	by Sir T.L. Heath. New York, 1956.	Pollux	*Onomasticon*
Euripides	*Ion*	Polyaenus	*Strategemata*. E. Woelfflin and J. Melber, eds.,
	Iphigenia in Tauris		1887
Herodotus	*Histories*	Sextus Empiricus	*Outlines of Pyrrhonism*
Herondas	*Mimes*, J. Arbuthnot Nairn, ed., L.Laloy, trans.,	Sophocles	*Ajax*
	Paris (1960)		
		Strabo	*Geography*
Hesiod	*Works and Days*		
		Thucydides	*History*
Homer	*Homeric Hymn to Aphrodite*		
	Homeric Hymn to Apollo	Vitruvius	*De Architectura*
	Odyssey		*On Architecture*. Edited and translated by
	Iliad		F. Granger. London and Cambridge, Ma., 1970.
	The Homeric Hymns and Homerica. Edited and		
	translated by H.G. Evelyn-White. Cambridge, Ma.		
	and London, 1967.		
Lucian	*Fugitivi (The Runaways)*		
	Herodotus		

MODERN WORKS

Akurgal, E. "Vom äolischen zum ionischen Kapitell." *Anatolia* 5 (1960).

Akurgal, E. *The Birth of Greek Art: The Mediterranean and the Near East.* London: 1968.

Akurgal, E. *Alt-Smyrna I.* Ankara: 1983.

Alberti, L.B. *De Re Aedificatoria.* 1440–50.

Alcock, S.E. and R. Osborne, eds. *Placing the Gods, Sanctuaries and Sacred Space in Ancient Greece.* Oxford and New York: 1994.

Alroth, B. "The positioning of Greek votive figurines." *Early Greek Cult Practice: Proceedings of the Fifth International Symposium at the Swedish Institute at Athens, June 26–29, 1986,* R. Hägg, N. Marinatos, and G.C. Nordquist, eds. Göteborg: 1986.

Amandry, P. "La Colonne des Naxiens et la Portique des Athéniens," *Fouilles de Delphes.*" Vol. 2. Paris: 1953.

Amandry, P. "La vie religieuse à Delphes." *BCH*, suppl. 36 (2000) 9–21.

Andrae W. "Die griechischen Säulenordnung." *IstForsch* 17 (1950).

Antonaccio, C.M. "Terraces, tombs, and the Early Heraion." *Hesperia* 61 (1992): 85–105.

Antonaccio, C.M. "Placing the Past: the Bronze Age in the Cultic Topography of Early Greece." In *Placing the Gods, Sanctuaries and Sacred Space in Ancient Greece.* S.E. Alcock and R.Osborne, eds. Oxford and New York: 1994.

Arnold, D. *Temples of the Last Pharaohs.* Oxford: 1999.

Ashby, C. *Classical Greek Theatre, New Views of an Old Subject.* Iowa City: 1999.

Auberson, P. *Temple d'Apollon daphnéphoros, Architecture.* Bern: 1968.

Augustinos, O. *French Odysseys: Greece in French Travel Literature from the Renaissance to the Romantic Era.* Baltimore: 1994.

Austin, M.M. *Greece and Egypt in the Archaic Age.* Cambridge: 1970.

Balanos, N. *Les monuments de l'Acropole, relèvement et conservation.* Paris: 1938.

Bammer, A. "Beiträge zur ephesischen Architektur," *ÖJh* 49 (1968–71): 1–40.

Bammer, A. " A Peripteros of the Geometric Period in the Artemision of Ephesus." *Anatolian Studies* 40 (1990): 137–60.

Bammer, A. "Les sanctuaires des VIIIᵉ et VIIᵉ siècles à l'Artémision d' Ephèse." *RA* (1991) 63–84.

Barletta, B.A. *Ionic Influence in Archaic Sicily: the Monumental Art* (*SIMA* 23). Göteborg: 1983.

Barletta, B.A. *The Origins of the Greek Architectural Orders.* Cambridge: 2001.

Barnes, J. *The Presocratic Philosophers.* London: 1986.

Bauer, H. *Korintische Kapitelle des 4. und 3. Jahrhunderts v. Chr.* (*AM*, suppl. 3). Berlin: 1973.

Baumeister, A. *Denkmäler des Klassischen Altertums.* Vols. 1-3. Munich and Leipzig: 1885–88.

Bergquist, B. *The Archaic Greek Temenos: a Study of Structure and Function.* Lund: 1967.

Bergquist, B. "The Archaic Temenos in Western Greece A Survey and two inquiries." In *Le Sanctuaire Grec* (*Fondation Hardt* 37) A. Schachter, ed. Vandoeuvres-Geneva: 1992.

Bergquist, B. "Feasting of Worshippers or Temple and Sacrifice?" *Ancient Greek Cult Practice from the Archaeological Evidence*: *Proceedings of the Fourth International Seminar on Ancient Greek Cult, October 22–24, 1993.* R. Hägg, ed. Stockholm: 1998.

Bernal, M.G. *Black Athena, the Afroasiatic Roots of Classical Civilization.* London and New Brunswick, N.J.: 1987.

Berve, H. and G. Gruben. *Griechische Tempel und Heiligtümer.* Munich: 1961.

Berve, H. and G. Gruben. *Tempel und Heiligtümer der Griechen.* Munich: 1978.

Betancourt, P.P. *The Aeolic Style in Architecture, a Survey of its Development in Palestine, the Halikarnassos Peninsula, and Greece, 1000–500 BC.* Princeton: 1977.

Bieber, M. *The History of the Greek and Roman Theater.* Princeton: 1939.

Biederman, I. "Visual Object Recognition." In *Visual Cognition, An Invitation to Cognitive Science.* Vol. 2, S.M. Kosslyn and D.N. Osherson, ed. Cambridge, Mass. and London: 1995.

Bietak, M., ed. *Archaische griechische Tempel und Altägypten.* Vienna: 2001.

Billot, M.-F. *L'apparition de l'acanthe dans les décors des toits du monde grec.* Acanthe: 1993.

Blondel, F. *Cours d'architecture.* Paris: 1675–83.

Blondel, J.-F. *Architecture française.* Paris: 1752–57.

Bloom, P., M.A. Peterson, L. Nadel, and M.F. Garret, eds. *Language and Space.* Cambridge, Mass. and London: 1999.

Blümel, C. *Greek Sculptors at Work.* London: 1969.

Boardman, J. "Chian and Early Ionic Architecture." *AntJ* 39 (1959).

Boardman, J. *The Greeks Overseas, their Early Colonies and Trade.* London: 1980.

Boardman, J. *Persia and the West: an Archaeological Investigation of the Genesis of Achaemenid Art.* London: 2000.

Boardman, J. and D. Finn. *The Parthenon and its Sculptures.* Austin: 1985.

Boardman, J., J. Griffin, and O. Murray, eds. *The Oxford History of Greece and the Hellenistic World.* Oxford: 1988.

Bodnar, E.W., and C. Mitchell, eds. *Cyriacus of Ancona's Journeys in the Propontis and the Northern Aegean 1444–1445.* Philadelphia: 1976.

Boersma, J.S. *Athenian Building Policy from 561/0 to 405/4 B.C.* Groningen: 1970.

Bommelaer, J.-F. and D. Laroche. *Guide de Delphes, le site.* Paris: 1991.

Bowen, M.L. "Three Attic Temples." *ABSA* 45 (1950).

Bowen, M.L. "Some Observations on the Origin of Triglyphs." *ABSA* 45 (1950).

Brijder, H.A.G., ed. *Ancient Greek and Related Pottery: Proceedings of the International Vase Symposium in Amsterdam, April 12–15, 1984.* Amsterdam: 1984.

Brockman, A.D. *Die griechische Ante.* Marburg: 1968.

Brommer, F. "Gott oder Mensch." *Jdl* 101 (1986): 37–50.

Broneer, O. *Isthmia I: Temple of Poseidon.* Princeton: 1971.

Brun, J.-P.,and P. Jockey, eds. *Technai, Techniques et sociétés en Méditerranée, Hommage à Marie-Claire Amouretti.* Paris: 2001.

Bruneau, P. and J. Ducat. *Guide de Délos.* Paris: 1983.

Buitron-Oliver, D.M., ed. *The Interpretation of Architectural Sculpture in Greece and Rome.* Hanover and London: 1997.

Bundgaard, J.A. *Mnesicles: a Greek Architect at Work*. Copenhagen: 1957.

Bundgaard, J.A. *The Parthenon and the Mycenaean City on the Heights*. Copenhagen: 1976.

Burckhardt, J. *The Greeks and Greek Civilization*. London: 1998.

Buren, E. D. van. *Archaic Fictile Revetments in Sicily and Magna Graecia*. London: 1923.

Burkert, W. *Greek Religion: Archaic and Classical*. Cambridge, Mass.: 1985.

Burkert, W. *The Orientalizing Revolution*. Cambridge, Mass. and London: 1992.

Burkert, W. "Greek temple-builders: Who, where and why?" *The Role of Religion in the Early Greek Polis: Proceedings of the Third International Seminar on Ancient Greek Cult, organized by the Swedish Institute at Athens, October 16–18, 1992*, R. Hägg, ed. Stockholm: 1996.

Burns, G. *Festschrift für Karl Weickert*. Berlin: 1955.

Buschor, E. *Altsamische Standbilder*. Vol. 2. Berlin: 1934.

Büsing, H.H. *Die griechische Halbsäule*. Wiesbaden: 1970.

Butler, E. M. *The Tyranny of Greece over Germany*, Cambridge, Mass.: 1935.

Cali, F. *L'Ordre Grec, essai sur le temple dorique*. Paris: 1958.

Camp, J., ed. *The Athenian Agora, a Guide to the Excavation and Museum*. Athens:1990.

Camp, J. and E. Fisher. *Exploring the World of the Ancient Greeks*. London: 2002.

Camp, J.M. *The Archaeology of Athens*. New Haven and London: 2001.

Cantarella, E. *Ithaque, De la vengeance d'Ulysse à la naissance du droit*. Paris: 2003.

Caratelli, G.P., ed. *Megale Hellas, Storia e civiltà della Magna Grecia*. Milan: 1983.

Caratelli, G.P., ed. *Sikanie, Storia e civiltà della Sicilia Greca*. Milan: 1985.

Carpenter, R. *Ancient Corinth: a Guide to the Excavations and Museum*. Athens: 1947.

Carpenter, R. *Esthetic Basis of Greek Art*. Bloomington: 1959.

Carpenter, R. *The Architects of the Parthenon*. Harmondsworth: 1970.

Cartledge, P. *The Greeks: a Portrait of Self and Others*. Oxford: 2002.

Cassimatis, H., R. Étienne, and M.-Th. le Dinahet. "Les autels, Problèmes de classification et d'enregistrement des données." *L'espace sacrificial, Colloque. Lyon 4-7 Juin 1988*, R. Etienne and M.-Th. le Dinahet, eds. Paris: 1991.

Catling, R.W. "A fragment of an Archaic Temple from Artemis Orthia, Sparta." *ABSA* 89 (1994): 269–275.

Cavalli-Sforza, L.L., P. Menozzi, and A. Piazza. *The History and Geography of Human Genes*. Princeton: 1994.

Cesariano, C. *De architectura*. Como: 1521.

Changeux, J.-P. and A. Connes. *Matière à pensée*. Paris: 1992.

Childs, W.A.P., et al. *Fouilles de Xanthos 8, Le monument des Néréides: le décor sculpté. Vol. 2: Illustrations photographiques et graphiques*. Paris: 1989.

Coldstream, J.N. "The meaning of the regional styles in the eighth century B.C." In *The Greek Renaissance of the Eighth century B.C., tradition and Innovation*, R. Hägg, ed. Stockholm: 1983.

Coldstream, N. *The Formation of the Greek Polis: Aristotle and Archaeology*. Wiesbaden: 1984.

Cole, S.G. "The Uses of Water in Greek Sanctuaries." *Early Greek Cult Practice: Proceedings of the Fifth International Symposium at the Swedish Institute at Athens, June 26–29, 1986*, R. Hägg, N. Marinatos, and G.C. Nordquist, eds. Göteborg: 1988.

Cole, S.G. "Demeter in the Ancient Greek City and its Countryside." In *Placing the Gods, Sanctuaries and Sacred Space in Ancient Greece*, S.E. Alcock and R.Osborne, eds. Oxford and New York: 1994.

Colonna, F. *Hypnerotomachia Poliphili*. Venice: 1499.

Connelly, J.B. "Parthenon and *Parthenoi*, a Mythological Interpretation of the Parthenon Frieze." *AJA* 100 (1996): 53–80.

Cook, J.M. and R.V. Nicholls. *Old Smyrna Excavations: the Temples of Athena (ABSA, suppl. 30)*. London: 1998.

Cook, J.M. and R.V. Nicholls. *Old Smyrna Excavations*. London: 1998.

Cook, R.M. "Origins of Greek Sculpture." *JHS* 87 (1967): 24–31.

Cooper, F.A. *The Temple of Apollo at Bassai: a Preliminary Study*. New York and London: 1978.

Cooper, F.A., with contributions by N.J. Kelly, eds. *The Temple of Apollo Bassitas. Vol. 1: The Architecture*. Princeton: 1996.

Cooper, F.A., *The Temple of Apollo Bassitas. Vol. 3: The Architecture: Illustrations*. Princeton: 1996.

Cornford, F.M. *From Religion to Philosophy*. New York: 1957.

Coulson, W.D.E. et al, eds. *The Archaeology of Athens and Attica under the Democracy (Oxbow Monographs 37)*. Oxford: 1994.

Coulton, J.J. "The Treatment of Re-entrant Angles." *ABSA* 61 (1966): 132–46.

Coulton, J.J. *The Architectural Development of the Greek Stoa*. Oxford: 1976.

Coulton, J.J. *Greek Architects at Work*. London: 1977.

Coulton, J.J. "Doric capitals as proportional analysis." *ABSA* 74 (1979): 81–153.

Coulton, J.J. "The Parthenon and Periklean Doric." In *Parthenon-Kongress Basel, Referate und Berichte*, E. Berger, ed. Mainz: 1984.

Coulton, J.J. "Modules and Measurements in Ancient Design and Modern Scholarship." *Munus non ingratum: Proceedings of the International Symposium on Vitruvius" De architectura and the Hellenistic and Republican Architecture (BABesch., suppl. 2)*. H. Geertman and J.J. de Jong, eds. (1989): 85–89.

Coulton, J.J. "The Toumba Building: Description and Analysis of the Architecture." In *Lefkandi II: The Protogeometric Building at Toumba, Part 2: The Excavation, Architecture and Finds*, M.R. Popham, P.G. Calligas, and L.H. Sackett, eds. Athens and London: 1993.

Coupel, P. et al. *Fouilles de Xanthos 3, Le monument des Néréides: l'architecture. Vol. 2: Études et restitutions*. Paris: 1969.

Courtils, J. des and J.-C. Moretti, eds. *Les grands ateliers d'architecture dans le monde égéen du VIe siècle avant J.-C*. Paris: 1993.

Danner, P. *Griechische Akrotere der archaischen und klassischen Zeit (RdA, suppl. 5)*. Rome: 1989.

Davis, J.H.R. *People of the Mediterranean: an Essay in Comparative Social Anthropology.* London: 1977.

De Coulanges, F. *La cité antique.* Paris: 1984.

Dekoulakou-Sideris, I. "A metrological relief from Salamis." *AJA* 94 (1990): 445–51.

De la Coste-Messelière, P. "Chapiteaux doriques du haut archaïsme." *BCH* 87 (1963).

Demand, N.H. *Urban Relocation in Archaic and Classical Greece, Flight and Consolidation.* London: 1990.

Demangel, R. *La frise ionique.* Paris: 1932.

Dennett, D.C. Jr. "Pirenne and Muhammed." *Speculum* 23 (1948).

Detienne, M. *Les Maîtres de vérité dans la Grèce Archaïque.* Paris: 1967.

Detienne, M. *Apollon le Couteau à la Main.* Paris: 1998.

Detienne, M., ed. *Les savoirs de l'écriture en Grèce ancienne.* Lille: 1988.

Detienne, M., and J.-P. Vernant. *Les Ruses de l'intelligence, La Métis des Grecs.* Paris: 1974.

Detienne, M., and J.-P. Vernant, eds. *La cuisine du sacrifice en pays grec.* Paris: 1979.

De Waele, J.A. "Le dessin d'architecture du temple grec au début de l'époque classique." *Le dessin d'architecture dans les sociétés antiques, actes du colloque de Strasbourg 26–28 janvier 1984.* Leiden: 1985.

De Waele, J.A. *The Propylaia of the Akropolis in Athens: the Project of Mnesikles.* Amsterdam: 1990.

Diels, H. *Die Fragmente der Vorsokratiker.* Berlin: 1934–54.

Dinsmoor, W.B. *Observations on the Hephaisteion* (*Hesperia,* suppl. 5). Cambridge, Mass.: 1941.

Dinsmoor, W.B. *The Architecture of Ancient Greece: an Account of its Historic Development.* London: 1950.

Ditlefsen, F. "Gedanken zum Ursprung des dorischen Frieses." *ActaAArtHist* 5 (1985).

Dodds, E.R. *The Greeks and the Irrational.* Berkeley: 1951.

Donohue, A.A. "The Greek Images of Gods, Considerations on Terminology and Methodology." *Hephaistos* 15 (1997): 31–45.

Dörpfeld, W. "Der Tempel von Sunion." *AM* 9 (1884).

Dörpfeld, W. et al. *Troja und Ilion.* Athens: 1902.

Dörpfeld, W. et al. *Alt-Olympia, Untersuchungen und Ausgrabungen zur Geschichte des ältesten Heiligtums von Olympia und der älteren griechischen Kunst.* Berlin: 1935.

Dothan, T. The Philistines and their Material Culture. Jerusalem: 1967.

Dougherty, C., and L. Kurke, eds. *Cultural Poetics in Archaic Greece: Cult, Performance, Politics.* Cambridge: 1993.

Doxiadis, C.A. *Architectural Space in Ancient Greece.* Cambridge, Mass. and London: 1972.

Drachmann, B., ed. *Scolia vetera in Pindari Carmina.* Vol. 1. Leipzig: 1903.

Drerup, H. "Zur Enstehung der griechischen Tempelrinhalle." In *Festschrift für Friedrich Matz.* N. Himmelmann-Wildschütz and H. Biesantz, eds. Mainz am Rhein: 1962.

Drerup, H. *Griechische Baukunst in geometrischer Zeit.* Göttingen: 1969.

Drerup, H. "Das sogenannte Daphnephorion in Eretria." In *Studien zur klassischen Archäologie zum 60. Geburtstag von F. Hiller.* K. Braun and A. Furtwängler, eds. Saarbrucken: 1986.

Durkheim, E.D. *The Elementary Forms of the Religious Life: a Study in Religious Sociology.* London: 1915.

Durm, J.W., H. Ende, and E. Schmitt. *Handbuch der Architektur 2. Teil: Die Baustile, 1. Band: Die Baukunst der Griechen.* Darmstadt: 1881.

Dyer, L. "Olympian Treasuries and Treasuries in General." *JHS* 25 (1905): 294–319.

Easterling, P.E. and J.V. Muir, eds. *Greek Religion and Society.* Cambridge: 1985.

Edmonds, J.M. *Lyra Graeca.* Vol. 3. London and New York: 1940.

Eilan, N., R. McCarthy, and B. Brewer, eds. *Spatial Representation: Problems in Philosophy and Psychology.* Oxford: 1999.

Étienne, R. "Autels et sacrifices." *Le Sanctuaire Grec* (*Fondation Hardt* 37). A. Schachter, ed. Vandoeuvres-Geneva: 1992.

Evans, A.J. *The Palace of Minos.* London: 1921–36.

Fagerström, K. *Greek Iron Age Architecture: Developments through Changing Times* (*SIMA* 81). Göteborg: 1988.

Farrar, C. *The Origins of Democratic Thinking: the Invention of Politics in Classical Athens.* Cambridge: 1988.

Fehr, B. "The Greek Temple in the early archaic period: meaning, use and social context." *Hephaistos* 14 (1996):165–191.

Fénelon, F. de Salignac de la Mothe. *Les Aventures de Télémaque.* The Hague: 1699.

Filarete (Antonio di Pietro Averlino). *Filarete's Treatise on Architecture.* Translated and edited by J.R. Spencer. New Haven: 1965.

Finley, M.I. *The Use and Abuse of History.* London: 1975.

Finley, M.I. *The World of Odysseus.* London: 1977.

Finley, M.I. *Politics in the Ancient World.* Cambridge and New York: 1983.

Fishman, J.A. "Language and Ethnicity." In *Language, Ethnicity and Intergroup Relations.* H. Giles, ed. London: 1977.

Fishman, J.A., ed. *Readings in the Sociology of Jewish Languages* (*Contributions to the Sociology of Jewish Languages.* Vol. 1. Leyden: 1985.

Foley, A. *The Argolid 800–600 B.C.: an Archaeological Survey.* Göteborg: 1988.

Frankfort, H. *The Art and Architecture of the Ancient Orient.* Harmondsworth: 1970.

Frederiksen, R. "The Greek Theatre, a typical Building in the Urban Centre of the Polis?" In *Even More studies in the Ancient Greek Polis* (*Papers from the Copenhagen Polis Centre* 6). T.H. Nielsen, ed. Stuttgart: 2002.

Freyer-Schauenburg, B. *Bildwerke der archaischen Zeit und des strengen Stils* (*Samos* 11). Bonn: 1974.

Friedländer, P. *Epigrammata, Greek Inscriptions in Verse from the Beginnings to the Persian Wars.* Berkeley: 1948.

Frontisi-Ducroux, F. *Dédale, Mythologie de l'artisan en Grèce ancienne.* Paris: 1975.

Furtwängler, A. *Aegina, das Heiligtum der Aphaia.* Munich: 1906.

Gebhard, E.R. "The Archaic Temple at Isthmia, Techniques of Construction." In *Archaische griechische Tempel und Altägypten.* M. Bietak, ed. Vienna: 2001.

Gebhard, E.R. and F.P. Hemans. "University of Chicago Excavations at Isthmia, 1989." *Hesperia* 61 (1992): 1–77.

Georgoudi, S. "La procession chantante de Molpoi de Milet." In *Chanter les dieux, Musique et religion dans l'Antiquité grecque et romaine.* P. Brulé and C. Vendries, eds. Rennes: 2001.

Gerkan, A. von. "Die Herkunft des Dorischen Gebälks." *JdI* 63–64: (1948–49).

Gerkan, A. von. *Milet I, 6. Der Nordmarkt und der Hafen an der Löwenbucht,* Berlin and Leipzig: 1922.

Gernet, L. *Droit et institutions en Grèce antique.* Paris: 1982.

Gernet, L. and R. Di Donato. *Les Grecs sans miracle.* Paris: 1983.

Giannisi, P. "Chant et Cheminement en Grèce archaïque." *QS* 46 (1997): 133–141.

Giles, H., ed. *Language, Ethnicity and Intergroup Relations.* London: 1977.

Giles, H., R.Y. Bourhis, and D.M.Taylor "Towards a Theory of Language in Ethnic Group Relations." In *Language, Ethnicity and Intergroup Relations.* H. Giles, ed. London: 1977.

Ginouvès, R., et al. *Dictionnaire méthodique de l'architecture grecque et romaine I: Matériaux, techniques de construction, techniques et formes du décor.* Athens and Rome: 1985.

Ginouvès, R. et al. *Dictionnaire méthodique de l'architecture grecque et romaine II: Éléments constructifs: supports, couvertures, aménagements intérieurs.* Athens and Rome: 1992.

Ginouvès, R. et al. *Dictionnaire méthodique de l'architecture grecque et romaine III: Espaces architecturaux, bâtiments et ensembles.* Athens and Rome: 1998.

Goethe, J.W. von. *Von Deutscher Baukunst.* Hamburg: 1772.

Goldstein, M.S. *The Setting of the Ritual Meals in Greek Sanctuaries, 600–300 B.C.,* Ph.D. diss. Berkeley: 1978.

Goodman, N. *Ways of Worldmaking.* Indianapolis: 1981.

Goodyear, W.H. *Greek Refinements: Studies in Temperamental Architecture.* New Haven: 1912.

Graf, F. "Pompai in Greece: some considerations about space and ritual in the Greek *polis.*" *The Role of Religion in the Early Greek Polis: Proceedings of the Third International Seminar on Ancient Greek Cult, Organized by the Swedish Institute at Athens, October 16–18, 1992.* R. Hägg, ed. Stockholm: 1996.

Green, J.R. *Theatre in Ancient Greece: Early Athenian Theatre Setting and Control.* London and New York: 1994.

Gruben, G. *Die Kapitelle des Heratempels auf Samos.* Munich: 1960.

Gruben, G. "Das archaische Didymaion." *JdI* 78 (1963): 78–182.

Gruben, G. "Die Sphinx-Säule von Aigina." *AM* 80. (1965): 170-208.

Gruben, G. "Naxos und Paros, Vierter Vorläufiger Bericht über die Forschungskampagnen 1972-80." *AA* (1982): 159–195.

Gruben, G. "Anfänge des Monumentalbaus auf Naxos." In *Bautechnik der Antike.* A. Hoffmann, ed. Mainz am Rhein: 1991.

Gruben, G. *Architektur auf Naxos und Paros.* Berlin: 1991.

Gruben, G. "Die insellionische Ordnung." In *Les Grands ateliers d'architecture dans le monde égéen du VIe siècle avant J.-C.* J. des Courtils and J.-C. Moretti, eds. Paris: 1993.

Gruben, G. "Griechische Un-Ordnung." In *Säule und Gebälk, zu Struktur und Wandlungsprozeß griechisch-römischer Architektur.* E.-L. Schwandner, ed. Mainz am Rhein: 1996.

Gruben, G. "Naxos und Delos, Studien zur archaischen Architektur der Kykladen." *JdI* 112 (1997).

Gullini, G. "Urbanistica e architettura." In *Megale Hellas, Storia e civiltà della Magna Grecia.* G.P. Carratelli, ed. Milan: 1983.

Gullini, G. "L'Architettura." In *Sikanie, Storia e civiltà della Sicilia Greca.* P. Carratelli, ed. Milan: 1986.

Haarmann, H. *Language in Ethnicity: a View of Basic Ecological Relations.* Berlin: 1986.

Haarmann, H. *Early Civilization and Literacy in Europe: an Inquiry into Cultural Continuity in the Mediterranean World.* Berlin: 1996.

Hägg, R. ed. *The Greek Renaissance of the Eighth Century B.C.: Tradition and Innovation.* Stockholm: 1983.

Hägg, R., ed. *The Role of Religion in the Early Greek Polis: Proceedings of the Third International Seminar on Ancient Greek Cult, Organized by the Swedish Institute at Athens, October 16–18, 1992.* Stockholm: 1996.

Hägg, R., and N. Marinatos, eds. *Greek Sanctuaries, New Approaches.* New York: 1993.

Hägg, R., N. Marinatos, and G.C. Nordquist, eds. *Early Greek Cult Practice: Proceedings of the Fifth International Symposium at the Swedish Institute at Athens, June 26–29, 1986.* Göteborg: 1988.

Hall, J.M. *Ethnic Identity in Greek Antiquity.* Cambridge: 1997.

Hamlin, T. *Architecture through the Ages.* New York: 1940.

Harris, D. *The Treasures of the Parthenon and Erechtheion.* Oxford: 1995.

Harrison, E.B. "The South Frieze of the Nike Temple and the Marathon Painting in the Stoa." *AJA* 76 (1972): 353–78.

Harrison, E.B. "The Glories of the Athenians, Observations on the Program of the Frieze of the Temple of Athena Nike." In *The Interpretation of Architectural Sculpture in Greece and Rome.* D.M. Buitron-Oliver, ed. Hanover and London: 1997.

Hartog, F. *Le Miroir d'Herodote.* Paris: 2001.

Haselberger, L. "Werkzeichnungen am Jüngeren Didymeion." *IstMitt* 30 (1980): 191–215.

Haselberger, L. "Bericht über die Arbeit am Jüngeren Apollontempel von Didyma." *IstMitt* 33 (1983): 90–123.

Haselberger, L. "Die Werkzeichnungen des Naiskos im Apollontempel von Didyma." In *Bauplanung und Bautheorie der Antike.* W. Hoepfner et al, eds. Berlin: 1983.

Haselberger, L. "The Construction Plans for the Temple of Apollo at Didyma." *Scientific American* 253 No. 6. (1985): 114–122.

Haselberger, L. "Aspekte der Bauzeichnungen von Didyma." *RA* (1991): 99–113.

Haugen, E.I. *The Ecology of Language: Essays.* Stanford: 1972.

Haussoullier, B. "La Voie Sacrée de Milet à Didymes." In *Cinquantenaire de l'École des Hautes Etudes, Sciences Historiques et Philologiques,* Fasc.138. Paris: 1921.

Havelock, E.A. *The Literate Revolution in Greece and its Cultural Consequences*. Princeton: 1982.

Heath, Sir T. *A History of Greek Mathematics*. Vol. 2. New York: 1981.

Heberdey, R. "Daitis: Ein Beitrag zum ephesischen Artemiscult." *ÖJh,* suppl. 7, coll. 44 ff. (1904).

Heckscher, W.S. "Relics of Pagan Antiquity in Medieval Setting," *Journal of the Warburg Institute* 1 (1937–38): 204–20.

Hedreen, G.M. *Capturing Troy: the Narrative Functions of Landscape in Archaic and Early Classical Greek Art*. Ann Arbor: 2001.

Heidegger, M. *Aufenthalte*. Frankfurt: 1989.

Heisel, J.P. *Antike Bauzeichnungen*. Darmstadt: 1993.

Hellmann, M.-C. *Recherches sur le vocabulaire de l'architecture grecque*. Athens and Paris: 1992.

Hellmann, M.-C. *L'Architecture grecque*. Paris: 1998.

Hellmann, M.-C., ed. *Choix d'inscriptions architecturales grecques*. Lyon and Paris: 1999.

Hellström, P. "The Planned Function of the Mnesiklean Propylaia." *OpAth* 17 (1988): 107–21.

Herrmann, H.-V. *Olympia Heiligtum und Wettkampfstätte*. Munich: 1972.

Herrmann, K. "Zum Dekor dorischer Kapitelle." *Architectura* 13 (1983).

Herzfeld, M. *Anthropology through the Looking-Glass: Critical Ethnography in the Margins of Europe*. Cambridge: 1987.

Highet, G. *The Classical Tradition, Greek and Roman Influences on Western Literature*. Oxford and New York: 1985.

Himmelmann-Wildschütz, N., and H. Biesantz, eds. *Festschrift für Friedrich Matz*. Mainz am Rhein: 1962.

Hodge, A. T. The Woodwork of Greek Roofs. Cambridge: 1960.

Hoepfner, W., ed. *Kult und Kultbauten auf der Akropolis, internationales Symposion vom 7. bis 9. Juli 1995 in Berlin*. Berlin: 1997.

Hoepfner, W. et al., eds. *Bauplanung und Bautheorie der Antike*. Berlin: 1983.

Hoffmann, A., ed. *Bautechnik der Antike*. Mainz am Rhein: 1991.

Holbl, G. "Ägyptischer Einfluss in der griechischen Architektur." *ÖJh* 55 (1984): 1–18.

Hollinshead, M.B. "'Adyton,' 'Opisthodomos,' and the inner room of the Greek temple." *Hesperia* 68 (1999): 189–218.

Howe, T.N. *The Invention of the Doric Order*, diss. Harvard University: 1985.

Humphrey, J.W., J.P. Oleson, and A.N. Sherwood, eds. *Greek and Roman Technology, a Sourcebook: Annotated Translations of Greek and Latin Texts and Documents*. London: 1998.

Hurwit, J.M. *The Art and Culture of Early Greece, 1100–480 B.C.* Ithaca, N.Y. and London: 1985.

Hurwit, J.M. *The Athenian Acropolis: History, Mythology and Archaeology from the Neolithic Era to the Present*. Cambridge: 1999.

Ito, J. *The Site Planning of Greece and Rome: Theory and Practice of Architectural Planning in the Sanctuaries of Classical Antiquity*. Kamamoto: 1988.

Ito, J. *Theory and Practice of Site-Planning in Classical Sanctuaries*. Fukuoka-shi: 2002.

Jackendoff, R. *Consciousness and the Computational Mind*. Cambridge, Mass. and London: 1989.

Jackendoff, R. *Languages of the Mind: Essays on Mental Representation*. Cambridge, Mass. and London: 1992.

Jacob, F. "Evolution and Tinkering." *Science* 4295, Vol. 196 (1977).

Jaeger, W. *The Theology of the Early Greek Philosophers*. Oxford: 1936.

Jaeger, W.W. *Paideia: the Ideals of Greek Culture*. Oxford: 1939.

Jakobson, R., C.G.M. Fant, and M. Halle. *Preliminaries to Speech Analysis*. Cambridge, Mass.: 1952.

Jammer, M. *Concepts of Space: the History of Theories of Space in Physics*. Cambridge, Mass.: 1970.

Janko, R. "From Catharsis to the Aristotelian Mean." In *Essays on Aristotle's Poetics*, A. Oksenberg Rorty, ed. Princeton: 1992.

Jeffery, L.H. *The Local Scripts of Ancient Greece*. Oxford: 1990.

Jenkins, I. *The Parthenon Frieze*. Austin: 1994.

Jeppesen, K. *Paradeigmata: Three Mid-Fourth Century Main Works of Hellenic Architecture Reconsidered*, diss. Aarhus: 1958.

Jeppesen, K. *The Theory of the Alternative Erechtheion: Premises, Definition, and Implications*. Aarhus: 1987.

Jeppesen, K. "The Superstructure: A comparative analysis of the architectural, sculptural and literary evidence." In *The Maussolleion at Halikarnassos, Reports of the Danish Archaeological Expedition to Bodrum*. Vol. 5. K. Jeppesen, ed. Copenhagen: 2002.

Jeppesen, K., ed. *The Maussolleion at Halikarnassos, Reports of the Danish Archaeological Expedition to Bodrum*. Vol. 5. Copenhagen: 2002.

Kalpaxis, A. *Früharchaische Baukunst in Griechenland und Kleinasien*. Athens: 1976.

Kalpaxis, A. *Hemiteles, akzidentelle Unfertigkeit und "Bossen-Stil" in der griechischen Baukunst*. Mainz am Rhein: 1986.

Kaminski, R.G. and C. Maderna-Lauter. *Die Geschichte der antiken Bildhauerkunst I, Frühgriechische Plastik*. Mainz am Rhein: 2002.

Karageorghis, V. *Excavations in the Necropolis of Salamis*. Nicosia: 1967. 1971. 1973.

Karageorghis, V. *Les Ancient Chypriotes, entre Orient et Occident*. Paris: 1991.

Karakasi, K. *Archaische Koren*. Munich: 2001.

Kauffman, S.A. *The Origins of Order: Self-Organization and Selection in Evolution*. New York: 1993.

Kempinski, A. and M. Avi-Yonah. *Syria-Palestine*. Geneva: 1979.

Kienast, H. "Samische Monumentalarchitektur—Ägyptischer Einfluß?" In *Archaische griechische Tempel und Altägypten*. M. Bietak, ed. Vienna: 1991.

Kienast, H. "Topographischen Studien im Heraion von Samos." *AA* (1992): 171–213.

Kienast, H. "Die rechteckigen Peristasenstützen am samischen Hekatompedos." In *Säule und Gebälk, zu Struktur und Wandlungsprozeß griechisch-römischer Architektur*. E.-L. Schwander, ed. Mainz am Rhein:1996.

Kilian, K. "Zum Ende der mykenischen Epoche in der Argolis." *JbZMusMainz* 27 (1980): 166–195.

Kirk, G.S. *Myth: its Meaning and Functions in Ancient and Other Cultures*. Cambridge and Berkeley: 1970.

Kirk, G.S. and J.E. Raven. *The Presocratic Philosophers: a Critical History with a Selection of Texts*. Cambridge: 1963.

Klein, N. "Excavation of the Greek temples at Mycenae by the British School at Athens." *ABSA* 92 (1997): 247–322, 373–400.

Klein, N.L. *The Origin of the Doric Order on the Mainland of Greece*, diss. Bryn Mawr College: 1991.

Klibansky, R. *The Continuity of the Platonic Tradition during the Middle Ages*. London: 1939.

Knell, H. "Iktinos: Baumeister des Parthenon und des Apollontempels von Phigalia-Bassae?" *Jdl* 83 (1968).

Koch, H. *Studien zum Theseustempel in Athen*. Berlin: 1955.

Kohte, J. *Die Baukunst des Klassischen Altertums und ihre Entwicklung in der mittleren und neueren Zeit, Konstruktions- und Formenlehre*. Braunschweig: 1915.

Koldewey, R. *Die antiken Baureste der Insel Lesbos*. Berlin: 1890.

Koldewey, R. *Neandria*. Berlin: 1891.

Koldewey, R. and O. Puchstein. *Die griechischen Tempel in Unteritalien und Sicilien*. 2 vols. Berlin: 1899.

Kondis, J. "Olympia.' In *Temples and Sanctuaries of Ancient Greece: a Companion Guide*. E. Kunze, ed. London: 1973.

Konigs, W. "Der Athenatempel von Priene." *IstMitt* 33 (1983): 134–176.

Kopcke, G. "What Role for Phoenicians?" *Greece Between East and West, 10th–8th Centuries BC: Papers of the Meeting at the Institute of Fine Arts, New York University, March 15–16 1990*. G. Kopcke and I. Tokumarau, eds. Mainz am Rhein: 1992.

Korres, M. "Der plan des Parthenon." *AM* 109 (1994): 53–120.

Korres, M. *Study for the Restoration of the Parthenon: The West Wall of the Parthenon and Other Monuments*. Vol. 4. Athens: 1994.

Korres, M. and Ch. Mpouras Μελέτη αποκαταστάσεως του Παρθενος, Τομ. 1 Athens, 1983.

Korres, M. *From Pentelicon to the Parthenon*. Athens: 1995.

Korres, M., G.A. Panetsos, and T. Seki, eds. *The Parthenon: Architecture and Conservation*. Athens: 1996.

Koufopoulos, P. *Study for the Restoration of the Parthenon: Restoration Project of the Opisthodomos and the Ceiling of the West Colonnade Aisle*. Vol. 3a. Athens: 1994.

Krauss, F. *Paestum, die griechischen Tempel*. Berlin: 1941.

Krauss, F., G. Gruben, and D. Mertens. *Paestum, die griechischen Tempel*. Berlin: 1978.

Krautheimer, R. "Introduction to an Iconography of Mediaeval Architecture." *Courtauld Institute* 5 (1942–43).

Kriesis, A. "Ancient Greek Town Building." *Acta Congressus Madvigiani* 4 (1958).

Krinsky, C.H. "Seventy-Eight Vitruvius Manuscripts." *JWCI* 30 (1967).

Kron, U. "Archaisches Kultgeschirr aus dem Heraion von Samos." *Ancient Greek and Related Pottery: Proceedings of the International Vase Symposium in Amsterdam, April 12–15, 1984*. H.A.G. Brijder, ed. Amsterdam: 1984.

Kyrieleis, H. *Führer durch das Heraion von Samos*. Athens: 1981.

Kyrieleis, H. "Offerings of the common men in the Heraion at Samos." *Early Greek Cult Practice: Proceedings of the Fifth International Symposium at the Swedish Institute at Athens, June 26–29, 1986*. R. Hägg, N. Marinatos, and G.C. Nordquist, eds. Göteborg: 1988.

Kyrieleis, H. *Der Grosse Kuros von Samo*. Bonn: 1996.

Lang, M.L. *The Athenian Agora: a Guide to the Excavations*. Athens: 1954.

Laugier, M.-A. *Essai sur l'architecture*. Paris: 1753.

Lawrence, A.W. "The Acropolis and Persepolis." *JHS* 71 (1951).

Lawrence, A.W. *Greek Architecture*. Harmondsworth: 1957, revised 1983, 1996.

Lawrence, A.W. *Greek Aims in Fortification*. Oxford: 1979.

Le Roy, J.D. *Les ruines des plus beaux monuments de la Grèce*. Paris: 1758, revised 1770.

Lebouteux, D. *Expédition Scientifique de Morée*. 1833 and 1853.

Lefaivre, L., and A. Tzonis, eds. *The Emergence of Modern Architecture: a Documentary History from 1000 to 1800*. London: 2004.

Lefas, P. "How many columns did Hermogenes remove?" *RA* (2001): 93–103.

Lefkowitz, M.R. *Not Out of Africa*. New York: 1996.

Lefkowitz, M.R. and G. MacLean Rogers, eds. *Black Athena Revisited*. Chapell Hill and London: 1996.

Lévêque, P., and P. Vidal-Naquet. *Clisthène l'Athénien*. Paris: 1964.

Lissarague, F. "Delphes et la céramique." *BCH* 36 (2000): 53–67.

Lloyd, G.E.R. *Methods and Problems in Greek Science*. Cambridge: 1991.

Logan, R.K. *The Alphabet Effect: The Impact of the Phonetic Alphabet on the Development of Western Civilization*. New York: 1986.

Loraux, N. *Les Enfants d'Athéna, idées athéniennes sur la citoyenneté et la division des sexes*. Paris: 1981.

Loraux, N. *L'Invention d'Athènes, histoire de l'oraison funèbre dans la cité classique*. Paris and New York: 1982.

Lord, A.B. *The Singer of Tales*. Cambridge, Mass.: 2000.

Madigan, B.C., with contributions by F.A. Cooper, *The Temple of Apollo Bassitas. Vol. 2: The Sculpture*. Princeton: 1992.

Malkin, I. *Religion and Colonization in Ancient Greece*. Leyden: 1987.

Malkin, I. *Myth and Territory in the Spartan Mediterranean*. Cambridge: 1994.

Malkin, I. "The polis between myths of land and territory." *The Role of Religion in the Early Greek Polis: Proceedings of the Third International Seminar on Ancient Greek Cult, Organized by the Swedish Institute at Athens, October 16–18, 1992*. R. Hägg, ed. Stockholm: 1996.

Malkin, I. *The Returns of Odysseus, Colonization and Ethnicity*. Berkeley: 1998.

Malkin, I. "La Fondation d'une colonie apollinienne, Delphes et l'Hymne Homérique à Apollon." *BCH* 36 (2000): 69–77.

Malkin, I., ed. *Ancient Perceptions of Greek Ethnicity*. Washington and Cambridge, Mass.: 2001.

Mallwitz, A. "Das Heraion von Olympia und seine Vorgänger." *Jdl* 81 (1966).

Mallwitz, A. "Kritisches zur Architektur Griechenlands im 8. und 7. Jahrhundert." *AA* (1981): 599–642.

Mansfield, J.M. *The Robe of Athena and the Panathenaic "Peplos,"* diss. University of California. Berkeley and Ann Arbor: 1985.

Marchand, S.L. *Down from Olympus. Archeology and Philhellenism in Germany, 1750–1970.* Princeton: 1996.

Margineau-Carstoiv, M. "La composition des chapiteaux ioniques." *BCH* 121 (1997).

Margineau-Carstoiv, M., and A. Sebe. "Remarques sur le tracé des volutes ioniques hellenestiques." *BCH* 124/1 (2000).

Marinatos, N. "Medusa on the Temple of Artemis at Corfu." In *Archaische griechische Tempel und Altägypten.* M. Bietak, ed. Vienna: 2001.

Marinatos, S., and M. Hirmer. *Crete and Mycenae.* New York: 1960.

Mark, I.S. *The Sanctuary of Athena Nike in Athens: Architectural Stages and Chronology.* (*Hesperia*, suppl. 26). Princeton: 1993.

Martienssen, R.D. *The Idea of Space in Greek Architecture, with Special Reference to the Doric Temple and its Setting.* Johannesburg: 1956.

Martin, J. *Architecture ou l'art de bien bâtir.* Paris: 1547.

Martin, R.E. *Recherches sur l'agora grecque, études d'histoire et d'architecture urbaines.* Paris: 1951.

Martin, R. *Problème des origines des ordres à volutes, Études d'archéologie classique I.* Nancy: 1955–56.

Martin, R. *L'Urbanisme dans la Grèce antique.* Paris: 1956.

Martin, R. *L'Art grec.* Paris: 1994.

Martini, W. "Vom Herdhaus zum Peripteros." *JdI* 101 (1986): 23–36.

Mavrikios, A.D. "Aesthetic Analysis Concerning the Curvature of the Parthenon." *AJA* 69 (1965): 264–268.

Mazarakis-Ainian, A. "Early Greek Temples: Their Origin and Function." *Early Greek Cult Practice: Proceedings of the Fifth International Symposium at the Swedish Institute at Athens, June 26–29, 1986.* R. Hägg, N. Marinatos, and G.C. Nordquist, eds. Göteborg: 1988.

Mazarakis-Ainian, A. "Late Bronze Age Apsidal and Oval Buildings in Greece and Adjacent areas," *ABSA* 84. 1989. pp.269–88.

Mazarakis-Ainian, A. *From Rulers' Dwellings to Temples: Architecture, Religion and Society in Early Iron Age Greece, 1100-700 BC* (*SIMA* 121). Jonsered: 1997.

Meiggs, R. *Trees and Timber in the Ancient Mediterranean World.* Oxford: 1982.

Melas, E., ed. *Temples and Sanctuaries of Ancient Greece: a Companion Guide.* London: 1973.

Meritt, L.S. "The Geographical distribution of Greek and Roman Ionic bases." *Hesperia* 38 (1969): 186–204.

Mertens-Horn, M. "Die archaischen Baufriese aus Metapont." *RM* 99 (1992): 1–122.

Métraux, G. P. R. Western Greek Land-use and City-planning in the Archaic Period. New York, London: 1978.

Milizia, F. *Dizionario delle belle arti del disegno.* Bassano: 1797.

Miller, J.G. "Temple and Image: Did All Greek Temples House Cult Images?" *AJA* 101 (1997).

Mitchell, L.G., and P.J. Rhodes, eds. *The Development of the Polis in Archaic Greece.* London and New York: 1997.

Mitchell, T.C. "Israel and Judah untol the revolt of Jehu (931–841 BC)", in *Cambridge Ancient History 3.1: The Prehistoric of the Balkans, the Middle East and the Aegean World, Tenth to Eighth Centuries BC,* J. Boardman et al., eds., Cambridge: 1982

Momigliano, A. *The Classical Foundations of Modern Historiography.* Berkeley: 1990.

Montesquieu, C.L. de Secondat, Baron de. *Essai sur le goût.* Paris: 1748.

Morgan, C. *Athletes and Oracles: the Transformation of Olympia and Delphi in the Eighth Century BC.* Cambridge: 1990.

Morgan, C. "The Archaeology of Sanctuaries in Early Iron Age and Archaic Ethne, a Preliminary View." In *The Development of the Polis in Archaic Greece.* L.G. Mitchell and P.J. Rhodes, eds. London: 1997.

Morris, I., ed. *Classical Greece, Ancient Histories and Modern Archaeologies.* Cambridge: 1994.

Morris, S.P. *Daidalos and the Origins of Greek Art.* Princeton: 1992.

Mossé, C. *La Grèce archaïque d'Homère à Eschyle, VIIIe-VIe siècles av. J.-C.* Paris: 1984.

Mossé, C., ed. *La Grèce ancienne.* Paris: 1986.

Mourelatos, A.P.D., ed. *The Pre-Socratics.* New York: 1974.

Müller, V. "Development of the Megaron in Prehistoric Greece." *AJA* 48 (1944).

Müller-Wiener, W. *Bildlexikon zur Topographie Istanbuls, Byzantion, Konstantinupolis, Istanbul, bis zum Beginn des 17. Jahrhunderts.* Tübingen: 1977.

Murray, O. *Early Greece.* Cambridge, Mass.: 1993.

Muss, U. *Die Bauplastik des archaischen Artemisions von Ephesos.* Vienna: 1994.

Mylonas, G.E. *Ancient Mycenae: the Capital City of Agamemnon.* Princeton: 1957.

Myres, J.L. *Herodotus: Father of History.* Oxford: 1973.

Nagy, G. *Greek Mythology and Poetics.* Ithaca: 1990.

Nagy, G. *Pindar's Homer: the Lyric Possession of an Epic Past.* Baltimore and London: 1994.

Nehamas, A. "Pity and fear in the *Rhetoric* and the *Poetics.*" In *Essays on Aristotle's Poetics.* A. Oksenberg Rorty, ed. Princeton: 1992.

Neils, J., ed. *Worshipping Athena, Panathenaia and Parthenon.* Madison: 1996.

Neils, J. *The Parthenon Frieze.* Cambridge: 1995.

Newton, C.T. *A History of Discoveries at Halicarnassus, Cnidus and the Branchidae.* Vol. 2, part 2. London: 1863.

Nilsson, M.P. *A History of Greek Religion.* New York: 1964.

Nilsson, M.P. *The Mycenaean Origin of Greek Mythology.* Berkeley: 1972.

Norman, N.J. *The "Ionic" Cella: a Preliminary Study of Fourth Century B.C. Temple Architecture,* Ph.D. diss. University of Michigan: 1980.

Ohnesorg, A. "Votive- oder Architektursäulen?" In *Säule und Gebälk, zu Struktur und Wandlungsprozeß griechisch-römischer Architektur.* E.-L. Schwandner, ed. Mainz am Rhein: 1996.

Oksenberg Rorty, A., ed. *Essays on Aristotle's Poetics.* Princeton: 1992.

Orlandos, A.K. *Les Matériaux de construction et la technique architecturale des anciens Grecs.* Vol. 1. Paris: 1966.

Orlandos, A. Η αρχιτεκτονική του Παρθενώνος. Αθηναι, τομος Β, Athens, 1977.

Orlandos, A. Η αρχιτεκτονική του Παρθενώνος. Αθηναι, τομος Γ, Athens, 1978.

Orthmann, W. *Der alte Orient*. Berlin: 1975.

Osborne, R. *Classical Landscape with Figures: the Ancient Greek City and its Countryside*. London: 1987.

Osborne, R. "The Viewing and Obscuring of the Parthenon Frieze." *JHS* 107 (1987): 98–105.

Osborne, R. *Greece in the Making, 1200–479 BC*. London: 1996.

Østby, E. "Der Ursprung der griechischen Tempelarchitektur und ihre Beziehungen mit Ägypten." In *Archaische griechische Tempel und Altägypten*. M. Bietak, ed. Vienna: 2001.

Palladio, A. *I quattro libri dell'architettura*. Venice: 1570.

Parke, H.W. *Festivals of the Athenians*. Ithaca, N.Y.: 1977.

Parker, R. *Miasma, Pollution and Purification in Early Greek Religion*. Oxford: 1983.

Parry, A.M., ed. *The Making of Homeric Verse: the Collected Papers of Milman Parry*. Oxford: 1987.

Partida, E.C. *The Treasuries at Delphi: an Architectural Study* (*SIMA* 160). Jonsered: 2000.

Paton, J.M. *The Erechtheum*. Cambridge, Mass.: 1927.

Payne, H. and G.M. Young. *Archaic Marble Sculpture from the Acropolis*. London: 1950.

Pedersen, P. *The Parthenon and the Origin of the Corinthian Capital*. Odense: 1989.

Pedersen, P. "Reflections on the Ionian Renaissance in Greek architecture and its historical background." *Hephaistos* 19/20 (2001–2002): 97–130.

Pennethorne, J. *The Geometry and Optics of Ancient Architecture*. London and Edinburgh: 1878.

Penrose, F.C. *An Investigation of the Principles of Athenian Architecture*. London: 1888.

Perrault, C. *Ordonnance des cinq espèces de colonnes selon la méthode des anciens*. Paris: 1668.

Petropoulos, M. "New Elements from the Excavation of the Geometric Temple at Ano Mazaraki (Rakita)." *Peloponnesiaka*, suppl. 22 (1996–97):165–192.

Pfaff, C.A. "Three-peaked Antefixes from the Argive Heraion." *Hesperia* 59 (1990): 149–156.

Picard, C. *L'Acropole I, L'enceinte, l'entree, le bastion d'Athéna Niké, les Propylées*. Paris: 1929–32.

Picard, C. *L'Acropole II, Le plateau supérieur, l'Érechtheion, les annexes sud*. Paris: 1929–32.

Picón, C.A. "The Sculptures of the Archaic Temple of Artemis at Ephesos", Πρακτικα του 12ου Διθεθνους Συνεδρίου Κλασσικής Αρχαιολογίας 3, p. 221-224.

Piranesi, G.B. *Diverse Maniere d'adornare i Cammini*. Rome: 1769.

Pirenne, H. *Mohammed and Charlemagne*. London: 1939.

Plommer, H. "Review: Herbert Koch, Studien sum Theseustempel in Athen." *Gnomon* 29 (1957): 33–38.

Plommer, H. "The Archaic Acropolis, Some Problems." *JHS* 35 (1960): 127–159.

Plommer, H. "The Old Platform in the Argive Heraion." *JHS* 104 (1984):183–184.

Plommer, W.H. "Three Attic Temples." *ABSA* 45 (1950).

Plommer, W.H. *Ancient and Classical Architecture*. London: 1956.

Poliakov, L. *Le mythe arien*. Paris: 1971.

Polignac, F. de. "Mediation, Competition, and Sovereignty: The Evolution of Rural Sanctuaries in Geometric Greece." *Placing the Gods, Sanctuaries and Sacred Space in Ancient Greece*. S.E. Alcock and R. Osborne, eds. Oxford and New York: 1994.

Polignac, F. de. *La Naissance de la cité grecque*. Paris: 1995.

Polignac, F .de. "L'installation des dieux et la genèse des cités en Grèce d'Occident, une question résolue? Retour à Mégara Hyblaea." In *La colonisation grecque en Méditerranée occidentale, actes de la rencontre scientifique en hommage à Georges Vallet, Rome–Naples 15–18 novembre 1995*. Rome: 1999.

Pollitt, J.J. *Art and Experience in Classical Greece*. Cambridge: 1972.

Pollitt, J.J. *The Ancient View of Greek Art: Criticism, History and Terminology*. New Haven: 1974.

Pollitt, J.J. "The Meaning of the Parthenon Frieze." In *The Interpretation of Architectural Sculpture in Greece and Rome*. D.M. Buitron-Oliver, ed. Hanover and London: 1997.

Pollitt, J.J. *The Art of Ancient Greece: Sources and Documents*. Cambridge: 1990.

Pollock, J.L. *Cognitive Carpentry, Blueprint for How to Build a Person*. Cambridge, Mass.: 1995.

Pontremoli, E. and B. Haussoullier. *Didymes, Fouilles de 1895 et 1896*. Paris: 1904.

Pope, A. *Moral Essays*. London: 1731.

Popham, M.R., and L.H Sackett. *Lefkandi I, The Iron Age*. Athens and London: 1979–80.

Popham, M.R., P.G. Calligas, and L.H. Sackett, eds. *Lefkandi II, The Protogeometric Building at Toumba, Part 2: The Excavation, Architecture and Finds*. Athens and London: 1993.

Poulsen, F. *Delphi*. London: 1920.

Poursat, J.-C. *La Grèce préclassique, des origines à la fin du VIe siècle*. Paris: 1992.

Puchstein, O. *Das ionische Capitell*. Berlin: 1887.

Puchstein, O. *Die ionische Säule als klassisches Bauglied orientalischer Herkunft, ein Vortrag*. Leipzig: 1907.

Putnam, H. *Renewing Philosophy*. Cambridge, Mass. and London: 1992.

Quatremère de Quincy, A.C. *De l'architecture égyptienne*. Paris: 1803.

Renard, L. "Notes d'architecture proto-géométrique en Crète." *AntCl* 36 (1967): 566–595.

Renfrew, C. *The Emergence of Civilisation: the Cyclades and the Aegean in the Third Millennium B.C.* London: 1972.

Renfrew, C., ed. *The Explanation of Culture Change*. London: 1973.

Renfrew, C. *Archaeology and Language: the Puzzle of Indo-European Origins*. London: 1987.

Renfrew, C. and E.B.W. Zubrow, eds. *The Ancient Mind, Elements of Cognitive Archaeology*. Cambridge: 1994.

Rhodes, R.F. *The Beginnings of Monumental Architecture in the Corinthia*, diss. University of North Carolina: 1984.

Rhodes, R.F. *Architecture and Meaning in the Athenian Acropolis*. Cambridge, New York, and Melbourne: 1995.

Ribart de Chamoust, M. *L'Ordre François trouvé dans la Nature*. Paris: 1783.

Richter, G.M. *The Archaic Gravestones of Attica*. London: 1961.

Richter, G.M.A. "Perspective, Ancient, Medieval, and Renaissance." In *Scritti in Onore di Bartolomeo Nogara*. Rome: 1937.

Richter, G.M.A. *Perspective in Greek and Roman Art*. London and New York: 1970.

Ridgway, B.S. *The Archaic Style in Greek Sculpture*. Chicago: 1993.

Riemann, H. *Zum griechischen Peripteraltempel, seine Planidee und ihre Entwicklung bis zum Ende des 5. Jhds*. Düren: 1935.

Robertson, D.S. *Greek and Roman Architecture*. London: 1969.

Robinson, D.M. et al. *Excavations at Olynthus*. Vols. 8 and 12. Baltimore: 1938–46.

Robinson, H. "Excavations at Corinth, Temple Hill 1968–1972." *Hesperia* 45 (1976): 203–239.

Rodenwaldt, G. *Korkyra I, Der Artemistempel*. Berlin: 1940.

Rodenwaldt, G. *Korkyra II, Die Bildwerke des Artemistempels*. Berlin: 1939.

Roebuck, M. "Archaic Architectural Terracottas from Corinth." *Hesperia* 59 (1990): 49.

Romano, I.B. *Early Greek Cult Images*, diss. University of Pennsylvania: 1980.

Romano, I.B. "Early Greek Cult Images and Cult Practices." In *Early Greek Cult Practice: Proceedings of the Fifth International Symposium at the Swedish Institute at Athens, June 26–29, 1986.* R. Hägg, N. Marinatos, and G.C. Nordquist, eds. Göteborg: 1988.

Ross, Sir W.D. *Aristotle*. London: 1923.

Roux, G. "Le chapiteau corinthien de Bassae." *BCH* 77 (1953): 124–130.

Roux, G. "L'architecture de l'Argolide aux IVᵉ et IIIᵉ s. avant J.-C." *BEFAR* 199 (1961).

Roux, G. *L'architecture de l'Argolide aux IVᵉ et IIIᵉ siècles*. Paris: 1961.

Roux, G. *Karl Haller von Hallerstein, Le temple de Bassae*. Strasbourg: 1976.

Roux, G., ed. *Temples et sanctuaires*. Lyon: 1984.

Roux, G. "Pourquoi le Parthénon?" *CRAI* (1984): 301–317.

Roux, G. "L'architecture à Delphes: un siècle de découvertes." *BCH* suppl. 36 (2000): 181–199.

Rupp, D. "Reflections on the development of altars in the eighth century B.C." In *The Greek Renaissance of the Eighth Century B.C.: Tradition and Innovation*. R. Hägg, ed. Stockholm: 1983.

Salmon, J.B. *Wealthy Corinth: a History of the City to 338 BC*. Oxford: 1984.

Sandys, J. *The Odes of Pindar*. London: 1968.

Schachermeyer, F. "Die ältesten Kulturen Griechenlands." *AJA* 41 (1937).

Schachter, A. "Policy Cult and the Placing of the Greek Sanctuaries." In *Le Sanctuaire Grec* (Fondation Hardt 37). A. Schachter, ed. Vandoeuvres-Geneva: 1992.

Schachter, A. *Le Sanctuaire Grec* (Fondation Hardt 37). Vandoeuvres-Geneva: 1992.

Schleif, H. "Der Zeusaltar in Olympia." *Jdl* 49 (1934): 139–156.

Schmoll, J.A., ed. *Das Unvollendete als Künstlerische Form*. Bern: 1959.

Schnapp-Gourbeillon, A. *Aux origines de la Grèce, La genèse du politique*. Paris: 2002.

Schneider, P. "Zur topographie der Heiligen Strasse von Milet nach Didyma." *AA* 1 (1987): 101–129.

Scholl, A. "Choephoroi, zur Deutung der Korenhalle des Erechtheion." *Jdl* 110 (1995): 179–212.

Schwandner, E.-L. "Überlegungen zur technischen Struktur und Formentwicklung archaischer Dachterrakotten." *Hesperia* 59 (1990): 192–291.

Schwandner, E.-L., ed. *Säule und Gebälk, zu Struktur und Wandlungsprozeß griechisch-römischer Architektur*. Mainz am Rhein: 1996.

Scranton, R. "Interior Design of Greek Temples." *AJA* 50 (1946).

Scranton, R. *Greek Architecture*. New York and London: 1962.

Scully, V.J. *The Earth, the Temple and the Gods: Greek Sacred Architecture*. New Haven: 1962.

Seiler, F. *Die griechische Tholos, Untersuchungen zur Entwicklung, Typologie und Funktion kunstmäßiger Rundbauten*. Mainz am Rhein: 1986.

Semper, G. *Der Stil in den technischen und tektonischen Künsten, oder Praktische Aesthetik, ein Handbuch für Techniker, Künstler und Kunstfreunde, Bd.1: Die Textile Kunst für sich betrachtet und in Beziehung zur Baukunst*. Munich: 1878.

Semper, G. *Der Stil in den technischen und tektonischen Künsten, oder Praktische Aesthetik, ein Handbuch für Techniker, Künstler und Kunstfreunde, Bd.2: Keramik, Tektonik, Stereotomie, Metallotechnik für sich betrachtet und in Beziehung zur Baukunst*. Munich: 1879.

Serlio, S. *I libri dell'architettura*. Venice: 1537–75. Complete edition 1584. Reprint. Ridgewood, N.J.: 1964.

Shaftesbury, A.A. Cooper, Earl of. *Characteristics of Men, Manners, Opinions, Times*. London: 1711.

Shear, I.M. "Maidens in Greek Architecture, the Origin of the Caryatids." *BCH* 123 (1999): 65–85.

Shear, J.L. *Polis and Panathenaia: the History and Development of Athena's Festival*, diss. Ann Arbor: 2002.

Shiloh, Y. "The Proto-Aeolic Capital and Israelite Ashlar Masonry." *Qedem* 11 (1979): 83–87.

Shiloh, Y., and A. Horowitz. "Ashlar Quarries of the Iron Age." *BASOR* 217 (1975): 37–48.

Shipley, G., and J. Salmon, eds. *Human Landscapes in Classical Antiquity, Environment and Culture*. London: 1996.

Shoe, L.T. *Profiles of Western Greek Mouldings*. 2 vols. Rome: 1952.

Shoe Meritt, L. "The Geographical Distribution of Greek and Roman Ionic bases." *Hesperia* 38 (1969).

Sichtermann, H. *Kulturgeschichte der klassischen Archäologie*. Munich: 1996.

Simon, E. *Festivals of Attica*. Madison: 1983.

Simopoulos, K. *Foreign Travellers to Greece*. Athens: 1970–75.

Snell, B. *The Discovery of the Mind*. Cambridge, Mass.: 1953.

Snodgrass, A.M. *Archaeology and the Rise of the Greek State*. Cambridge: 1977.

Snodgrass, A.M. *Archaic Greece: The Age of Experiment*. London: 1980.

Sokolowski, F. *Lois sacrées des cités grecques, Supplément.* Paris: 1962.

Somolinos, J.R. "Le Plus ancien oracle d" Apollon Didymeen." *EpigrAnat* 17 (1991): 69–71.

Spengler, O. *The Decline of the West.* London: 1926.

Stais, V. Το Σούνιον και οι ναοί Ποσειδώνος και Αθηνάς.70 Athens, 1920.

Stevens, G.P. "The Periclean Entrance Court of the Acropolis of Athens." *Hesperia* 5 (1936): 443–520.

Stevens, G.P. *The Setting of the Periclean Parthenon* (*Hesperia*, suppl. 3). Princeton: 1940.

Stevens, G.P. "The Curves of the North Stylobate of the Parthenon." *Hesperia* 12 (1943).

Stevens, G.P. "The Northeast corner of the Parthenon." *Hesperia* 15 (1946):1–26.

Stevens, G.P. "Remarks upon the Colossal Chryselephantine Statue of Athena in the Parthenon." *Hesperia* 24 (1955): 240–276.

Stevenson Smith, W. *The Art and Architecture of Ancient Egypt.* Harmondsworth: 1958, revised 1965.

Stevenson Smith, W. *Interconnections in the Ancient Near-East: a Study of the Relationships between the Arts of Egypt, the Aegean, and Western Asia.* New Haven: 1965.

Stone, I.F. *The Trial of Socrates.* Boston: 1988.

Strauss Clay, J. *The Politics of Olympus: Form and Meaning in the Major Homeric Hymns.* Princeton: 1989.

Stuart, J., and N. Revett. *The Antiquities of Athens, Measured and Delineated.* London: 1762–1830.

Svenbro, J. *Phrasikleia: an Anthropology of Reading in Ancient Greece.* Ithaca, and London: 1993.

Tanoulas, T., M. Ioannidou, and A. Moraitou. *Study for the Restoration of the Propylaea* 1. Athens: 1994.

Tanoulas, T. "The Ionic stylobate and the building process of the Propylaia." In *Säule und Gebälk, zu Struktur und Wandlungsprozeß griechisch-römischer Architektur.* E.-L. Schwandner, ed. Mainz am Rhein: 1996.

Themelis, G. "Ξένοι ταξιδιώτες στην Ελλάδα," *ASAtene* 61 (1983): 237–244.

Theodorescu, D. *Le chapiteau ionique grec.* Geneva: 1980.

Tomlinson, R.A. "The Doric Order: Hellenistic critics and criticism." *JHS* 83 (1963): 133–145.

Tomlinson, R.A. *Argos and the Argolid: from the End of the Bronze Age to the Roman Occupation.* Ithaca, N.Y.: 1972.

Tomlinson, R.A. *Greek Sanctuaries.* London: 1976.

Tomlinson, R.A. "The Sequence of Construction of Mnesikles" Propylaia." *ABSA* 85 (1990): 405–413.

Tournikiotis, P., ed. *The Parthenon and its Impact in Modern Times.* Athens: 1994.

Travlos, J. Πολεοδομική Εξέλιξις των Αθηνών. Athènes, 1960.

Travlos, J. *Athènes au fil du temps, atlas historique d'urbanisme et d'architecture.* Bologna: 1972.

Travlos, I. *Pictorial Dictionary of Ancient Athens.* New York: 1980.

Travlos, J. *Bildlexikon zur Topographie des antiken Attika.* Tübingen: 1988.

Trevor Hodge, A. *The Woodwork of Greek Roofs.* Cambridge: 1960.

Tuchelt, K. *Vorarbeiten zu einer Topographie von Didyma.* Tübingen: 1973.

Tuchelt, K. "Tempel - Heiligtum - Siedlung- Probleme zur Topographie von Didyma." In *Neue Forschungen in griechischen Heiligtümern.* U. Jantzen, ed. Tübingen: 1976.

Tuchelt, K. "Didyma - Bericht über die Arbeiten der Jahre 1980–1983." *IstMitt* 34 (1984): 214–225.

Tuchelt, K., P. Schneider, T. Schattner and H.-R. Baldus. "Didyma - Bericht über die Ausgrabungen 1985 und 1986 an der Heiligen Strasse von Milet nach Didyma." *AA* (1989): 143–217.

Tzonis, A., and L. Lefaivre. *Classical Architecture: the Poetics of Order.* Cambridge, Mass. and London: 1986.

Tzonis, A. "Il bastione comme mentalità." In *La Città el mura.* C. de Seta and J. le Goff, eds. Rome: 1989.

Tzonis, A. "Hutten, Schiffe und Flaschengestelle, Analogischer Entwurf für Architekten und oder Maschinen." *Archithese* May–June (1990).

Tzonis, A. *Le Corbusier.* New York: 2001.

Ullman, S. *High-Level Vision, Object Recognition and Visual Cognition.* Cambridge, Mass. and London: 1996.

Umholtz, G. "Architraval arrogance? Dedication Inscriptions in Greek Architecture of the Classical Period." *Hesperia* 71 (2002): 261–293.

Van Buren, E.D. *Archaic Fictile Revetments in Sicily and Magna Graecia.* London: 1923.

Van Buren, E.D. *Greek Fictile Revetments in the Archaic Period.* London: 1926.

Van Straten, F. "Votives and Votaries in Greek Sanctuaries." In *Le Sanctuaire Grec* (*Fondation Hardt* 37). A. Schachter, ed. Vandoeuvres-Geneva: 1992.

Vasari, G. *Le vite de' più eccelenti pittori, scultori ed architettori.* Florence: 1550, 1568.

Vatin, C. "Marques de chantier et organisation du travail dans un grand sanctuaire." In *Technai, Techniques et sociétés en Méditerranée, Hommage à Marie-Claire Amouretti.* J.-P. Brun and P. Jockey, eds. Paris: 2001.

Vermeule, E.T. *Greece in the Bronze Age.* Chicago: 1972.

Vernant, J.-P. *Les Origines de la pensée grecque.* Paris: 1962.

Vernant, J.-P. *Mythe et pensée chez les Grecs.* Vols. 1 and 2. Paris: 1965.

Vernant, J.-P. "A la table des hommes, Mythe de fondation du sacrifice chez Hésiode." In *La cuisine du sacrifice en pays grec.* M. Detienne and J.-P. Vernant, eds. Paris: 1979.

Vernant, J.-P. "The Birth of Images." In *Mortals and Immortals, Collected Essays.* F. Zeitlin, ed. Princeton: 1991.

Vernant, J.-P., and P. Vidal-Naquet. *La Grèce ancienne 2, L'espace et le temps.* Paris: 1991.

Vernant, J.-P. *Entre mythe et politique.* Paris: 1996.

Veyne, P. *Les Grecs ont-ils cru à leurs mythes? Essai sur l'imagination constituante.* Paris: 1983.

Vidal-Naquet, P. *Le chasseur noir, formes de pensée et formes de société dans le monde grec.* Paris: 1981.

Vidal-Naquet, P. *La Démocratie grecque vue d'ailleurs, essais d'historiographie ancienne et moderne.* Paris: 1990.

Vidal-Naquet, P. *Les Grecs, les historiens, la démocratie: le grand écart.* Paris: 2000.

Vidal-Naquet, P. *Fragments sur l'art antique.* Paris: 2002.

Vidal-Naquet, P. *Le Monde d'Homère.* Paris: 2002.

Walbank, F.W. *The Hellenistic World.* Cambridge, Mass.: 1981.

Walter, H. *Das griechische Heiligtum, dargestellt am Heraion von Samos*. Stuttgart: 1990.

Walter-Karydi, E. "Geneleos." *AM* 100 (1985): 89–103.

Weickert, C. *Das lesbische Kymation, ein Beitrag zur Geschichte der antiken Ornamentik*. Leipzig: 1913.

Weiss, R. *The Renaissance Discovery of Classical Antiquity*. New York and Oxford: 1973.

Welter, G. *Aigina*. Berlin: 1938.

Werner, K. *The Megaron during the Aegean and Anatolian Bronze Age: a Study of Occurrence, Shape, Architectural Adaption and Function* (*SIMA* 108). Jonsered: 1993.

Wesenberg, B. *Kapitelle und Basen, Beobachtungen zur Entstehung der griechischen Säulenformen*. Düsseldorf: 1971.

Wesenberg, B. "Panathenäische Peplosdedikation und Arrhephorie, zur Thematik des Parthenonfrieses." *JdI* 110 (1995):149–178.

Wesenberg, B. "Die Enstehung der griechischen Säulen und Gebälkformen in der literarischen Überlieferung der Antike." In *Säule und Gebälk, zu Struktur und Wandlungsprozeß griechisch-römischer Architektur*. E.-L. Schwandner, ed. Mainz am Rhein: 1996.

West, M.L. *The East Face of Helicon: West Asiatic Elements in Greek Poetry and Myth*. Oxford: 1997.

Weynants-Ronday, M. *Les Statues vivantes*. Brussels: 1926.

White, J. *Perspective in Ancient Drawing and Painting* (*Society for the Promotion of Hellenic Studies*, suppl. 7). London: 1956.

Wiebenson, D. *Sources of Greek Revival Architecture*. London: 1969.

Wiegand, T. *Didyma*. Berlin: 1941.

Wikander, C. "Opaia Kiramis: Skylight Tiles in the Ancient World." *OpRom* 14 (1983).

Wikander, C. *Sicilian Architectural Terracottas: a Reappraisal*. Stockholm: 1986.

Winckelmann, J.J. *Anmerkungen über die Baukunst der Alten*. Leipzig: 1762.

Winter, F.E. *Greek Fortifications*. London and Toronto: 1971.

Wittkower, R. *Architectural Principles in the Age of Humanism*. London: 1962.

Woodruff, P. "Aristotle on Mimesis." In *Essays on Aristotle's Poetics*. A. Oksenberg Rorty, ed. Princeton: 1992.

Wren, Sir C. *Tracts on Architecture*. 1670.

Wright, G.R.H. *Ancient Building in South Syria and Palestine*. 2 vols. Leyden and Cologne: 1985.

Wright, J.C. "The Old Temple Terrace at the Argive Heraeum and the Early Cult of Hera in the Argolid." *JHS* 102 (1982): 186–201.

Wright, J.C. "The Spatial Configuration of Belief, the Archaeology of Mycenaean Religion." In *Placing the Gods, Sanctuaries and Sacred Space in Ancient Greece*. S.E. Alcock and R. Osborne, eds. Oxford and New York: 1994.

Wycherley, R.E. *How the Greeks Built Cities*. New York: 1949.

Wycherley, R.E. *The Athenian Agora III: Literary and Epigraphical Testimonia*. Princeton: 1957.

Yalouris, N. "Problems relating to the temple of Apollo Epikourios at Bassai." *Greece and Italy in the Classical World: Acts of the XI International Congress of Classical Archaeology, London 1978*. J.N. Coldstream and M.A.R. Colledge, eds. London: 1979.

Zanker, P. *The Mask of Socrates: the Image of the Intellectual in Antiquity*. Berkeley: 1995.

Παπαθανασόπουλος, Θ. "Ο ναός του Επικουρίου Απόλλωνα", *Αρχαιολογία* 29, 1988, p. 12-26.

Παπανικολαου, Ι.Α. "Ζητήματα των Μεγάρων Α και Β του Θερμου", *Aeph* (1990): 191–200.

INDEX

PHOTOGRAPHIC CREDITS

The images reproduced in this book are from Alexander Tzonis' archives, with the exception of the following:

AKG-images, 146, 221

AKG-images/Erich Lessing, 72 top, 72 bottom, 82 top, 86 top, 104, 132 left, 166

AKG-images/John Hios, 147

AKG-images/Robert O'Dea, 82 bottom

Archives Boissonas, 8, 12, 14, 16, 17, 23, 100, 114, 120, 121, 156, 178, 179, 236

Athènes, École française/Georges de Miré, 20 left, 20 rigth, 88 left, 88 right, 89, 170

Athènes, Deutsches Archäologisches Institut, 26, 27, 28, 42, 78, 79 top, 79 bottom, 80, 81, 92, 93, 96, 106, 108, 109, 110, 112, 118, 119, 124, 125, 126, 127, 162, 215, 222, 232, 235

Genève, Musées d'Art et d'Histoire/Waldemar Deonna, 22, 99, 134, 169

Serge Moulinier, 57, 60, 70, 113, 145, 180, 182, 183, 186, 187, 188, 189, 190, 191, 194, 196, 208, 214, 228, 230, 234

Paris, Lucien Hervé, 6

Mark Edward Smith, 102